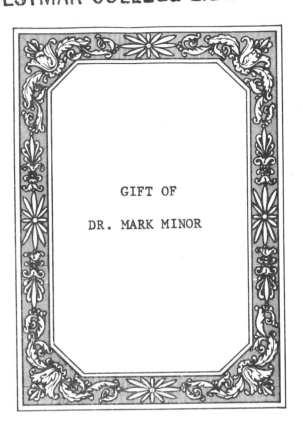

PROFIT WITH DELIGHT

PROFIT WITH DELIGHT

Richard I. Pervo

THE LITERARY GENRE
OF THE
ACTS OF THE APOSTLES

89-694

FORTRESS PRESS   PHILADELPHIA

Library of Congress Cataloging-in-Publication Data

Pervo, Richard I.
  Profit with delight.

  Bibliography: p.
  Includes index.
  1. Bible. N.T. Acts—Criticism, interpretation, etc.
2. Bible. N.T. Acts—Criticism, Form. 3. Narration
in the Bible. 4. Narration (Rhetoric) I. Title.
BS2625.2.P39   1987   226'.6066   86–45220
  ISBN 0–8006–0782–1

2555B87   Printed in the United States of America   1–782

For Karen
deliciae
animae meae

Omne tulit punctum qui miscuit utile dulci,
Lectorem delectando pariterque monendo.

The one who combines profit with delight,
equally pleasing and admonishing the reader,
captures all the plaudits.

—Horace *Ars poetica* 343–44

CONTENTS

PREFACE

Behind this study lies a bulky Harvard University dissertation of 1979 ("The Literary Genre of the Acts of the Apostles") accepted by a committee including the late George W. MacRae, S.J., John Strugnell, Albert Henrichs, and the chair, Dieter Georgi. Helmut Koester was then on sabbatical. These and other teachers had taught me to be skeptical about "assured results," not because our forebears were so stupid but because of the need for each generation to formulate its own answers to enduring questions. In particular, I learned to consider New Testament writings within a broad environment.

Koester and Georgi inspired my research into popular narrative writings of the Greco-Roman world. In this book I emphasize a kind of form-critical insight, the essence of which is distilled in the elegantly conventional quotation from the Roman poet Horace's *Ars poetica* 343–44, from which I appropriated my title, *Profit with Delight*. My object is to contribute to the contemporary quest for links between early Christian and other narrative literature. For over two millennia representatives of the most refined cultural strata have resisted the impetus to provide "improving" books with attractive covers. Ancient arbiters of taste rejected mixing the business of serious reading with pleasure. Even Plato's dialogues were regarded as a less than serious condescension to popular taste. Elevated style and exquisite rhetoric provided pleasure enough when mastered. This battle has never been won, of course, but the values endure to such an extent that even today professors may be defensive about their light reading. Exegetes, motivated by both cultural prejudice and religious reverence, have tended to treat canonical texts as thoroughly grave, if literarily defective, productions.

Critics notwithstanding, there are those who *do* like literature with lots of anecdotes and pictures. One of the characteristics of "popular" literature is its unabashed presentation of edifying messages in attractive form. This is true even of masterpieces like the plays of Euripides and Aristophanes, writings aimed at a broad public, and not only of the cautionary tales recited by nurses to their charges. Although few would quibble at the description of the Gospels and Acts as "popular," most studies have concentrated upon the profit and ignored the delight.

A major task of this book is to elucidate the entertaining nature of Acts.

Since one customary means for rejecting popular literature has been to label it pure entertainment, I wish to make clear that there is no intent here to deny Luke's serious theological program. If, however, Acts is popular in that it cloaks its message in a pleasant package, this will have implications for Luke's theology, some of which I seek to elucidate.

Through comparison of Acts with ancient popular narratives I seek not only the identification of literary affinities but also clarification of the religious and social values of the milieu in which it emerged. It is my desire that those engaged in social analysis and description of the early Christian world will find in this study stimuli for their own writing and research. Interest in the application of literary critical methods to New Testament writings has grown enormously since this work first began to take shape. Although intrigued by many contemporary approaches (none of which I pretend to have mastered), I have determined to keep traditional historical criticism in the forefront. The subject of this book is controversial enough. Time will judge the wisdom of this decision.

Although the citations given here are in English, this work is based upon the original texts. It is from these Greek and Latin documents that my perception of the literary world of the ancient novel derives. Translations are useful, however, and the forthcoming publication of a long-needed complete series of ancient novels in contemporary English, a project of the University of California Press, should make them available to a wider audience. Plans for a new collection of the Apocryphal Acts in English and the recent appearance of *The Old Testament Pseudepigrapha*, edited by James H. Charlesworth for Doubleday, reflect current interest in some texts central to this study and should enhance their accessibility. Even as this work was in preparation some new editions of ancient novels emerged in print, and the efforts of Swiss scholars are coming to fruition with the completion of critical texts of the Apocryphal Acts. These patient and welcome labors of many should offer numerous opportunities to correct and supplement my proposals.

Like other authors I am greatly indebted to numerous teachers, colleagues, and students whose contributions the references all too inadequately acknowledge. For the milieu needed to prepare the manuscript I am most grateful to the people of the Church of the Transfiguration, Bois Blanc Island, the Straits of Mackinac, especially to the late H. Earl Hoover and his wife, Miriam U. Hoover. Gratitude is also due to the clergy and people of St. Luke's Church, Evanston, where I have learned much about their patron on quiet weekdays and splendid feasts. Newland F. Smith and other staff of the United Library have been extremely helpful. Cathleen Chittenden assisted in the proofreading and preparation of indexes and located an elusive reference.

I am proud to be associated with the program of Fortress Press and owe a great deal to the support and guidance of John A. Hollar.

RICHARD I. PERVO

Seabury-Western Theological Seminary
Evanston, Illinois
The Feast of Saint Luke the Evangelist, 1986

1. LUKE-ACTS

The Eye of the Storm

PERSPECTIVES ON THE GENRE OF ACTS

As the second of two volumes composed by the writer of the Third Gospel, the Book of Acts has been subjected to the same techniques of historical criticism employed in Gospel studies. As the only narrative presentation of early church history to find a place within the canon, Acts comes into comparison with the rest of the New Testament, particularly the letters of Paul. Although there is no general consensus about the historical merits of this controversial book, not even the most conservative critics can overlook the presence of vexing historical problems.[1] To a large extent, researchers take their cue from their view of Paul and his theology. Whereas conservatives incline to find in Acts the "real Paul," liberal exponents of the Continental Reformation tradition frequently reject the "Paulinism of Acts" and many, if not all, of its works and ways.[2] Since the Enlightenment, Acts has lived mainly under a Pauline cloud.

I do not seek to demonstrate once again the presence of historical problems in Acts. If such problems are at points underlined, this is not in order to administer yet one more beating to "Luke"[3] but to support my proposal to view the document of Acts from a different perspective. Likewise, the following review of scholarship intends to illustrate the problem motivating this study rather than to resolve questions.

One approach, whose patron saint is the late Sir William Ramsay, has accepted the Book of Acts as a factual account of high quality, probably written by a participant in many of the events. History, rather than philology, has until recently dominated the investigations of this "school."[4] After an initial advance during the ebb of the Tübingen proposals, the disciples of Ramsay (and Theodor Zahn) have been locked in a series of rearguard actions.

Another important trend, exemplified by the work of Martin Dibelius and

---

*See W. C. van Unnik, "Luke-Acts, a Storm Center in Contemporary Scholarship," in *SLA* 15–32.

to an even greater degree by that of Henry J. Cadbury, tacitly sets historical questions to one side and focuses upon Luke as a writer and expounder of Christianity.[5] The concept of "Luke the theologian" is an implicit heritage of the Tübingen school now accepted by the vast majority of scholars. Dibelius played an important role in mediating this concept from one generation to another. Cadbury concentrated upon the questions of style, structure, and personal interests of the author. Many now reap what Cadbury sowed, and build upon foundations erected by Dibelius. What the two thought the historical value of Acts to be is by and large of secondary interest to their procedures. It is as preacher (following Dibelius) and writer (following Cadbury) that Luke is viewed today. The understanding of Luke as a historian, whether good, bad, or indifferent, occupies only third place in today's thinking about Acts.

The aggressively skeptical approach exemplified by the Tübingen school has traditionally stressed the tension between Acts and the Epistles, with the object of illuminating Luke's tendencies. In theology this method has carried the day. Skepticism has also become the moderate posture, to which a large number of post-conciliar Roman Catholic exegetes bear witness. Principal symbol of this general accord is the vast respect given to the commentary of Ernst Haenchen,[6] which still remains the point of departure in contemporary discussion.[7]

One reason for Haenchen's dominance is that his was the first large-scale commentary to make full and consistent application to Acts of the several methods developed during this century for the analysis of early Christian literature. Briefly stated, Acts has like the Gospels been subjected to, consecutively, text, source, form, and redaction criticism, although in each case without the emergence of the kind of consensus that permitted and required Gospel study to move into new fields.[8] The text problem appears to require positing more than one edition,[9] the question of sources is wide open,[10] and few of the units fall into the formal categories that pervade the Gospels.[11] Comparison of sources and awareness of formal considerations, both based upon a more or less secure text, serve to regulate and control the various proposals offered by redaction-critical studies of the Gospels, but the application of redaction-critical techniques to Acts will, given the uncertainty of the book's sources and forms, expose its practitioners to charges of wanton subjectivity.[12]

Haenchen illustrates this problem. By brilliantly exposing the frequently inept proposals of earlier researchers regarding source and form, he triumphantly led the reader to agree that "what Luke wanted to write" is central. This is a great strength: sustained, acute attention to the actual text and its author's objects. As his critics have hastened to observe,[13] however, judgments thus achieved may be arbitrary and subjective.

Most of the external controls Haenchen rejected deserved refutation. Haenchen was thus thrown back upon his understanding of Luke's ideas and techniques as the chief key for unraveling his compositions. For Haenchen, Luke was more of an "edifying" than an accurate historian. Eager to instruct the church in vivid and concrete fashion and blinded by fixed conceptions of the past, Luke was unable to perceive that some of his statements were untrue—a matter that was in any event of limited concern to his readers.[14] The use of the term "edifying" thus becomes a means for retaining the traditional epithet "Luke the historian." Crisply put, Luke was well intentioned but dumb.

LUKE AS HISTORIAN

For Luke as author, on the other hand, Haenchen needed to formulate no apologies. With consummate skill he revealed Luke's capacity to conjure up exciting episodes with creative ingenuity and a sound dramatic instinct. Haenchen convincingly elucidated Luke's bewitching ability to foist upon his readers one inconsistency after another and convert the most dreary material into good reading. But Haenchen apparently did not contemplate the enigma thus produced: a Luke who was bumbling and incompetent as a historian yet brilliant and creative as an author.

This two-headed Luke is partly the creature of Haenchen's method. By asserting, without reference to evidence, that Luke was a historian, Haenchen resolved historical questions by resorting to conjectures concerning what the author knew or thought or cared about. This technique is dangerously close to "psychologizing," peering into the mind of an author. Haenchen did not even in the course of his lengthy introduction address the question of genre. Luke was, by implication, a bad historian, but he was full of good intentions. On that conclusion Haenchen seemed content to let the matter rest. This is unfortunate, for the purpose of form criticism is to resolve just such dilemmas as those raised by Luke the stupid historian and brilliant writer. The unfinished form-critical task left by Haenchen is the classification of works that are bad history but good writing.

In the case of the NT Gospels there are four specimens, and their major sources may be isolated to a tolerable degree of satisfaction. With regard to Acts one must look to other models. The conventional basis for comparison has been historiography. But that ground, once chosen, must be a battleground. Upon it have been waged all the conflicts about accuracy and fact, source and intention. Those who take that ground can hold it only at tremendous cost, whether they are Theodor Zahns or Ernst Haenchens.

Just why Acts is thought to be historiography is unclear. From the viewpoint of Gospel criticism, such a view has an old-fashioned ring. The notion that the Gospels are immanent, objective history has few contemporary adherents. Discovery of the nonhistorical character of the Gospels gave impetus to form-critical investigation of Gospel forms and genre(s). The result of this research was to affirm that the evangelists were evangelists, proponents of a religious message, theologians rather than historians. Although there is no lack of data to suggest that Acts is something other than history, relatively little has been done to account for this phenomenon in terms of literary forms.

This is even more surprising when one recalls that the writer of Acts also wrote one of the Gospels. Despite such external marks of historiography as a preface and synchronism (Luke 1:1–4; 3:1–2), few attempt to maintain that Luke was really a better (i.e., more accurate) historian that Matthew, Mark, or John. On the contrary, critics observe that the Third Evangelist edited passages to suit his ideas, rearranged events at will, and invented at least a few episodes.[15] Transition to the second volume somehow requires a change of costume. Instead of folklore, the classics are invoked. Luke the evangelist gives place to Luke the historian.

Behind this somewhat perplexing presumption of a change of masks stands an important truth: that Luke and Acts represent different genres. Acts contains relatively few of the traditional pericopes, gives more place to apostolic adventure than apostolic instruction, and includes a number of integrally structured speeches. Luke apparently used different types of sources for Acts. He certainly employed different compositional techniques. There is a formal difference between the two books.

The use of historiography in Acts is thus posited to account for the apparent divergences between the two books. This solution is perhaps logical enough, but the basis for it is a bit more fragile than the quavering crust of learned consensus might indicate. Prominent critics have often hedged their bets.[16] Haenchen was even willing to concede Luke the historian the freedom of a contemporary historical novelist.[17] The new costume handed Luke by critics to wear in his second act begins to resemble the emperor's clothes.

The Preface

One major pillar of the dogma that Acts is ancient historiography comes from the use of a preface, the employment of speeches, and of course, the sustained narrative of events, including references to secular history. For those nurtured on the classics, Acts looks like a bit of somewhat familiar ground. These formal trappings make Luke a literary personage. Despite such blandishments one must not forget that the same sort of preface—with its claims for energetic research, great fidelity, and correct order—precedes the Gospel as well. If this single Greek period can convert a work into history, it must do so for both books. The synchronism, which is not without problems,[18] also belongs to the Gospel, as do some of the references to historical persons and events.[19] Observation that the much-studied[20] prefaces resemble those of Flavius Josephus implies no more than that they conform to late first-century C.E. historical *style*.

Prefaces were highly conventional. Composition of them may have been taught in school. Their claims could be the object of parody.[21] Not only historians but medical writers, astrologers, dream interpreters, and novelists made use of such marks of erudition.[22] The use of a preface does not settle the question of genre, for such devices could be employed by novelists to create verisimilitude.[23]

Nor does chronology settle the question. Luke's absolute chronology is so thin that one of his defenders was driven to assign chronological data to a projected third volume by Luke and another to blame the problem on sources.[24] Relative chronology is also problematic. Only those readers supplied with data from other sources perceive that the book records events that took place over an entire generation.[25] If chronology, both external and internal, was an important concern for historians, it was not so for Luke.

Speeches

Ancient Greek and Roman historians were famous for their composition of speeches. Since the speeches in Acts do not resemble those in the Gospel, they are conventionally attributed to a historiographical intent. Dibelius did not find the analogies at all persuasive.[26] It is not acceptable, therefore, to regard Acts as history merely upon the basis of the preface, temporal and historical references, and the speeches.

Greek and Roman fashions of writing history by themselves represent a broad spectrum. When oriental and biblical modes are also, quite properly, taken into account, very little generalization about the writing of history is possible.[27] Although one dare not, given Luke's familiarity with the Septuagint,[28] overlook the older biblical models, Hellenized Jewish historiography seems to provide the most fertile area for comparison. The most common name invoked is that of Flavius Josephus, but detailed comparison of his major works with Acts reveals vast differences. Both the *Jewish War* and the *Antiquities* made use of Greek prototypes.[29] Use of such models reflected literary tastes of the day. Those who wished to compose "real" history imitated the structure and style, often even the viewpoint, of an appropriate authority.[30] Style was essential, not peripheral.

Other Models

One cannot point to such an extant learned Greek model for Luke. This is by no stretch of the imagination an *Antiquitates Christianae* of Lucius (Antio-

chenus). No educated Greek would place such a poorly written account of the
missionary activities of a newfangled oriental cult during its first thirty years
on the shelf beside the *Antiquities* of Dionysius of Halicarnassus. Julian's contemptuous "Let them repair to the churches of the Galileans and interpret
Matthew and Luke"[31] shows how insignificant the difference between Luke
and the other NT writers appeared to a cultivated Hellene of late antiquity.

One suggestion is to liken Acts to *hypomnemata,* unpolished vernacular
memoirs touched up with an elegant preface.[32] The surviving examples of
such memoirs, mainly fragmentary, are unpretentious enough in style and
structure. A survey of the *Spanish War* in the works of Caesar will point to
some significant contrasts. Memoir style was mainly crisp and simple. Acts is
rarely if ever dull. More than poor style is required to constitute memoir
diaries.

Much stronger claims can be made for likening Acts to the then-fashion-
able monograph. Ramsay may have been the first to make this suggestion,
taken up more recently by Hans Conzelmann and his students.[33] A brief description of the possibilities of this genre may be found in Cicero's well-
known bid to Lucceius:

> The fact is that the regular chronological record of events in itself interests us as
> little as if it were a catalogue of historical occurrences; but the uncertain and var-
> ied fortunes of a statesman who frequently rises to prominence give scope for
> surprise, suspense, delight, annoyance, hope, fear; should those fortunes, how-
> ever, end in some striking consummation the result is a complete satisfaction of
> mind which is the most perfect a reader can enjoy. (Cicero *Letters to His Friends*
> 5.12.5)[34]

Sallust's monographs and the *Agricola* of Tacitus confirm that monographs
could focus upon the most important phase of an individual's public career.
Although not biographies, monographs often focused upon a person. "Character studies" of this type in antiquity almost inevitably included encomium
and invective, with the corresponding acceptance of untruth. The monograph is an important formal category for comparison with Acts. Not all
monographs were historical. The structure could be used for outright fiction
or other purposes. Monography refers more to a structure and design than to
a specific genre.[35]

However the structure and design of Acts may resemble monographs or
other writings, the criteria of style and content must be taken carefully into
account. Legitimate pieces of historiography needed, like all literary works,
to reflect unity of style, vocabulary, and syntax, as well as proportion and balance.[36] Minor skirmishes had no right to pose as the battle of Marathon.
Speeches were to be appropriate to the circumstances, and all reporting
should be suitable to its station in human affairs. Acts does not suit such

requirements! Its inconsistent style and inclination to treat insignificant happenings as world-historical events would offend learned readers. Educated persons would regard a comparison of Peter to Socrates as an exhibition of shockingly poor taste.[37] Historians often referred to supernatural phenomena, in particular, portents, but were expected to qualify their reports by appending the ancient equivalent of "it was reported."[38] Their primary task, however, was to reconstruct the most plausible description on the basis of reasonable criteria.[39] Luke's congeries of miracles, impossible statistics, and constant improbabilities exceeded even the most permissive limits.[40]

Ancient historians were expected to explain the causes and effects of significant events. The beliefs, attitudes, and even the fortunes of ordinary people rarely qualified for inclusion in a history. Political and military history did, social matters intruding only in cases of upheaval or revolution, and then in only the most stereotyped ways. Newly formed oriental sects need not apply for treatment in a monograph.

As an example of how the kinds of events presented in Acts were treated in ancient historiography there is Livy's account of the Dionysiac mission in Italy.[41] This writer, who shrank from neither propaganda nor little bits of fiction, would not for a moment have considered Luke a colleague. Livy's point of view and the space devoted to the important incident of the Bacchanalia brightly illumine the great gulf fixed between Luke and the learned historians of his era.[42]

Another possible analogy is with the *Bacchae* of Euripides. Here the perspective is more "sympathetic." *Mythos* (myth) and *pseudos* (falsehood) were fitting material for poets and dramatists. Those who wished to record the wondrous origins of a cult employed one of the poetic genres, and their readers would not cavil at the presence of the supernatural within such contexts. Luke thus had no real classical prose model for his work because his subject was not suitable for historians.

Both the style and content of Acts urge the consideration of Jewish prototypes. Second Maccabees, with its dramatic scenes, stunning miracles, and edifying message, offers an obvious basis for comparison. This book has, moreover, the scope and quality of a monograph. Despite the similarities in vocabulary style and episodic composition there are important differences. Second Maccabees is stylistically superior to Acts. Political and military history are its subject. One may well presume that a cultivated critic would recognize this as a piece of tendentious and grossly propagandistic history. It is in fact precisely the kind of writing taken to task by Lucian in his essay on historiography.[43]

Although it would be relatively simple to demonstrate that Acts violates nearly every single canon advanced by Lucian, that is not material. Lucian ridiculed works he regarded as poor specimens of history writing. A book like Acts did not even meet the standards of the works he despised. To discover what Lucian thought about literature like ours one must turn to such essays as *Alexander*,[44] *Peregrinus*, *The Lover of Lies*, and *A True Story*. Second Maccabees could be scolded for, among other things, including *pseudos*. Acts was simply falsehood through and through.

Those who would align this book with some type of ancient history or another must therefore recognize the limitations of such proposals. At best they can appeal to no more than slight structural resemblances and a thin veneer of formal apparatus. Nor should it be overlooked that the more closely Acts is linked to historiography, the more acute the tension between volume one (Luke) and volume two (Acts) will be.[45]

There are some other avenues for exploration. One useful suggestion invokes *praxeis* literature.[46] The vast majority of works called *Praxeis* (Acts of . . .) do not survive, but the available evidence does not point to one specific genre with recognizable form, style, and point of view. The term seems to reflect the cultural preference of the Hellenistic and Roman eras for admiring the great deeds (*praxeis, acta*) of the mighty. To that extent, at least, research on material described as *praxeis* will help illuminate the milieu of Acts.

Perhaps Luke created a new genre, "ecclesiastical history," in response to the needs of a new social body. At the very least, church historians might quite properly treat the history of Christian life and mission, and one would not expect them to abstain from the topic of miracles—not in antiquity. The evidence does not, however, establish Luke as "father of church history" in a formal sense. Eusebius's predecessors, Hegisippus, Julius Africanus, and Hippolytus, devoted themselves to chronology, heresiology, and lists of succession—procedures they did not learn from Luke. When Eusebius composed his *Ecclesiastical History* he developed a new genre, based upon the *antiquitates* format together with the design employed for sketching the histories of the schools. His extensive quotation of sources represents a decisive break with ancient tradition.[47] Luke did not constitute his prototype.

For many the chief obstacle to viewing Acts as a work of history arises from its content rather than its style and form. After all excuses have been made for the presumed lack of ancient concern for strict truth, Acts is still lacking. More than a few of the incidents appear to have been invented, good sources were not used even if available,[48] and the characterization of both people and events can often be shown to be either highly improbable or contrary to known facts. The various matters may still be debated, and there is no absolute consensus, but the very volume of apologetic efforts to defend Luke testifies in itself to the gravity of the problem.[49] To illustrate its magnitude, I offer a review of Acts 19.

ACTS 19

Acts 19 disturbed Ramsay. Here he saw his beloved historian behaving more like a retailer of gossip than like the Thucydidean figure of his admiration. The Ephesian ministry was one of the most important phases of Paul's missionary career,[50] and this portion of Acts lies within the arena of the Aegean, the chapters framed by the use of "we." Hence, one is hard pressed to excuse Luke on the grounds of sources. The writer may indeed have come from Ephesus.[51] Neither the space devoted to this locality nor the quality of events related suggests that Luke did not see Paul's work in Ephesus as of prime importance. What he says, how he says it, and what he apparently chooses not to say are very revealing.

Acts 19 opens with a perplexing description of some adherents of John the Baptist. These individuals, who, like Apollos, know only the baptism of John and, unlike John, have never heard of the Holy Spirit, have been allowed to pray in blissful ignorance by the Christians in Ephesus until Paul appears, examines and corrects their beliefs, and imposes his hands upon them, producing the accustomed ecstasy (19:1–7). There are a few links between this episode and the issues treated in 1 Corinthians.[52]

The three following verses treat the stereotyped separation of Paul from the synagogue and briefly allude to a two-year mission that reached the entire population of Asia. After this terse note, Luke turns to spiritual and social accomplishments. Second-class relics of Paul work wonders (vv. 11–12). Certain religious quacks are driven out of business, left wounded and nude (vv. 13–17). Encouraged by this example, the Ephesians renounce magic (vv. 18–19). Commercial exploiters of the great shrine of Artemis begin to feel the pinch, Christian preaching having provided a falloff in the sale of devotional souvenirs (vv. 23–27). Through them the urban rabble is maneuvered into an ultimately futile demonstration of unrest (vv. 28–40).

Opposition to Paul derives from undesirable elements: magicians, Jews, itinerant exorcists. His supporters include the very foremost men of the province (v. 31). One can scarcely deny that in Acts 19 Luke has pulled out all the stops to describe the peak of Paul's mission in the Aegean region. There is not another chapter in the Book of Acts which can match this for color, variety, excitement, and sheer unmitigated success. Paul converts sectaries at the touch of a finger, cures disease with castoff rags, humiliates opponents who merely seek to misuse his name, convinces myriads to renounce superstition, and hobnobs with Asiarchs.

This is impressive. No less impressive is the complete lack of information about a community of believers, or a clear statement of actual converts (other than ex-disciples of the Baptizer), or a single name of a new believer. Our author also severs all ties between Paul and Apollos. While the latter was active in Ephesus and Corinth, Paul was absent—on a pilgrimage to Jerusalem.[53]

Paul experienced some serious difficulties in Ephesus. He may have been imprisoned;[54] there were serious conflicts with some of his congregations, in particular, with Corinth. Acts 19:21—20:1, together with 20:17–38, makes it difficult to maintain that Luke had no idea of these problems. He will go so far as to admit that there was a riot in Ephesus; he devotes nearly twenty verses in one of the most popular and famous episodes of Acts to it (chap. 19). Be that as it may, Paul was not driven out of town because of this disturbance, for he had planned to leave anyway (v. 21). Nor was he involved, although, as a gesture of concern for law and order, he did attempt to intervene in order to quiet the crowd,[55] until dissuaded from doing so by the Asiarchs, who took time at this moment of grave crisis to reassure themselves of the apostle's personal security. Who caused the riot at Ephesus? Pagan trash, agitated by aggrieved pagan craftsmen. Where was Paul? Sipping sherry with the high priests of the imperial cult. Paul was able to resume his travel as soon as conditions had returned to normal (20:1).

The actual Paul would have found this account quite fascinating, to say the least. Comparisons with 2 Corinthians are extremely instructive.[56] Attempts to defend Luke's accuracy may miss the point. Both Acts and Paul's Epistles agree that this stay in Ephesus was one of the longest and most productive of Paul's projects. Luke differs in the way he selects to narrate this triumph, a way that includes improbable and probably concocted episodes and allegations about Paul's associates and virtues that strongly contrast with Paul's own testimony. Haenchen, who disputes none of this, suggests that Luke did not want the Ephesian mission to end on a downbeat.[57] But more than a penchant for happy endings, scarcely an admirable trait in historians, appears to be at issue. Acts 19 is the pièce de résistance of Luke's narrative power, his way to bring the Aegean mission to a climax. Here Luke emerges at the top of his form, not the lowest, as Ramsay claimed.

Attempts to explain such passages as Acts 19 have led many able critics to tie themselves in knots. These efforts to rationalize Acts began at least as early as Codex Bezae and will doubtless continue.[58] They are far from valueless.

A NEW APPROACH

My work will follow a different path. Rather than attempt to extricate Luke from his situation or revile him for misrepresenting facts, I wish to let Acts speak for itself. In order to be heard over the din of centuries, the text sometimes requires amplification. At times this will look like distortion. Yet the effort needs to be made, and then remade.

One cannot rest upon the observation of Dibelius, followed by Conzelmann, that Luke was really a preacher.[59] Vital as this insight is, it will not excuse every error, nor does it obviate the need for form-critical research. Because affiliation with historiography presents serious difficulties,[60] it is necessary to cast a broader net.

Comparison with ancient historiography produces limited results for the simple reason that Luke did not write a learned treatise. He was a "popular" writer. This observation, common as it is,[61] has not always received the attention it deserves.[62] Popular writers were not always concerned to follow the rules laid down by their cultured betters, who sneered at the notion of lowbrow history.[63]

Popular works were doubtless often *edifying*, the quality Haenchen found dominant in Acts. They were also quite frequently intended *to entertain*, an object that did not at all diminish their value for illumination and improvement. Only recently has the presence of entertainment in Acts been accorded some of the appreciation it merits. The major portion of this book will be devoted to demonstrating how pervasive the element of entertainment actually is. I do not argue that Luke wishes only to entertain,[64] but I try to establish the basis for a fresh examination of the genre of Acts, and of the relation between Acts and the Apocryphal Acts (hereinafter Apoc. Acts) and other literature.

2. WHEN ALL SEEMS LOST

Adventure in the Acts of the Apostles

The great new middle-class public was to dominate the age, docking its literature of the old thin-blooded cynicism and drenching it with morality and sentiment. . . . They wanted to satisfy their emotions without outraging their conscience; and they liked nothing better than the spectacle of endangered virtue. . . . They might . . . relish morality far more when it was tied to a plot than when it was preached from a pulpit. There was, at any rate, a sincere desire to be moved and edified.

—Louis Kronenberger,* on the emergence of a new reading public in eighteenth-century England

Acts' succession of interesting, "action-packed" stories has long made it one of the more interesting works to study in Sunday school. There are arrests and escapes, stonings and beatings, trials and riots, travel to various places, and as a grand finale, a shipwreck in the middle of the Mediterranean. These adventures distinguish Acts from Luke and raise the question of literary genre.[1]

Until recently there has been little attention to the entertaining character of the apostolic escapades narrated by Luke. Biblical scholarship since the Renaissance has been at some pains to reject the stimulation of pleasure as a worthy object of inspired writings. Biblical criticism of the modern variety arose in circles influenced by Rationalism and Pietism, movements disinclined to approve of the frivolous and amusing, especially in the Bible.[2] Martin Dibelius's disapproval of the intrusion of "secular" themes into Acts was but a continuation of such earlier biases. Entertainment has evolved from a bane of Pietists to a tool of higher critics. When scholars discover anything aimed to please, they take umbrage. The presence of entertainment in the Apoc. Acts serves as prima facie evidence for relegating those works to an inferior status.[3]

This bias may explain why Ernst Haenchen so often seems to imply that Luke wrote, in part, to entertain his readers, but avoids saying this in so

---

Kings and Desperate Men (New York: Alfred A. Knopf, 1942), 275.

many words. He prefers to speak of "edification," invoking this term so often that one may ultimately come to believe that by "edifying" Haenchen really means "unedifying" because untrue or bad theology or frivolous or all three.

Classical standards transmitted to the contemporary world through the Renaissance have played their part also. Educated people should appreciate their culture neat. No sugarcoating of important themes was needed, certainly not in the study of history. Biblical critics have tended to identify with this classical, Thucydidean position.[4]

Popular literature happily ignored such canons. The twin goals of pleasure and instruction were taken for granted in material designed to enlighten the common folk. Few would challenge the edificatory intent of the *Aesopica*, the *Apothegmata patrum*, Midrashim, or Talmud, writings sprinkled with enjoyable and memorable stories. Longer works, including "lives," like those of Aesop and Secundus the Silent Philosopher, as well as various types of novels, some quite serious, others intended chiefly to please, reflected the same perspective. Highbrow writings proudly displayed unsullied instruction. Lowbrow productions were clothed in forms that would cause the less motivated to pay attention.

In speaking of historiography, Lucian of Samosata maintains the hard line: "History has one task and one end—what is useful—and that comes from truth alone." When he turns to the mime, on the other hand, a popular genre, he lauds dance because it "brings not only pleasure but benefit to those who see it; how much culture and instruction it gives; how it imparts harmony into the souls of its beholders." Drama was equally popular:

> The one who combines profit with delight equally pleasing and admonishing the reader, captures all the plaudits. (Horace *Ars poetica* 343–44)[5]

As a popular document, Acts may well be expected to contain some entertaining stories. Determination of what readers of ancient times might have found pleasing can be difficult. I have attempted to reduce subjectivity by basing my observations upon criteria derived from ancient novels, in particular, romantic novels. Themes and motifs frequently recurring in such works may reasonably be assumed to have been found pleasing. If particular attention is given to the novels of Chariton and Xenophon of Ephesus, that is because their style and contents make them especially appropriate to audiences of the same sort to whom much early Christian literature was directed.

Adventurous material, since it is identified with comparative ease and is likely to be accepted as entertaining, will be treated first. Table 1 indicates both the scope of adventure in Acts and the variety of incidents.

Even a cursory review of the table shows that Acts focuses, to a surprising degree, upon the personal experiences of missionaries. Twenty-three of the

TABLE 1
ADVENTURE IN ACTS

	Text	Characters	Danger	Issue/cause	Deliverance/result
1.	4:1–3	Peter and John	Arrest	Teaching, miracle, growth	4:21. Release with warning
2.	5:17–18	All the apostles	Arrest	Jealousy	5:19–20. Miracle
3.	5:21b–27	All the apostles	Rearrest	Jealousy	5:34–39. Gamaliel's speech 5:40. Release after being beaten
4.	6:11–12	Stephen	Arrest	Miracles, success	7:55–60. Execution
5.	8:1b	Whole church	Persecution	Miracles, success	8:1b, 4; 11:19. Flight (inspired)
6.	8:3; 9:1–2	Whole church	Persecution (by Paul)	Miracles, success	9:3–9. Conversion of persecutor
7.	9:23–24	Paul	Plot to kill	Conversion preaching	9:25. Escape by trick
8.	9:29	Paul	Plot to kill by Hellenists	Conversion preaching	9:29. Flight to Tarsus
9.	11:28	Everyone (Jerusalem?)	Famine	—	Prophecy, collection
10.	12:1–24	"Some," Peter, James	Persecution by Herod	Placation of "Jews"	12:1. Killing of James 12:6–18. Miraculous escape by Peter

	Text	Characters	Danger	Issue/cause	Deliverance/result
11.	13:50	Paul and Barnabas	Persecution	13:45. Jealousy	13:50. Expulsion 13:52. Happy ending
12.	14:2–6	Paul and Barnabas	Attempted stoning	Slander by unbelieving Jews	14:6. Flight (learned)
13.	14:19	Paul	Stoning	Stirring up of mob by Jews from Antioch and Iconium	14:20. Superhuman survival
14.	16:16–40	Paul and Silas	Imprisonment	Stirring up of mob by economic rivals, political charges	14:25–26. Miracle 14:35–36. Release
15.	16:27–32	Jailer	Threat of suicide	Fear of disgrace, execution	Maintenance of security by apostles
16.	17:5–10	Paul, Silas, and others	Arrest	Jealousy, political charges of Jews and mob	Nocturnal escape, with case against others continued
17.	17:10b–14	Paul and Silas	Mob action	Jealousy of Jews from Thessalonica	Sending on of Paul
18.	17:18–33	Paul	Trial by Areopagus	Introduction of new gods	No decision, no detention
19.	18:12–17	Paul	Trial by Gallio	Illegal activity	Dismissal by Gallio

TABLE 1—Continued
ADVENTURE IN ACTS

	Text	Characters	Danger	Issue/cause	Deliverance/result
20.	19:23–40	Paul and others	Riot	Economic jealousy, claims of threatening ancestral religion	Dissuasion of Paul by Asiarchs, stopping of crowd by *Grammateus*
21.	20:3	Paul	Jewish plot	Jealousy, etc.	Change of route
22.	21:27–32	Paul	Mob in temple	Claim Gentiles introduced	Rescue by tribune
23.	22:22–24	Paul	Mob in temple	Gentile converts	Removal to barracks
24.	22:24–29	Paul	Torture	Attempt to obtain information	Revelation of Roman citizenship
25.	22:30—23:10	Paul	Trial by Sanhedrin	Paul's activity and beliefs	Escort of Paul to safety by tribune
26.	23:12–35	Paul	Plot by 40 +	Paul's activity and beliefs	Mounting of successful operation by tribune to take Paul away
27.	24:1–23	Paul	Trial by Felix	Jerusalem charges	Suspense, with case continued

	Text	Characters	Danger	Issue/cause	Deliverance/result
28.	24:27	Paul	Continued imprisonment	Placation of "Jews"	Removal of Felix
29.	25:1–6a	Paul	Plot by high priests and leading citizens	Hatred	Rejection of plan, by Festus
30.	25:6b–12	Paul	Trial by Festus	Jerusalem charges	Appeal by Paul when Festus wishes to "please Jews" and change venue to Jerusalem
31.	27:1–44	Paul and others	Shipwreck	Storm	Divine protection of personnel
32.	28:1–2	Paul and others	"Natives" who might kill	Plunder	Divine protection of personnel
33.	28:3–7	Paul	Viper	God, to prove divine nature of apostle	Divine protection of personnel

thirty-three episodes listed occur in Acts 13—28, where the author is believed to have had his best sources. No fewer than twenty-six include Paul as
a major figure.

Luke presents his story of the early church largely as a series of escapades,
from nearly all of which the leading characters escape great danger. Critical
study must do more than analyze this or that incident to extract a historical
kernel. The sheer number of adventure stories must also be given its due.

These episodes have often received piecemeal analysis based upon the canons of rational historiography. These criteria may not always be the most useful. In particular, distinction between "natural" and "supernatural" introduces a misleading anachronism. For Luke each of the incidents listed (and
many others within the book) are powerful demonstrations of God's powerful
and guiding hand.[6] All are marvelous deeds narrated not only to stimulate
their readers but also to proclaim the mighty providence of God.

SACRED INCARCERATIONS

Arrests dot the pages of Acts. From beginning to end the danger of sudden
seizure—on false charges—is a constant threat. What Luke presents is far
from a dull catalogue of legal incidents. Despite the similarity of theme and
the limited number of possible outcomes, Acts, for whatever reason, somehow produces a remarkable variety of detail and outcome. One arrest leads to
an exciting trial; another ends with a marvelous escape. Legal vindication
may produce relief and pride; a brave martyrdom might rouse the heart and
strengthen the soul. Careful study of these several incidents leads to the all
but inevitable conclusion that variation for literary reasons was important to
Luke. The most likely literary explanation for the variety is a desire to hold
the interest of the audience.

The apostles depicted in early Christian literature spent time enough in
prison. Many, like Paul, could scarcely visit a city without doing a tour in the
local lockup. Even before her baptism the noble Thecla discovered what jails
were like—in both Iconium and Antioch. Thomas, arrested as it were by
God, went to India as a slave. There he would be incarcerated by two kings.[7]

The same fate lay in store for heroes of ancient novels, for pirates and robbers no less than magistrates and kings. False arrest, seizure by malevolent
ruffians, detention in vile dungeons, caves, even brothels, were pretty much
routine. The experience of Lucius could easily stand in some apostolic tale:

> In a moment the entrance was thrown open. . . . The whole house was packed
> with magistrates and their servants and a nondescript herd of people. At once
> two of the lictors clapped me on the shoulder "In the Name of the Law" and be-
> gan to haul me off. . . . It seemed the whole city had turned out. . . . [The popu-
> lace] streamed out and filled the pit of the theatre. (Apuleius 3.2)[8]

This was not his only brush with the law.[9] Romantic leads fared no better. Chaireas was arrested for the presumed murder of his wife, later for attempting to escape from slavery, and like Paul was held in custody for much of the book.[10]

In both Acts and novels arrests serve a similar plot function. They introduce great danger while evoking sympathy from the readers. Frequently detention provides the reason for travel to some distant locale. The ultimate trial (at which the facts must finally emerge) may be delayed time and again. Thus Luke uses arrest, or the threat of arrest, as the mainspring by which Paul is propelled from Damascus to Jerusalem and on through Pisidian Antioch, Philippi, and Corinth, and from Jerusalem to Rome. Readers of Acts would not discover from reading about arrests how to obtain recognition in an alien environment.

Acts 3—7. The cycle of arrests in Acts 3—7 reveals Luke's literary skill no less than his particular view of church history. At the basis is a rather typical and widespread pattern of missionary aretalogy,[11] a pattern that may be outlined as follows:
1. Missionaries of a new god appear.
2. They achieve success (usually with women, foreigners, slaves, or some other less "respectable" group).
3. The establishment is jealous, and opposition develops.
4. That leads to persecution and punishment (arrests, martyrdoms, suits, etc.).
5. The mission is vindicated by what believers see as a miracle.
6. There follow the defeat and punishment of the opponents, possibly ending with their conversion.

The particular patterns of Acts 3—7 may be outlined as follows:
A. Miracle, which draws attention and followers
B. Teaching addressed to those attracted by the miracle
C. Arrest of the missionary by jealous Jewish officials
D. Trial of the missionary
E. Miraculous vindication of the mission

Luke repeats this sequence in three consecutive reports, varying the contents in each and structuring the sequence so that it becomes a crescendo of violence climaxing in the final episode. Each sequence in the cycle features different characters, resulting in a literary tour de force.

Cycle I. Peter (and John)
      (2:42–46. Community life—communalism.)
      (2:47. First note on growth.)
      A. 3:1–11. A healing. Crowd forms.

    B. 3:12–26. Missionary address.
    C. 4:1–3. Chief of temple police and
        Sadducees arrest.
        (4:4. Second note on growth.)
    D. 4:5–21. Trial. Magic and philosophers
        vs. tyrants.
    E. 4:21ff. Released with warning.
        4:31. Miraculous affirmation.
        (4:32 — 5:11. Interlude on communalism.)

Cycle II. All the apostles

    A. 5:12a, 15–16. Summary of miracles.
    B_1. 5:12b. Apostles teach in temple like philosophers.
        (5:13–14. Third note on growth.)
    C_1. 5:17–18. High priest and Sadducees arrest.
    E_1. 5:19–20. Released by miracle.
    B_2. 5:21a. Return to teaching.
    D_1. 5:21–25.Trial aborted.
    C_2. 5:26–27a. Rearrest.
    D_2. 5:27b–39. Trial: Let God decide.
    E_2. 5:40–41. Beaten and released, saved by Gamaliel.
        5:42. Return to teaching.
        (6:1–7. Interlude on community life, communalism.)
        (6:8. Fourth note on growth.)

Cycle III. Stephen

    A. 6:8. Works miracles.
    B. 6:9–10. Teaches (see 7:2–53).
    C. 6:11–12. Arrested and brought before
        Sanhedrin (false charges).
    D. 6:13—7:57. Trial (only full-length of three accounts).
    E. 6:15; 7:55–56, 59–60. Martyred. Vindication
        by signs of divine approval and heavenly reward.

The climax is a general persecution, which only leads to further teaching and missionary travel. Ironically the plan to suppress this movement leads only to its extension. Through persecution by Jerusalem authorities the followers of Jesus are motivated to reach out to Gentiles.

Despite the shopworn and restricted nature of his basic outline, Luke has created a dramatic sequence. Each episode leads to greater violence and mounting tension. The officials first warn, then whip, and finally kill. The first section affects two apostles, the second all twelve, and the last extends into the circle of the Seven and the laity. Both cycles I and II describe an orderly trial after a night of detention, but in cycle II escape and rearrest intervene. Death threatens in cycle II, averted by the timely intervention of Gamaliel. Cycle III depicts the apex of rage: no deliberation, no due process. Stephen is dragged from the street to face a Sanhedrin already assembled and ravenous for blood.[12]

Alert readers will observe the gradual moral deterioration of the opposition. Frustration at their inability to muzzle the apostles, whose preaching and miracles make them jealous, leads them from legal nicety to lynching. Beginning with sincere questions, they conclude with concocted evidence (4:7; 6:11–14). All in vain, for the wider and more devious the snares and nets of the persecutors, the more quickly the mission grows.

This segment of Acts brings to light the author's talent for repeating basic patterns with enough variation of detail to keep interest high.[13] In general, Luke presents just one full-scale account of a particular type of incident. So here the personnel of the Sanhedrin are fully described only at their first appearance. Within this series of pericopes there is one exemplary apostolic miracle of healing, one missionary speech, one judicial debate, and one full-size defense oration. Wonders abound, including a transfiguration, a nature epiphany, and a prison miracle. So accomplished is the variation that one may easily overlook the sameness of structure. Can such variation be attributed to the fortuitous circumstances of the sources? If, as appears all but certain, it is due in large part to the author, then the creation of dramatic excitement and pleasing narrative must be given a high place on Luke's list of discernible priorities.

This is not to suggest that Luke does not have ideological points to make. He does, but he makes them by telling vivid stories. Five times within five chapters (Acts 3—7) we learn that the Jewish leaders were responsible for the death of Jesus. We further observe his followers teaching like philosophers, disciples even of Socrates, rather than like magicians or quacks.[14] Luke's characters wear either white or black hats.

The prison-escape scene in Acts 5 participates, along with related incidents recorded in chapters 12 and 16, in one of the most widespread stock incidents of aretalogical literature. More than thirty such tales can be studied, in Acts and Apoc. Acts, Dionysiac literature, Jewish narrative, historical and romantic novels, and novellas.[15]

The apparent home of this type was the Dionysiac tradition. So appealing was it that proponents of other religions, including Jews and Christians, made similar demonstrations of the vindicating power of their gods, and storytellers and novelists transformed them for their purposes.[16] The Dionysiac tales, best known through the *Bacchae* of Euripides, reflect no interest in legal vindication, set as they are in the mythical past. Resistance to the mission is *theomachia* (obstinate flouting of a god), and such opposition receives its just due. With the exception of Peter's release in Acts 12,[17] however, Luke consistently pairs miraculous support to repentance by the authorities.[18]

Other prose tales of the imperial age, including those found in *The Life of Apollonius of Tyana* (*Ap. Ty.*) and the Apoc. Acts, tend to be both apologetic and aretalogical. The combination of miraculous signs with legal vindication reflects this dual interest. Luke's preference for both miraculous signs and legal vindications thus reflects the viewpoint typical of contemporary and later religious propagandists.[19]

Although many of the prison delivery scenes found in ancient novels would appear to reflect a kind of "secularized aretalogy,"[20] the opposite may be true.[21] In romantic novels a fortuitous event may stand in the crucial spot held by a miracle in religious works. The view of novels as "secularized aretalogy" will be considered later.[22] Here it should be noted that the romantic novels and miraculous stories appear to have appealed to similar readers through the use of similar tales. What is the action of a particular god in one may pass as plain good luck or a general sort of providence in another, but in both, the stories serve to entertain. When Achilles Tatius can compose a scathing parody of the episode,[23] its popularity is established. Like Lucian, Achilles knew how to pillory hackneyed conventions of popular writing and belief. The issue is not the separation of miraculous rescues from "natural"[24] incidents but recognition of a category of ancient "escapist" entertainment.

Luke blends his materials with characteristic artistry. The legal release of Acts 4 is joined to a splendid epiphany, showing where God stands. Acts 5:17–20 includes a wonderful instance of angelic liberation, but that amounts to no more than a pleasant interlude. Gamaliel's shrewd and inspired little oration brings final delivery. When the walls collapse and the chains fall away, Paul and Silas do not flee but wait in quiet confidence (restraining less devout captives) for Roman justice to come into play. Extraordinary miracles are only the most outward and visible of God's signs.[25] Haenchen's efforts to sift source material on the basis of miracle seems to misperceive the author's intention.[26]

Luke's several prison escapes are wonderfully varied through the addition of suspense, local color, trials, allusions to literature, crowd scenes, torture, martyrdom, threatened suicide, and speeches, no less than in the use of different plot structures. Their function is to portray the triumph of a new religion over all opposition. They are religious propaganda. Literarily, they frighten and amuse, excite and surprise. Rescue always comes in a novel way, at the most dismal moment—*when all seems lost*. Passages so rich and diverse require more than the gleanings of faded memories and scraps of source material, more even than an author with a taste for aretalogy. They display the hand of a writer interested in pleasing his audience. They build upon one another, each more detailed and dramatic than the last. In Acts 4 a liberation miracle is "available," so to speak, but not required. The earthshaking epiphany is a taste of things to come. Acts 5 shows miraculous release and legal deliverance walking hand in hand. By chapter 12 things have come to such an impasse that lawful discharge is out of the question. Only a miracle will save Peter. It does. Acts 16 has it all: crowd, officials, beating, earthquake, a conversion, recantation by the magistrates. The grand climax thus comes as Paul reaches the European side of the Aegean.

Acts 16:19–40. The formal complexity of Acts 16:19–40, with its parallels not only to *desmolyta* (prison escapes) but also to a type of conversion story and a friendship novella,[27] indicates Lukan composition. The close resemblance to Lucian's story, in particular, suggests that the passage should be classified as a fictional episode, not because the events are improbable (as indeed they are) but on formal grounds. The strands do not all hold together. When the jailer threatens suicide, he is certainly indulging in one of the most threadbare devices of ancient fiction, but this disrupts the flow of the conversion account. One expects his religious query to follow upon the earthquake. Here, however, the most striking epiphany is that Paul (and, of course, Silas) has restrained the prisoners. His subsequent hospitality, although parallel to theoxenies, is more akin to the friendship novella. Most anomalous is the conclusion, when the officials take no notice of the earthquake but move on strictly legal paths.[28] This is somewhat characteristic of Luke. At times he introduces more material than he can master and resolves tensions before they are given adequate time to mature.[29] If, however, Luke sometimes attempts to weave more threads than he can remember, he is nonetheless master enough of his craft to pull the wool over his readers' eyes. So engaged is the reader at each moment of the narrative that rarely will one pause to notice inconsistencies.

The themes of this tale—Roman vindication, respect for law and order, high social status—are Lukan. Luke is thus almost certainly responsible for transforming a traditional *praxis Paulou* (Act of Paul), which may well have included a liberation wonder, into this complex piece of engaging historical fiction.

Acts 16 contains Luke's showpiece prison story. Within twenty verses the missionaries rise from beaten and despised hucksters of a new foreign cult to respected burghers worthy of official solicitude. They gain the support of their jailer, a local worthy,[30] and leave the entire colony in their debt, since

Philippi has one fewer religious fraud (16:16–18) and no escaped prisoners for whom to account. Most astonishing is that, amid all this good will, they also leave. There are, to be sure, some problems of law and logic.[31] Since Luke is quite capable of writing sequential and logical narrative, I conclude that he did in Acts 16:19–40 just what he wanted to do. Historical probability was not this writer's highest priority. Composition of appealing stories was not his lowest.

Luke agreed with his fellow evangelists, and with Paul, that prison was one fate in store for believers. Most of his chains serve to decorate a theology of glory rather than to express identification with the humility and rejection experienced by Jesus. Until Acts 21, only once[32] must anyone spend so much as an entire night in prison. Release and relief come quickly, often attended with wonder. Suffering is unheard of, even in the face of beatings and torment. Once released, the missionaries return to work without so much as an hour's sick leave. Readers of such tales were doubtless inspired, inspired not by direct exhortation to courage, such as one reads in the Gospels and Epistles, but inspired by accounts of thrilling adventures, adventures not less entertaining than those described in the Apoc. Acts and in the pages of romantic and other novels.

PERSECUTION AND MARTYRDOM

Rosa Soeder introduced her study of persecution in the Apoc. Acts with this contrast:

> And thus the persecutions [in the canonical Acts] are of a different type than in the Apocryphal Acts. They always refer to the Apostles as members of the Christian sect, which ought to be extirpated. Thus general persecutions or those of more than one apostle are described . . . whereas the Apocryphal Acts deal with the successive persecutions and sufferings of one hero.[33]

Acts is responsible church history. The Apoc. Acts are fantastic entertainments. Soeder's views are standard. They also need reexamination. Luke's approach to persecutions gives no consistent and especial emphasis to the history and life of the community. Membership in the Christian sect is no less attributed to the apostles of the Apoc. Acts than to the characters of Acts. Nor are the apostles of Acts any less likely to be persecuted for individual deeds than the apostles of the Apoc. Acts. Thus, in 4:1–22 Peter and John are seized for working a miracle, not for sectarian affiliation. Acts 5:17–42 likewise focuses upon the wonderworking name of Jesus. Envy of this power was the cause, as it was also of Stephen's arrest, in 6:11–12. Paul's powerful preaching aroused opposition in Damascus and Jerusalem (9:23–24, 30). After the attempt to kill Peter in 12:1, it is always the actions of Paul that spark the flames of persecution. James can live comfortably in Jerusalem with myriads of co-sectarians, until Paul comes to town (21:18–22). Whenever Paul leaves, the believers seem able to live in peace and quiet (13:52; 16:40; 17: 10–14; etc.). The apostle is the source of uproar. In all the Acts persecution centers on the powerful personality of the missionary whose teaching and deeds ignite entire cities.

Persecution is part of Luke's basic aretalogical scheme.[34] Missionary religions use persecution as an instrument of propaganda:

> Fellows like these are believed if they've been in some far-off prison, shackled hand and foot: if he hasn't a prison record, then he has no renown, but a sentence to one of the islands, a narrow escape from death, procures him a reputation. (Juvenal *Satire* 6.560–64)[35]

Acts is, if anything, a bit more rigid in its adherence to this format than are the Apoc. Acts. Where Acts and the Apoc. Acts differ is in motifs. In the Apoc. Acts sex is likely to light the blaze.[36] The cause is, in very fact, quite often nothing other than some good woman's adherence to the Christian sect. The merits of Encratism may be as they are. All of the Acts describe persecution as due to the anger or jealousy generated by success. All proclaim final vindication.

Soeder's contention that persecutions in Acts are general is equally objectionable. The only general persecution took place subsequent to Stephen's martyrdom.[37] There are no details other than reference to the heroic resistance of the apostles, who alone were brave enough to avoid flight. Granted that this is a Lukan invention, its purpose was not to bring the community to the fore.[38] At the core of this outburst was none other than Saul, no less zealous in persecuting than in proclaiming. Once he came over, nothing more was mentioned about general persecutions. The church enjoyed peace (9:31).

Persecutions of groups of apostles are not possible in the Apoc. Acts, because in those works the Twelve scattered to the ends of the earth (as Acts 1:8 implied they might well do).[39] In both Apoc. Acts and Acts the missionary might have a silent partner to share his fate. As for the persecution of converts, this experience is much more important a part of the Apoc. Acts than of Acts. Both canonical and noncanonical Acts thus use religious persecution as a medium for proclaiming their message. Persecution serves to display the heroic prowess of the leading characters and God's benefactions for believers. All exploit the possibility of deriving some entertaining episodes from persecution.

The prolific tradition of Christian hagiography provides ample evidence that the subject of persecution was the major staple of Christian entertainment for a millennium and beyond. Acts stood at the beginning of what would be a rich and productive literary heritage. Where the Apoc. Acts may seem deficient is in the quantity and variety of persecution stories. Prison walls break, guarded rooms fail, honest judges refrain from pressing charges, persecutors suffer horribly, and mobs seek to stone in vain. By prowess and providence Paul and the others elude their final fate time after time.

Acts 14:1–23. Two incidents help clarify how Luke makes persecution into opportunities for entertainment. Success in Iconium incited Jewish opponents. They, together with gentile supporters, plotted to stone Paul and Barnabas. Uncovering this wicked plan, the missionaries were able to escape to Lystra (14:5). Literally, the reference to stoning foreshadows what is to come. What will happen next? Can the wily opponents be foiled? Indeed, persistent in their malefaction, the Iconium mob, reinforced by an Antiochene contingent, irrupt into Lystra and, undaunted by the distance they have traveled, quickly whip up the local rabble into a frenzy of hatred. Seizing stones, they batter the apostle to the point of apparent death.[40] Roughly pitching the battered corpse outside the city limits, they, we may presume, rub their hands in satisfaction and go on, pleased with a good day's work and the death of a noxious menace. Luke then summons from offstage a crowd of believers, origin unknown, who, now that it is safe, gather to gaze with dejection at the lacerated carcass of their hero. But possibly even before they can begin to formulate plans for the requiem, lo and behold, Paul leaps to his feet and heads right back into town, the very lair and den of his enemies! The next day, apparently none the worse for wear, he completes his mission work, scoops up the faithful and unmolested Barnabas, then hastens on to convert a new city (14:19–20). Paul here appears as the typical superhero, able to shrug off a beating that would have killed any ordinary man, then return without hesitation or delay to his appointed task. Paul's equals are alive and well in western and detective books and films.[41] Ancient readers had often to enjoy, or merely endure, the apparent death of some vital character. A novel without an apparent death was all but unthinkable.[42]

Acts 21:27—22:29. The next adventure took place in Jerusalem. Paul had so impressed the arresting officer, C. Lysias, with his Hellenic status and erudition that the tribune acceded to his request for permission to address the seething mob (21:31–40). Battered as he was, Paul could still turn on enough oratorical charm (thus demonstrating a facility in Aramaic equal to that of his speeches in Greek) to calm the seething mob. All to no avail, however, for once he raised the topic of gentile believers, the ire of the crowd reerupted. Lysias (no half measures there) abandoned the procedures applicable to gentlemen of culture and ordered torture. After the apostle had been stripped and bound for flogging, as the first blow was about to strike, Paul calmly introduced a point of law: Are Roman Citizens to be treated so? All was left hanging until the officer could be summoned. In due course he arrived and learned from Paul's statement that Paul was indeed a citizen, and had been from birth. Lysias, who had bribed his way onto the rolls, was duly impressed. His soldiers shrank away from the scene of their near misdeed (22: 24–29).

Logically, this story is deficient. The time to establish citizenship was at the moment of arrest. By having Paul play first the card of Tarsian citizenship and thus display his culture, and then reveal at the very last possible moment his Roman status, Luke fills this dismal scene with drama and glitter. He has presented his readers with the perennially popular last-second rescue.

Compare Achilles Tatius, where the hero Clitophon is about to be tortured for information:

> I was therefore at once fettered, stripped naked of my clothes, and slung up on the cords, the attendants were some of them bringing the scourges, some the fire and wheel. (Achilles Tatius 7.12.2–3)[44]

Not a moment too soon, chance intervened: the priest of Artemis appeared on an embassy, causing a technical delay. So too a chance remark overheard led to removing Chaireas from the cross on which he was to die. Anthia was likewise hanged as a human sacrifice, but at the moment of greatest peril, the police arrived to rescue her.[44] These examples indicate, if proof is required, that Luke's portrayal of Paul under imminent threat of torture sounded to ancient readers, as it does to moderns, like a sensational account of last-second delivery.

Theologia Gloriae

Suffering does not really exist in these tales. Paul was indeed stoned (2 Cor. 11:25) and otherwise persecuted. For Luke, however, such experiences become opportunities to display heroic qualities. One cannot claim that Luke did not know that stoning hurt, nor can it be denied that he was aware of persecution in his own day.[45] This is indeed a theology of glory, a theology expressed in vivid and gripping popular form that would entertain no less than edify.

The leading characters of ancient novels were equally frequent victims of persecution. Popular literature often reflects the self-understanding of immature people, people of any age who see themselves as constant victims, who assign their problems to the machinations of others. This is the essential world view of the adolescent, but there are many unwilling to forsake it in later years. Thus the romantic novels, in which wicked forces and people attempt with great cunning and diligence to thwart the consummation of true love, are perfect reflections of the adolescent world.[46] The attraction of persecution in hagiography and religious novels suggests that such works were read or heard by kindred souls. At bottom the cause is envy. "Why are they doing this to me? Because they are jealous." It is thus symptomatic and typical that in Artapanus the conflict between Moses and Pharaoh Chenephres is quite personal and based upon the latter's envy.

Persecution, based upon rivalry or beauty, is the catapult that launches many romantic heroes onto their course of travel.[47] The old epic serenade is played through in a largely personal key.[48] When the persecution is for religious or political reasons, this need not represent an essential difference. Persecution, as a plot device and symptom of the spirit of the ancient novel, tends to function in similar ways despite differences in causation.[49] All who attribute the unfairness of life to external forces and love to root for the underdog can find something pleasing in tales of persecution.

Thus in Acts as well as the Apoc. Acts[50] oppression tends to be highly personal, motivated by malicious envy. Jealousy over Stephen's ability to preach and work miracles would bring him to the grave. Jews envious of Gentiles' gaining the benefits of the privileged formed raging mobs in Jerusalem, Asia, and Achaea. Economically embarrassed entrepreneurs launched persecution in Philippi and Ephesus. There is little theology here, but lots of excitement. Luke does not wrestle sympathetically, as Paul does in Romans 9—11, with the nuances of religious controversy. Those who read Acts from this viewpoint will be no less disappointed than those who watch old-time westerns expecting a sympathetic portrayal of the fate of native Americans. In both instances one is dealing with popular narration. What we do find in Acts is good guys versus villains. Neither doctrinal issues nor community experience plays a major role. Attention focuses upon the figure of the apostle engaged in dire struggle with ruthless enemies. The community comes on stage, if at all, to serve as nameless props, extras, and foils, such as the nameless hordes of Christians with whose bodies Paul had fairly littered the streets of Jerusalem and environs.

In Acts, as in ancient novels, persecution is often the springboard for travel. Missionaries move from place to place not by plan so much as through the compulsion of hostile powers. Luke describes, with apparent ingenuousness, how Paul, innocent of any political threat or intention hostile to the social order, is somehow driven from place after place by the authorities. If scholars know or suspect better, this is not because Acts has been quite candid. Persecution is for Luke a literary opportunity and a literary device.

Hagiography

Twice opposition results in death. Luke devotes seven words to the martyrdom of James, which serves to create suspense for the following episode about Peter: this Herod really will have people put to death![51] Stephen's death will get the full treatment (6:8—7:60; cf. 8:2). Just as Luke prefers in general to describe only one example of each type of incident in detail, leaving the reader to fill in the rest, so he does not seek to describe, or even mention, every martyrdom of which he has heard, but describes only those which serve his program.

Stephen's execution comes as the grand climax of the events narrated in Acts 3—7.[52] The literary stress falls upon his "trial" and death. Summary description of his skill at preaching and healing (6:5, 8) helps evoke the impression of a brief, meteoric career. Having briefly outlined his work and then narrated the arrest, Luke retards his plot at this juncture with the longest and most breathtaking speech in the book (7:2–53). The transfigured Stephen holds the Sanhedrin spellbound through a review of Bible history. Critique of cult and temple passes without demurrer, but when Stephen turns to the law, the judges rise in fury. In their zeal for the law, they lawlessly disregard even the trappings and appearance of justice. Stephen is simply hauled out and killed. But how magnificently he expires! Still transfigured,[53] battered by rocks but unbowed, the erect Hellenist offers a pious prayer for a good and noble death (*mors bona et nobilis*). That done, he carefully kneels amid the swirling stones, prays once more, this time for his enemies, then dies. His passion, like that of Jesus in Luke,[54] is more of a heroic scene than an ugly incident.

Both language and structure closely resemble the martyrological material of Apoc. Acts and hagiography.[55] Luke, rather than some source, is responsible for the shape of the episode. This is hagiography inspired by classic accounts of the deaths of statesmen and philosophers.[56]

The deaths of martyrs can be a source of inspiration. Accounts of them may also entertain. Liturgical tradition has regarded them as celebrations, leading to numerous laments from church leaders about the carousing and lovemaking that often marked the observance of "heavenly birthdays."[57] If the vigils gave the young people a chance to drink and neck, the literary form of martyrs' deaths rapidly became the most acceptable outlet for narrating sex, violence, and various sorts of adventure in the service of Christian edification.[58] Death by martyrdom is the happy ending of such works, occasional denials notwithstanding. What makes an ending happy is that it conforms to the intended reader's expectation of bliss. There are many, after all, who would not be enthralled by galloping off into the sunset trailing a woman or following a victorious horseman, but such views do not mean that westerns have tragic conclusions.[59]

In his "Life and Passion of the Holy Stephen" (Acts 6—7) Luke offers a narrative no less lurid and thrilling than many of his other episodes. The nature and manner of such narration demonstrate that the author of Acts used such material to provide his audience with inspiring adventures in which the heroes emerge victorious against awesome odds and triumph over death it-self. The death of Stephen can be repeated by others. Thereafter there will al-ways be the threat of another martyrdom. Suspense increases, and because of persecution, danger lurks at every turn. Acts stands at the beginning of a type of Christian light reading that will flourish for more than a millennium and survive into the present day.

PLOTS, CONSPIRACY, AND INTRIGUE

Addressing, for the last time, a group of presbyters from Ephesus, Paul could summarize his career as a series of "trials which befell me through the plots of the Jews" (20:19). In reality, "the Jews" had scarcely begun to plot. Even the most unobservant reader of Acts will learn that Paul's career was tumultuous not, to be sure, because he preached an incendiary gospel but be-cause of the network of intrigue erected on an ecumenical basis to discredit his activity and, if possible, destroy him. Paul's message, purged of all but the most innocuous elements, could not have caused trouble, had not jealous scions of Abraham pursued him from place to place, enraged that Gentiles might share in their blessings.[60]

Jesus and Stephen had earlier been the victims of evil high priests who ma-nipulated Pilate and suborned false witnesses. No sooner was Paul converted and preaching than a murder plot was fomented in the synagogues of Damas-cus. This was a bit strange, given the view of Acts that Jerusalem authorities could have dispatched a letter ordering his detention and extradition (9:2). The plot was even stranger. Rather than, say, execute him in his residence or cut him down on the street, "the Jews" elect, with apparent connivance from the authorities, to guard the city gates in order to slay him as he leaves town. Uncovering this vile scheme, the resourceful Paul, aided by brave disciples, makes a daring nocturnal escape (9:19b–25).

Improbabilities abound. In addition to the political problems,[61] and the strange decision to wait for Paul to win his converts and leave, there is little logic in fleeing to Jerusalem to elude a Jewish plot. Paul dashes from frying pan to fire.[62] Those who wish to defend Luke point to the agreement of this passage with 2 Cor. 11:32. There, however, Paul states that Aretas's Eth-narch attempted to capture him by securing the Damascus gates. Unable to enter another jurisdiction, it would seem, the guards patiently waited outside to make a civil arrest. Paul's story makes sense. It is also a rather un-self-complimentary joke. Not so Acts, which portrays the whole incident as a shrewd and valiant exploit. To meet apologetic and novelistic objectives, Luke has turned this story upside down.[63] This is not a commendable use of sources—not for historians.

Paul is no sooner in Jerusalem than his preaching sparks another plot (9:

25–30). This is probably editorial.[64] Presuming that Luke had a story about the Damascus episode, one can observe his use of sources here: turning that episode into a Jewish plot from which Paul cleverly escapes, he sends Paul on a trip to Jerusalem (a trip never made; Galatians 1—2) to meet with apostles (denied by Paul; Galatians 1—2), and cooks up yet another conspiracy, from which Paul is extricated by being whisked off to Tarsus, where he will apparently sit on the shelf until fetched by Barnabas (of Jerusalem). The idea that missionaries know only success which leads to persecution that sends them whirling deeper into the lions' den is the kind of thinking for which the Apoc. Acts are so often chastised. In Acts 9:19b–30 Luke inverted one incident to make it reflect credit upon his hero and then invented another.

Jewish intrigue also led to expulsion from Pisidian Antioch, headed by wealthy women and leading citizens (13:50). Jealousy was the cause. Pagan ire in Iconium likewise sprang from Jewish skulduggery (14:2). All this was to reach its peak at Lystra.[65]

Heathen conspirators got their turn at Philippi. Some religious hucksters had their life of ease rudely terminated by Paul (16:16–18). In retaliation they stirred up the mob.[66] A similar rabble at Thessalonica could not resist the blandishments of Jewish villains. Paul (and Silas) were able to evade their net (17:5–10). There was some of the same at Berea (17:13), and still more at Corinth (18:12–17).[67]

Ephesian pagans took the next round, and quite a fracas it was (19:21–41).[68] Within three verses (20:1–3) yet another Jewish cabal compelled Paul and company to proceed overland.[69] For this last incident there are some very interesting sources, showing that Luke has once again cooked up a conspiracy to gloss over what he evidently regarded as a blot in Paul's copybook.[70]

Having escaped all these entrapments, Paul goes to Jerusalem, "not knowing," as he advises the good clergy of Ephesus, "what might be in store for him" there (20:22).

Much is there in store for him (Acts 21:15–32). Having met to exchange greetings and self-congratulations with James, he would seem to have accomplished the apparent purpose of his chat (21:18–19). But there is just one small thing: Would Paul be willing to dissipate any vestiges of criticism by discharging a vow together with some other Torah-observing Christians? He would be delighted, of course. That will take a week, time enough for mischievous hands to knit a web of treachery. For six days all goes well. One may begin to breathe a sigh of relief. Then, on that seventh and final day (21:27), just as the ritual is drawing to a close (leaving Paul free to depart for Rome), some Jews from Asia Minor incite a riot that will quickly end in death. Only the intervention of the attentive soldiery of Rome saves him (21:31–33).

The very next day, unwittingly delivered to the Sanhedrin (a body that, as all who have read of Stephen's end know, will kill him, legally or otherwise), Paul counters with a little intrigue of his own (22:30—23:10). Livid at yet one more humiliation, more than forty zealots concoct a desperate conspiracy.[71] How they are foiled constitutes the most elaborate account of a conspiracy in Acts (23:12–25). Just here, when Paul goes permanently into confinement, Luke goes into an unusual degree of elaboration. Had he merely noted that Paul had been dispatched to Caesarea, left to languish there for a couple of years, and then been dispatched to Rome for the resolution of his legal problems, the author would be open to no censure as a historian. Had he devoted a good bit of ink to unraveling the complex legal knots, that would have been ink well spilt. Instead we are regaled with nine chapters (20—28) demonstrating how much Paul impressed his captors, how his opponents failed to kill him, and how he survived shipwreck to get to Rome. The final third of Acts is probably the most entertaining segment of the work. Its contributions to the specific history of the Christian mission are rather limited. Any definition of its genre needs to take these items into account.

Acts 23:12–35. This is a timeless tale of high adventure which, in any other work, would be called pure entertainment. Paul will be ambushed when brought before the Sanhedrin on the pretext of a theological examination.[72] Fortunately, a nephew learns of their scheme and has the presence of mind to visit his uncle at once. Paul receives him without delay and listens with attention, then beckons a centurion with orders to convey the lad to the tribune. Lysias, quickly perceiving the need for secrecy, allays the young man's anxiety and escorts him to a private spot.[73] Nephew gives him the oath, verbatim. Lysias springs into action. He dismisses the boy with an admonition to silence, summons two tribunes, and with professional ease dictates orders for a rescue mission. Urgency and security both recommend a nocturnal operation. So it will be. The requisite force will trim the tribune's garrison to the danger point, but the value of the prisoner seems worth the risk. Pausing in the midst of these crisp commands, Lysias dashes off a communication to his superior, Felix, giving him a cogent résumé of the case as he sees it. Lysias's well-planned and ably executed combination of speed, force, and surprise succeeds. After a night march of forty miles, the infantry may return to base. From that point a seventy-horse escort will be adequate. "Operation Paul" was a bold move. Jerusalem could have gone up in smoke. It required 470 men and two days to rescue Paul from the hands of his co-religionists.

Numerous contradictions and improbabilities aside, this tale is a rousing success. "A dreary matter of routine is transformed into a narrative full of breathless suspense,"[74] noted Haenchen. While enjoying the excitement, the reader is assured, not for either the first or the last time, that Paul is a VIP. Through giving us a chance to read Lysias's letter Luke lets us know what this official thought about Paul's guilt. Direct speech and precise details also contribute to the vividness of this military adventure. Those who envision Luke patiently taking careful notes of all this have surely missed the woods for the trees.

Opponents like Paul's will not give up easily, of course. When a new procurator, Festus, arrives, the "high priest and leading citizens" try to renew their old game. Behind an apparently thoughtful suggestion lurks a plot to ambush Paul on the highway. Festus, who has assumed his office with high ideals, will not succumb. Another plot is thwarted (25:1–6a). Luke appears to have painted himself into a corner here. The idea of an ambush on the open road (minus the 470 escorts) is the author's explanation for the necessity of Paul's appeal, even when all in authority affirm his innocence. To achieve this he seems to have cooked up one more conspiracy and had Festus unintentionally quash it. Festus will not, alas, live up to his initial promise and release Paul after a hearing. The explanation for this appears shortly: Festus is more intent upon currying favor from his subjects than in showing justice to a wronged citizen.[75] In both 24:26–27 and 25:9 Luke shifts gears and thereby the characters of the respective governors. Initially honest, they are ultimately corrupt. Present-day readers, influenced by Josephus and Tacitus, are inclined to see the procurators as rascals and overlook Luke's quick shifts in characterization. Having persons change characters like coats as a means of cutting literary knots is a license taken by popular writers.[76]

The net result is that Paul's imprisonment in Palestine is redolent of intrigue. The consistent policy of the Sanhedrin was the extrication of this prisoner from Roman hands in order to do away with him. For both Sanhedrin and imperium Paul constituted a major priority. He was first on the subjects' agenda for a new governor, and the case was of no small interest to Rome. While regaling his readers with a potpourri of splendid adventures, Luke has also managed to make these conspiracies explain why Paul was not discharged and thus why he went as a prisoner to Rome. He has presented a piece of historical fiction.[77]

Ancient novelists found intrigue and conspiracy no less useful. In Jewish novels the gentile schemers differ in no essential way from the adversaries faced by Paul. In *Joseph and Asenath*, for example, there is a conspiracy to ambush Asenath on the road, the chief architect of which is heir to the throne, moved by jealousy that Joseph "got the girl" (23–28). Needless to say, the plot is foiled, God stepping in to lend the heroes a hand. There is enough harem scheming, court intrigue, and conspiracy in the book of Esther to satisfy even the most avid appetite for oriental soap opera.[78]

Artapanus borrowed from the novelist's repertory to enrich his account of the life of Moses by introducing conspiracies aimed at the hero. Evil Chenephres, jealous because of Moses' civilizing innovations, tries to do away with him by ordering that he invade Ethiopia with an army of untrained peasants. After Moses is nonetheless victorious, Pharaoh strips him of this command and alienates his Egyptian lieutenants. Assassins are secretly sworn. They back out. Pharaoh does not. Having gained the allegiance of one Chanethothes, he dispatches Moses on a diplomatic mission, planning to ambush him on the road. An insider reveals the plot. In flight (on advice from Aaron) to Arabia, Moses meets and kills Chanethothes in single combat.[79] The resemblance to Acts requires no comment.

Romantic novelists also knew how to make use of such a good thing. The storybook nuptials of Chaireas and Callirhoe had scarcely ended before certain jealous rival suitors began to plot (Chariton 1.2.4ff.). Their endeavors caused the unlucky couple to begin a long series of adventures, each phase of which was sparked by yet more intrigue. Chariton used such intrigue to motivate his plot.[80]

Heliodorus's pair of lovers barely escaped a net of amorous intrigue cast by an Egyptian princess in a nocturnal escape reminiscent of Acts 23:12ff. (Heliodorus 7–8). Clitophon likewise had to overcome a dire conspiracy designed to rob him of his beloved. Various novelists wrote novels cut to quite different patterns from various types of material, but for nearly all of them, plots and conspiracies served to generate action and create adventure.[81]

Apollonius of Tyana's experiences closely resembled Paul's. Intrigue in the court of Nero brought him into grave peril. The sage countered Tigellinus's evil maneuvers by helping launch the conspiracy that would unseat Nero (*Ap. Ty.* 4.35–47, 5.7–13). Domitian used every dirty trick known to tyrants (7.27ff.). Apollonius had, therefore, to battle charges of wizardry and subversion. By strength of character and piety he was able to win the allegiance of good people and even receive aid from on high.

Conspiracies thus served Luke literarily to propel his plot along its appointed course. Thematically, reference to intrigue explains why such characters had such nasty things said about them. Excellent analogies to his practice may be found in the works of historical, and even romantic, novelists.

CROWDS, MOBS, RIOTS, AND ASSEMBLIES

The fickle crowd of the ancient Mediterranean is never far offstage in Acts. Whether to flood the streets or fill a synagogue, to listen to a sermon or conduct a lynching, the masses stand ready. Wherever they exist, the crowds represent the potential for riot, disorder that will reduce Roman rule to chaos. Luke found in the urban mob a handy tool, either for glorifying the apostles or for villifying them. As an antithesis to the unruliness of pagan and Jewish crowds there emerges the orderly structure of Christian meetings, in which crowds behave just as the imperial masters believe they ought to act.

The constant presence of the mob reflects Acts' urban orientation. Missionaries do not hesitate to perform public healings and thereby attract a crowd, which, lured by the spectacle, may be enticed to remain and hear some good preaching. Pagan clergy may lure gullible hordes with fraudulent marvels, pass the hat, and then pull out. Not so the apostles.[82]

From the outset the crowds attracted represent every nation under heaven: Jews from everywhere, learned Greeks, Roman colonists, polished provincials, and the yokels of upcountry Asia Minor. Quantity was no less impressive than variety. Audience reaction to the preaching of Peter and Paul established these speeches as scarcely less marvelous in their character than healings.[83]

As an accomplished orator, Paul could soothe an unruly crowd with speech. At Lystra he and Barnabas were able to elevate the religious outlook of some superstitious countryfolk through administration of an emergency dose of natural theology (Acts 14:14–18).[84] Paul calmed the Jerusalem mob with a gesture, and would have done the same at Ephesus had he not been dissuaded by the Asiarchs (21:40; 19:30–31). Vergil describes the species:

> When rioting breaks out in a great city,
> and the rampaging rabble goes so far
> that stones fly, and incendiary brands—
> for anger can supply that kind of weapon—
> if it so happens they look round and see
> Some dedicated public man, a veteran
> whose record gives him weight, they quiet down,
> Willing to stop and listen.
> Then he prevails in speech over their fury
> By his authority, and placates them.
> (*Aeneid* 1.148–53)[85]

No less dignified was Apollonius, who like Paul could quell a riot by "manual gesture or by look upon his face."[86]

Just as hostile crowds might goad officials into punishing the innocent, so friendly supporters could require circumspection. Popular support hampered the efforts of the Sanhedrin against the apostles (4:21; 5:25–26), and the Corinthian herd apparently switched sides to mob Paul's accuser (18:17).

Romantic novels portray remarkably similar crowds. In them beauty is the cause of admiration. The appearance of a heroine is an epiphany. We learn of her beauty by observing the reaction of the crowd:

Because of the girl's [Callirhoe's] beauty and her unfamiliar appearance the more humble class of people was persuaded that she was some nymph . . . or . . . a goddess. . . . All, however, had but one desire and that was to see Callirhoe. . . . She looked out. . . . All of them shouted, "It is Aphrodite who is the bride! . . . Not a person, young or old, was left inside the houses. . . . The crowd climbed up to roof tiles . . . [and later] whole cities came out; . . . the streets were crowded . . . and to all the girl seemed even to surpass the report made of her. (Chariton 3.12.17, 4.7.5)[87]

To see such glamour or to celebrate reunions, to witness trials and make their views known, and for many other reasons, the crowds pour into streets or theater.[88] Such scenes reflect an important facet of civic life. Where crowds gather, there factions may form. This proclivity to factionalism, stringently resisted by appeals to *homonoia* (oneness of mind, unanimity) is mirrored in the text of Acts. City or audience may divide, sometimes violently so, for or against the message.[89]

Novelists exploit the same device:

When Clinias had finished this speech, the majority . . . were convinced by his argument; but Thersander's Counsel, and those . . . with him, shouted for the sentencing of the murderer. (Achilles Tatius 8.7.1)[90]

It will come as no surprise to discover that supporters of the protagonist are normally decorous, whereas those in opposition may be so unseemly as to foment unrest.[91]

Luke is not reluctant to explain much of the difficulty experienced by primitive Christian missionaries as due to the volatile *Lumpenproletariat* of the cities. On at least eleven occasions mob or riot scenes are described:

1. 6:12; 7:56–58. Stephen stoned
2. 14:4–5. Attempt to stone at Iconium
3. 14:19–20. Paul stoned at Lystra
4. 16:19–23. Mobs at Philippi
5. 17:5–9. Mob at Thessalonica
6. 17:13. Agitation in Berea
7. 18:12–17. Mob at Corinth
8. 19:21–40. Riot at Ephesus
9. 21:26—22:24. Lynch mob in temple
10. 23:7–10. "Riot" in Sanhedrin
11. 25:24. Festus pressured by crowds

If one of Luke's two villains is "the Jews," the urban rabble is the other. Since the ruling class did not regard such gatherings as desirable manifestations of popular democracy, pointing the finger at them would in no way discredit the Christian movement. Like Gallio, Luke does not admit refined discussions of halachic controversies. Instead of such potentially tiresome and disturbing debates, he much prefers to describe an exciting riot.

Attentive readers will soon discover that Jewish legal process is scarcely different from pagan lynchings. This subtle principle is manifestly operative in the "trial" of Stephen. Rather than deliberate issues, the Sanhedrin will, later, turn into a real donnybrook (23:7–10). So violent are the judges that Lysias fears for Paul's life. For Luke the Sanhedrin is a lynch mob with official sanction and permanent standing. Where the sway of the Sanhedrin does not extend, Jewish provocateurs will have to do, and they do very well. To demonstrate his lack of bias Luke does not hesitate to depict gentile disturbances. The two climactic riots are evenly balanced: one at Ephesus, one at Jerusalem. Not until that final disruption is Paul ever seriously delayed or severely injured. Despite all of this violence, he could by the end of the story still preach unhindered at Rome. The mob may have delayed his progress, but they got him a free ticket.

The facts, naturally, are less tidy. Luke does not portray Paul's acceptance of synagogue discipline (2 Cor. 11:24) nor the anguish of lengthy imprisonment (as in the opening of Philippians). Not all of Paul's problems came from rowdies. Readers of his letters hear much more about internal dissent and rival Christian interpretations. Luke's substantial simplification of Paul's and others' situations reveals his tastes and objectives. Hostile mobs provide exciting reading and cast mud upon the opposition. Views are not given a serious canvass. This is vulgar propaganda.

For variety of detail and incident the author must get the usual high marks. No two events are quite alike. Causes and outcomes differ, and the potentially boring sequence of riots does not pall. Rather than state that civic unrest often required Paul to seek a new base, Luke likes to have his riots bring a missionary visit to a rousing climax. In place of the *via crucis* (the Way of the Cross) there stands a literary device.

Acts 19:21–40. The famous riot at Ephesus is the showcase exhibit of social disorder. This justly famous passage gains high praise for its verisimilitude.[92] There are many good parallels in novels.[93] Granted that the passage deserves merit for its vivid and exciting evocation of urban life, one must still ask why Luke, who has devoted so little space to Paul's pastoral and missionary work in this, one of his most important centers, spends twenty verses on a spectacular display of fireworks, the net effect of which is to deflect attention from the serious trouble into which Paul got at Ephesus.[94] The use of a similar ploy at Jerusalem two chapters later (chap. 21) supports the contention that this obscurity is due to Luke. If early church history must be seen through a glass darkly, that is in part due to this "historian"'s fondness for smokescreens rather than mirrors.

Civil disorder was a continual problem for Rome, although religion was not often its cause.[95] The mob was a pressure group and seems to have been responsible for initiating many of the pre-Decian persecutions.[96] Magistrates must often have held Christians responsible for disorder and not just its victims.[97] Luke may well have experienced and heard of such violent outbreaks. He chose instead to narrate scenes depicted with the palette of the emergent hagiographic tradition: angry crowds, bold Christian witnesses, honest and sympathetic officials, fixed vocabulary, and recurrent motifs.[98]

These goals resemble those of the Apologists. The methods are those of martyrological romancers. When trouble erupts over Christianity, this is the scream of *barbara superstitio*[99] threatened with extinction. Good rulers will hold their ground, but weak ones fold and tyrants cannot be trusted to deliver justice. The same technique appears in Philostratus's treatment of Apollonius.[100]

This topic provides an apt point for comparison of Acts with ancient historiography. Two of Erich Auerbach's leading illustrations of ancient writers' lack of concern for the behavior and motives of ordinary people are mob scenes from Latin historians.[101] Realistic language was scorned by learned authors. Verisimilitude is quite seductive, but a critical perspective must recognize that verisimilitude does not guarantee accuracy. Fiction requires some conventions of realism, to be acceptable. But the sort of realism to which modern readers are accustomed is rather recent. Such realism was not an ancient expectation, particularly not of historians. In the case of Luke's Gospel it is possible to observe that the writer often contributes realistic details to his source (see esp. Luke 4:16–30). The "western text," especially Codex Bezae, is fond of adding realistic details. These warnings need to be taken seriously. Verisimilitude does not guarantee accuracy of reporting. With regard to ancient literature, the opposite is likely to be the case, in particular where the matters reported have to do with the experiences of the common people.

Spontaneous assemblies in the local theater were a favorite convention of ancient novelists. Such events brought the readers into the scene as participants:

> Here they [the masses] experienced excitement, here they felt their power a little, and a kind of patriotism. . . . Lesser folk made their weight felt in the theatre by disciplining their cheers to a unison. . . . The connection that existed between the people as an audience and the people as an assembly in the constitutional sense [was] a connection made express in the use of theatres for mass meetings.[102]

Evidence for that sense of excited participation abounds in the pages of ancient novels. Crowds flock to the theater, often to try some legal issue, rather than debate politics. Like the Ephesians they may shout acclamations. Even in the romantic novels a hostile crowd may prevent justice from taking its course. Fickle crowds may be stampeded into a hasty execution of participatory capital punishment:

"On your honours, fellow Roman citizens . . . take severe vengeance on this wickedly plotting woman. . . ." The mob grew restive, excited into crediting the charge on mere grounds of probability; they shouted for firebrands; they looked for stones; they encouraged the lads to lynch the woman. (Apuleius 2.27)[103]

Stoning was the common means for such justice,[104] and the innocent could be threatened no less than the guilty. Chaireas, convinced of his own guilt, begs the assembly to stone him to death (Chariton 1.4). Apollonius of Tyana led the entire electorate of the city to the theatre and had them stone a demon (*Ap. Ty.* 4.10).

Admirers of popular Greek literature would find nothing deficient in the tale of Susanna. Wicked elders convene the assembly to condemn the beautiful and innocent heroine, but after God has come to her rescue, the whole assembly shouts as one (and has done to them what they would have done to her).[105] *Third Maccabees* features both Jewish crowds at Jerusalem and a pagan mob at Alexandria.[106]

The excitable crowd, unpredictable and changing, is thus a regular feature in Greek and Latin novels, as well as in Acts, the Apoc. Acts, and hagiography. It functions as a composite character, one with which the readers may sometimes identify. In Acts, as in these other works, crowds enhance the entertainment value of the work.

Church Councils and Meetings

Cicero—and he was not alone in this matter—did not find the procedure of Greek assemblies orderly:

Thus he extorted those "elegant" decrees read to you—decrees passed neither by formal vote nor proper authority, nor even hallowed by oath, but carried by the upraised hands and loud shouts of an excited mob. (Cicero *Pro Flacco* 15–16)

Acts takes pains to illustrate the contrast between the tumultuous clamor of those assemblies, the Jewish "senate," and the decorous action of the Christian *ekklesia*. In addition to Acts 15 there are several "church councils," for Luke wishes to make clear how seemly the Jerusalem church is—"an idealized version of . . . many other Hellenistic religious associations."[107]

Acts 1:15–26: Replenishment of the apostolic college.[108] Peter arises to address the postascension assembly of 120 persons.[109] His formal (*andres adelphoi;* v. 16) speech, cast in LXX style, crisply summarizes the fate of Judas and the need to fill the vacant office (*episkopē;* v. 20b).[110] After qualifications are stated, two qualified candidates emerge and the assembly prays in unison. Luke had no interest in conjuring up some harebrained sect. *Synkatepsephisthe,* "he was enrolled" (v. 26), has an electoral ring to it. Lots were often cast in constitutional assemblies to choose officials,[111] and the church here operates like a Greek city council. Luke no doubt made use of traditional elements, but he has shaped them to fit his purpose.[112] The picture of a young church acting like a formal senate with fixed criteria, stated rules, and the like is not the result of a reconstruction so much as it is a pleasing invention. The first Christians were dignified and respectable.[113]

Acts 6:1–6: Bureaucratic reform. Food supply was a problem for many ancient cities. Rapid growth and expansion of the community of believers led to allegations of ethnic bias. The Twelve convene the citizen body, as it were.[114] The solution emerges promptly in a brief but elegant speech. Once again qualifications for office are stated. Seven are chosen. Christians could quickly and efficiently handle so sensitive a matter by developing a new layer of bureaucracy staffed by competent persons democratically selected.

Once chosen, these Seven do not for a moment resemble welfare officials but go directly to the people, preaching great sermons and working great miracles, venturing to far-off places. Bureaucrats were not expected to perform miracles nor to be martyred for their principles. The perceptible dissonance between Luke's Seven and their appointed task stems, of course, from his desire to subordinate this group to the Twelve and assign them innocuous tasks. In reality the Seven were a rival group with a different theological program.[115] Two birds fall with a single stone: the church glows with undivided gentility, and a competing group evaporates into a group of grocery boys.

Acts 11:2–18: Dress rehearsal for the apostolic council. Without reference to the trappings of a formal assembly, Luke narrates how the gentile issue will be settled. Peter has returned from his conversion of Cornelius to learn that "those of the circumcision"[116] are displeased. After a speech "comprehensible only to the readers of the book,"[117] all are satisfied. God can even save Gentiles. Luke has composed this incident with an eye to the problem of the gentile mission, responsibility for which belongs to God, who attested divine favor in the presence of Peter "long before" the trouble at Antioch brewed.

Acts 15:1–29: The apostolic council. Having settled the issue, Luke can now present a moving account of the crucial encounter of the apostolic council. The account is splendid, so long as one is not seeking facts.[118] Paul and Barnabas return from a mission to learn that anonymous accusers have appointed themselves judges. The community solemnly dispatch Paul, Barnabas, and some others.[119] These ambassadors do not slink hastily down to Jerusalem but stop for visits at other sites. At Jerusalem they meet with an equally solemn assembly of all orders who listen to their report, a medley of miracles. Christian Pharisees politely demand obedience to the Torah. The audience receives this proposal as if it were a brand-new notion. Orderly debate, managed by the leaders, ensues until, "when excitement and conflict have reached their peak, Peter intervenes and with one stroke clarifies the situation."[120] Reminding them of the evidently overlooked case of Cornelius and dismissing the Torah as impossible of observance, Peter closes with a touch of "Paulinism" (v. 11). Awesome silence prevails, after which Paul and Barnabas rise to supplement Peter's theology with some aretalogy (v. 12). James then steps forward for a brief speech (vv. 13–21), followed by a formal resolution, the wording of which apes the diction of civic and other corporate organizations (v. 22).[121] Like many governmental directives, this "decree" is couched in the form of a letter (vv. 23–29), to be delivered by selected ambassadors, "prophets."[122] Another potential danger dissolves in a glittering conclave of good will and fine manners.

Acts 15 is indisputably Luke's most compelling account of a church meeting. Narrative suspense, elegant rhetoric, and correct procedure justify its traditional title.[123] Despite violent contradictions with Galatians 2, this attractive account continues to exert seductive force. Early readers would sense the same attraction and revel in the stateliness of their ancestral assemblies.

Acts 21:18–25: Paul and the Jewish Christians. Vicious rumors against Paul persist, so James and the elders formally consult with Paul and his entourage. They present a plan for cleansing the gentile missionary of all stigma. This may in fact have been the most spirited meeting of all. Its actual purpose was presentation of "the Collection." Luke certainly knew more than he chose to share, with the result that the outcome of this meeting is probably permanently obscured.[124] Historians have no reason to be grateful about any of these reports.

Each of the five meetings reported in Acts comes at a significant point in the community's life and growth. Not one resolves pressing historical issues or commands much credibility. The first treats of the Twelve, who then slowly fade into an early obscurity. The rest deal with the gentile mission in a way that really illuminates only the problems faced by Luke. Literarily, they provide nice changes of pace from the constant cycle of adventures and give scope for some pleasing oratory. Socially, they enhance the image of the church as an organization able to control the unstable masses, "teach 'em some manners," and subordinate obedient followers to strong rulers. The Christian community enjoys *homonoia* and eschews unproductive *stasis*.[125] Factionalism (*stasis*) is not a problem for Christians. Historically, the reports of the meetings gloss over very important conflicts and transitions.[126]

The early church displayed in Acts is a place where *amor vincit omnia* (love conquers all things) and people live happily in unity, harmony, and peace. The usual term for such depiction is "romantic," and that term is certainly apt here. The romantic portrayal was due to neither ignorance nor naiveté. Luke did have at least a faint glimmering that things had been otherwise. He wrote what he wanted to write.

Even in the novels with love stories at their basis, the assembly may often gather to hear reports, give judgment, and approve courses of action. The *ekklesia* of Syracuse regularly meets to deal with each major development of Chariton's plot. No issues of policy seemed more pressing to them than the fate of Chaireas and Callirhoe.[127]

In Chariton 3:4–5 the *ekklesia* is convoked to hear about a search for the heroine. Different ideas come forth, Hermocrates speaking for strict adherence to legal practice and the dispatch of an embassy, and before

> he had finished speaking, the members of the Assembly shouted . . . but Hermocrates said . . . so they decided and this it was decreed and thereupon he dismissed the assembly. (Chariton 3.4)[128]

This representative scene[129] indicates how the first audience of Acts might relate to its accounts of assemblies. As a literary device the accounts strike today's readers as highly artificial, but frequent use suggests that ancient audiences must have loved to read of such meetings of the *plēthos* (entire community). From the ideal perspective they show wholly decent people taking their place in community life, quite unlike the herds that packed arenas to view massacre and mime.[130] All testify to the end of older Greek civic life. In Acts the rootless citizens of the Mediterranean create for themselves a new community and people. The audiences of the romantic novels meet to debate purely individual matters, including the pursuit of erotic adventures.

Crowds therefore play an important part in both the literary and the ideological structure of Acts. Friendly crowds attest to the appeal of the young movement. Opposition is often foisted off upon the notorious rabble, not in the least to its credit. Mob action sparks adventures and provides a frequent excuse for embarrassing legal embroilments. The orderly convocations of Christian leaders with their docile disciples make a pleasant contrast to the idlers about Aegean agoras and the temperamental congregations of the Jerusalem temple.[131]

TRIALS, LEGAL ACTIONS, AND PUNISHMENT

Callirhoe lamented, "This is the one thing which was yet lacking in my misfortunes—to be dragged into court!" (Chariton 5.5, Blake). She would have many companions in grief before the ancient novel had seen its last. The dramatic opportunities inherent in courtroom scenes were no more over-looked by ancient writers than by their successors down to the present time. Innocent victims wrongly accused, lovers, travelers, missionaries, philoso-phers, and politicians must face tyrants and seek vindication.

Trials have been exploited for their propaganda value since antiquity.[132] They allow the presentation of weighty ideas in exciting dress. About one-fifth of Acts treats juridical conflicts:

1. 4:5–22. Peter and John by the Sanhedrin
2. 5:28–42. The Twelve by the Sanhedrin
3. 6:12—7:54. Stephen by the Sanhedrin
4. 17:18–33. Paul by the Areopagus
5. 18:12–17. Paul by Gallio
6. 22:30—23:11. Paul by the Sanhedrin
7. 24:1–23. Paul by Felix
8. 25:6–12. Paul by Festus
9. 25:23—26:32. Paul by Festus and Agrippa

Other legal actions include

10. 8:1b (cf. 9:1–2). Official persecution by the Sanhedrin
11. 16:19–24. Arraignment and punishment in Philippi
12. 17:5–9. Hearing in Thessalonica
13. 22:24. Interrogation in Jerusalem

Moreover, Paul's legal difficulties are the focus of the text from Acts 21:27 to the end. Legal struggles are a major interest of Luke, gaining much more attention than a host of doctrinal and ecclesiastical issues of concern to mod-ern historians. The net result of all this is perhaps disappointing, since no clarity emerges. If the accounts do little to illuminate the legal situation of early Christians, they do make for pleasant diversion.

Acts 4:5–22.[133] Peter and John, seized for offending the Sadducees (who came along to lend a hand in the detention), spent a night in custody and were released with an admonition to desist. In the hagiographic tradition, they boldly resisted tyranny and made a propaganda speech, like philoso-phers.[134] Dismissed by the judges, they waited outside for the Sanhedrin to find a solution. In omniscient style, Luke reports the deliberations. The judges look like bullies, but the apostles resemble Socrates. Despite the real-istic details, difficulties abound.[135] As drama, it is a rousing success. The stage is set. The apostles are not magicians but honest teachers. Their oppo-nents are a pack of fascist clowns, reduced to silence with a few inspired words. Haenchen's insistence that Luke was convinced of the accuracy of his report is dubious.[136] The distinction between fantasy and reality is no less important for historians than for others.

Acts 5:28–42.[137] Round two: The injunction disregarded, the Sanhedrin arrests all the Apostles. Except for the inconvenient delay of a miraculous release, the earlier charges and defenses are reiterated. The judges fume. Enough is enough. "In these dire straits, with martyrdom all but certain, the apostles are saved by the intervention of Gamaliel."[138] Spared from execution, they receive another warning, punctuated with a touch of the whip. This trial, which is probably a Lukan composition, also possesses glaring flaws.[139] Inconsistent as it is, there are within twenty-five verses a frightening arrest, a marvelous delivery, a thrilling trial, two good speeches, some real suspense, bold opposition to oppression, and a soupçon of violence. The position is now apparent. The early Christians, supported by the Pharisees and the crowd, are hated by the Sadducees for preaching resurrection. Their leaders are wholly admirable. Their opponents are not.

Acts 6:12—7:54.[140] Official villainy reached its peak in the murder of Stephen. In this material there are traces of sources, into which Luke inserted the speech and made certain other modifications.[141] Since Acts 6:8–11(?12) does not refer to the Sanhedrin, and the charges, when repeated, are borrowed from Mark 14:57–58, the inclusion of the Sanhedrin appears secondary. Detailed study of the martyrdom scene suggests that the source spoke of a lynch mob rather than a trial.[142] The outcome of this is a travesty of justice. The Sanhedrin hastily assemble at the prospect of Hellenist blood, sit back to listen to the longest address in Acts, and then degenerate into a mob armed with stones. No respect for the Sanhedrin as an instrument of justice can remain. The stirring sermon[143] gives Luke's readers the chance to enjoy seeing the enemy told off in the most effective way, by a prospective martyr whose face literally glows with inspiration. The more attentive would also have observed that, as hints of the gentile mission increase, violence expands.

Acts 17:16–33.[144] Fondly ruminating about Paul in Athens, Sir William Ramsay stated,

> Here alone he stands amid the surroundings of a great university, disputing with its brilliant and learned teachers; and here, as in every other situation, he adapts himself with his usual versatility to the surroundings and moves in them as to the manner born.[145]

All very well, but just what did happen here? Was Paul tried, given an informal hearing, examined for orthodoxy, or merely invited to offer a guest lecture? The best answer is probably to see this as a trial of the faith itself. The new movement is *paideia* (education), not superstition, as determined by its reception in this most educated of settings.

The Areopagus is one of those Athenian motifs "which at that time nearly every half-educated person recognized as specifically Athenian."[146] This patina of classical nostalgia is found in other popular writings.[147] The prestige of the Areopagus could not be overlooked.

Opening with an evocation of Socrates, and its concomitant threat of danger, Luke turns to a proper setting for this case, the elite Areopagus. The apparatus of a trial is present, with all the excitement thereunto attending, but here as elsewhere there is no suggestion of a verdict.[148] Inconsistency does not disturb this author. Insofar as a trial contributes to the excitement, he will suggest that it took place. At the point of difficulty, the hearing seems to become a lecture. "What we see here is an 'ideal scene' which baffles every attempt to translate it into reality."[149] "Ideal" is, of course, a euphemism for "fictional."

Luke apparently intended Paul's speech (17:22–31) to be his best rhetorical effort. He succeeded. The thought of Paul holding the rapt attention of Greek philosophers in these august surroundings surely delighted early audiences no less than it did Ramsay.[150] It is impressive testimony to what Luke could accomplish without the assistance of evident sources.[151]

Acts 18:12–17. On Paul's first appearance before a Roman bench, the only question is whether Roman law need take notice of Christianity. Unlike others,[152] Gallio answers with such an emphatic no that the plaintiffs are mobbed. The account is legendary in form and contains humor, propaganda, and suspense. The historical and legal questions are fuzzy.[153]

Hitherto the trials have served to advance the plot or bring a phase of mission to a close. From this point on the legal situation will be central. Isolation of Paul's trials in Judea does not do justice to their inclusion within a carefully constructed literary whole. For the last eight chapters of Acts, Paul maneuvers to evade the clutches of the Sanhedrin until, all else having failed, he files an appeal and thus lands, at the book's conclusion, safely in the haven of Rome.

Acts 22:30—23:11. The Sanhedrin will regain no prestige as they fall out over Paul. Summoned into order by a Roman tribune,[154] they are to examine the Roman prisoner and citizen. Paul, no doubt familiar with Sanhedrin procedure from his service in that body, seizes the floor to proclaim his innocence. The high priest has one of his lackeys fetch the apostle a slap.[155] Undaunted by such brutality, Paul boldly rebukes this practice, but repents when advised that he has abused the pontiff.[156] More than a slap is in the offing, so Paul ingeniously seizes the initiative a second time with a claim that starts a brawl (v. 7). Fearing for Paul's safety, Lysias summons additional troops to rescue the missionary. This incredible story[157] depends upon the presumed result: a sentence of death. As in Corinth, the opposition is laughed off the stage. As for the Sanhedrin, it is capable of anything.

Acts 24:1–23. Rescued by Rome from a conspiracy, Paul is taken to Felix, who promises prompt action. Five days later, it comes. The accusers, with one Tertullus, a rhetor, sagely in tow, arrive to make their case. Their attorney leads off with a sparkling little speech (vv. 2b–8), not nearly long enough to be realistic but long enough to show that Paul must face major-league talent.[158] Suspense is raised. Paul has been charged with being a scab on the body politic, who, most recently, desecrated the temple. Paul, who can hold his own against trained Greek orators, speaks for himself (vv. 10–21), until, when his apology has begun to resemble a missionary sermon, Felix interrupts. The trial will resume when Lysias puts in a personal appearance. Things begin to improve for Paul, and this suggests that Felix must be dubious about the charges. He would grant no privileges to an ecumenical menace. But somehow Lysias never comes and Felix begins to backslide. Justice will have to await a new procurator.

Acts 25:6b–12. One arrives by and by, M. Porcius Festus. Things begin all over again. Lysias has been forgotten, but Paul now begins to deny offense against Jewish law, temple, and Caesar. Why Caesar? At any rate, the trial is over. The verdict is . . . a request for the case to be tried in Jerusalem! Paul, in desperate straits, since journey there means certain death, lodges an appeal.

Once more the historical situation is an unmanageable tangle.[159] No sense can be made of the results or the process as presented. The longer Luke's spotlight shines upon Paul's trial, the more his readers are in the dark.

Acts 26:1–32. So Paul is bound for Rome, but not until some visiting royalty drop by to provide a suitable setting for yet another information-gathering session, the very object that Rome has pursued since Paul's arrest. Although this is not a trial, it does have a verdict of sorts. Although this is not a trial, Paul makes use of the occasion to give his most comprehensive defense yet. With Agrippa, expert on Judaica, present, Paul gives the most atticistic of his speeches. It is all a cozy scene, ending with a wistful "This man could have been set free if he had not appealed to Caesar" (v. 32). Only seekers after facts will leave the hall disappointed.

F. F. Bruce, no carping skeptic, commented that "artistic and powerful as the conclusion is, it is strange that Luke has not told us explicitly what the result of Paul's appeal was."[160] After eight chapters (Acts 21—28) focused upon Paul's legal problems, the reader no longer understands why he is under arrest, of what he is really charged, why he appealed in the first place, or why he did not withdraw his appeal later. As an apology for Paul and for the faith, and as a stirring and appealing narrative, the last third of Acts leaves little to be desired. Here Luke has lavished his atttention and skill, but it is also here that he will receive some of his worst marks as a historian. He appears by a historical criterion to be doing his worst when at his best. The criterion may be at fault.

Extracanonical parallels. Trials and legal difficulties play similar roles in the Apoc. Acts. About one fourth of the *Acts of Thomas* (126–170) and *Acts of Peter* (30–41) describe the last trials. These Acts do end with the death of their heroes, which, although not the stopping point of the canonical work, is nonetheless a reasonable place to stop. H. Delehaye and H. A. Musurillo point out that in hagiography, elaborate, fictitious accounts of trials are more popular than genuine reports. Delehaye's "epic" genre includes among its recurrent features a fondness for detailed descriptions of the judge and his entourage, personal confrontations between judge and defendant, verisimilitude (when magistrates are good), stereotypes like wicked judges, and a tendency to multiply incidents, prolong interrogations, and move from place to place.[161] So similar is this practice to Luke's that it should be important evidence for evaluating the proclivity of Acts.[162]

Another noteworthy parallel from later literature is the story of Apollonius, who went to Rome in the face of gloomy warnings (*Ap. Ty.* 7.9–16, esp. 12). Falsely accused of crimes both religious and political, Apollonius was sustained by right-thinking officials and despised by tyrants (7.9, 7.11, 7.16). In his case, also, the defense led to protracted proceedings that constitute a good fourth of the book. Apollonius defended himself in the best speech his biographer could muster (8.7). The trial ended with a confusing acquittal (8.5). This sample of substantive parallels[163] suggests that, despite the difference in date and style, the two works have a similar purpose and draw from a common pool of motifs.

Trials were no less a part of the conventional repertory of romantic and other novels. In addition to being a sure-fire technique for producing suspense, they were excellent settings for astonishing revelations, recognitions, and denouements, as well as impressive oratory.

Denouements also emerge in the course of trials in Achilles Tatius and Heliodorus. The last part of Chariton is surrounded by the nimbus of the trial begun in book 5.[164] The dramatic structure of Luke's work would make good sense to the readers of ancient novels.

Trials can produce surprises galore. When all seems lost, a new speaker may arise to set things right:

They became infuriated and determined to kill them. Then there arose in the Sanhedrin a Pharisee by the name of Gamaliel. . . . (Acts 5:33–34)

With these words Dionysius aroused the emotions of the audience and he unquestionably had their vote. The king, too, [was] moved to anger; . . . while he [Mithridates] was still speaking, . . . Chaereas himself stepped forward. (Chariton 5.7–8)

The trial ended, and not one of the senators remained disposed to express any doubt of the youth's guilt . . . but, at this juncture, an aged member of the senate . . . (Apuleius 10.7–8)[165]

Slander and superficial evidence of guilt, circumstance and the work of evil plotters—these are the pitfalls that produce so many juridical close calls. The Apoc. Acts, the various novels, Acts all use a similar repertory. Without such devices the cases would not even reach court. Because of them the heroes' acquittal is by no means certain.

Luke turned Acts 21—28 into a cliffhanger by withholding the verdict again and again, despite assurances that this time it would be final. Chariton did the same. The grand trial takes place in book 5. Mithridates is exonerated, but the union of Chaireas and Callirhoe, the heroes, remains in doubt. The king sets a new trial five days hence. When that day finally arrives the entire city is gripped in suspense, but His Majesty delays fifty more days (hoping not, like Felix, for money but for Callirhoe). When the agony of that wait is at last over, revolt breaks out in Egypt, shipping the whole cast out west. There never is a resumption, but fear of the king's lust-biased justice hangs over the last third of the novel.[166] So, too, in the *Acts of Thomas* it is many chapters before the evil king Misdaeus will be able to accomplish that action contemplated in chapter 106.[167] *Third Maccabees* also has some impressive examples of retardation, including having a king fall asleep and thus delay the massacre.[168]

Historical criticism has struggled with little success to explain the delays and postponements recorded in Acts. Reference to the technique of retardation at least illustrates their literary function. By such devices and techniques, found also in the Apoc. Acts and in novels, Luke has transformed a potentially depressing account of Paul's incarceration into a narrative of high suspense and broad appeal.

Torture and Punishment

With reference to ancient novels, A. D. Nock spoke of

the popular pleasure in sensational incident and a common pleasure in reading of cruelty, heightened when the victim is young and beautiful. The sensational Hellenistic historians . . . offer a good parallel; so do the elaborate stories of martyrs' deaths. . . . They illustrate popular taste; and though it coarsened undoubtedly during Roman Rule and after, the basis is the same. [In Martyr Acts], as in the Greek novel, we have a continued heightening of interest by suspense; we know the end of the story in advance, the martyr's beheading, the young couple's happy reunion. But we are in the meanwhile continually brought to the point of thinking "This is the end" and then given a respite.[169]

Part of the phenomenon noted is due to cultural change, to a civilization that delighted in the cruelty of gladiators and animal slaughter. A second factor is the generalization of education and the accompanying production of mass culture resulting in the rule of popular taste. Popular lore has never shied from the violent and sadistic. In folklore and fairy tale there is often a frank acceptance of sexual and aggressive feelings. Bourgeois popular literature accepts such material with certain premises, adequately summed up in the thesis "Crime does not pay." One can depict nearly any amount of sex and violence so long as transgressors reap their due reward. In cultures where sex is suspect, torture and rape become acceptable outlets, for they reinforce the notion that sex is bad. Enforced sexual submission permits readers to identify in fantasy since one need not feel responsible for what is beyond one's personal control. Jewish, Christian, and pagan popular literature of ancient times contains a good amount of sex and violence that conform to these uplifting criteria.[170]

Desire for popular appeal accounts for the narration of Judas's horrible death (Acts 1:16–20), the sudden demise of Ananias and Sapphira (5:1–11), the blinding of Elymas (13:6–12), the beating of Sosthenes (18:12–17), and the brutal humiliation of the sons of Sceva (19:13–17). Reading of such suffering in Acts permits the audience to enjoy their violence and inculcate the implicit moral advice.

Apostles also suffer, from whips and stones (5:40; 16:22–23). Paul knew both ends of the whip, as persecutor and as victim (22:19; 16:22–23). There's an irony here for the discerning. To the same world of ideas, as it were, belong stoning and mob assaults. Between the temporal punishment for sin suffered by the wicked and the meritorious afflictions of the just, there is a fair supply of personal violence in Acts.

Likewise, no hero of an ancient novel seems immune from the lash.[171] The threat, even the reality, of gruesome torture is never far away, and sometimes the heroes are scarcely seconds from the agony of the rack:

> Without more ado the instruments used for torture among the Greeks were produced: fire and wheel, and every variety of scourge . . . but the old woman exclaimed . . . (Apuleius 3.9)[172]

Paul, likewise, was spared at the last second (Acts 22:24–25), and such rescues would happen again.[173]

Nor were the horrors of crucifixion ignored.[174] Regarding such scenes in ancient novels, Martin Hengel has commented,

> Crucifixion made for exciting entertainment and sensationalism. Here the suffering was not really taken seriously. The accounts of the crucifixion of the hero served to give the reader a thrill: the tension was then resolved by the freeing of the crucified victim and the obligatory happy ending.[175]

The "theology" of the novels is that of Mark 15:29–32: "Save yourself by [miraculously] coming down from the cross." This is not a facetious statement, for the romantic view of life presented in the novels to which Hengel refers is a secular equivalent to the "theology of glory" espoused by Luke. His heroes can walk away from a beating in good health. They, like the lead characters in novels, are *theioi andres* (divine men). Those who read of their exploits can enjoy the violence without having to take it seriously, just as the proponents of various theologies of glory declined to take the cross seriously, as Paul (and Mark, among others) continually reminded them. Both novels and so-called aretalogies have the same kind of attraction and appeal to the same large public, the people who have heard and known enough of unhappy endings. Luke's theological and literary programs go hand in hand, and one should not wonder if what Luke says of Paul's career and his ideas disagrees with what the apostle himself had to say. Whatever else the study of ancient entertainment literature may have to contribute to the study of the NT, it does give depth and scope to the world in which certain theological ideas flourished. Comparison with such literature strongly supports the case that one of Luke's objectives was the construction of entertaining narrative.

SHIPWRECK AND TRAVEL

Although travel constitutes the structural basis for both Luke and Acts, the theme functions differently in the two works. Acts' journeys may be traced on a map, as every Sunday-school child knows. This is not true of Jesus' journey to Jerusalem (Luke 9:51—19:44). In the Gospel the journey is devoted to the teaching of Jesus. Apostolic adventures fill the pages of Acts. Source alone cannot explain the problem,[176] nor are the forms of the sources unimportant for the genre of the work in its entirety.

Travel narrative in Acts[177] is concentrated at three vital points:

1. 16:6–12. Inception of the "European" mission
2. 20:1–7, 13–16; 21:1–9, 15–17. Last voyage to Jerusalem
3. 27:1—28:16. Voyage to Rome

The travel sequences in chapters 16 and 21—22 form a bracket around Paul's most important labors.[178] These share the "itinerary style,"[179] direction by the Spirit, and prophecy.[180] The series of stations reads like mirror images: Troas, Philippi, Macedonia, Achaea, Achaea, Macedonia, Philippi, Troas. These portals enshrine Paul's central activity.[181] Such symmetry does not easily come by the accident of sources.

Sixty of the ninety verses are devoted to the trip to Rome. Why? Paul had made many voyages before this, and had experienced shipwreck (2 Cor. 11:25). Why does the author spend sixty verses on this trip when nothing was said about the beginnings of Christianity in Galilee, Rome, Alexandria, Illyricum, "North Galatia," Laodicea and environs, Cilicia, Pergamum, Smyrna, and other places? If nine verses suffice for Thessalonica, seventeen for Corinth, and (at most) twenty for Asia, why sixty for this trip? Why not edit this sequence a bit to permit describing what Peter did after converting Cornelius, how Paul died, what heresies arose, what came of the Collection, and kindred subjects of great interest then and now? Even if Acts is classified as a biography of Paul, this lack of balance is not very defensible.

One answer is that storm and shipwreck stories were a staple of ancient adventure writings.[182] Historians had no need to liven up their material with a shipwreck, but composers of fiction did,[183] often enough to inspire parodies.[184] The evidence suggests that ancient audiences would not have seen voyage and shipwreck as the kind of set pieces historians like to include, such as accounts of a siege or an oration for the nation's dead soldiers.

Voyage to Rome

In opposition to this view, Haenchen waged a vigorous campaign.[185] He argued for the presence of an underlying reminiscence, shaped by Luke and larded with interpolations. Maintaining, against J. Wellhausen and Dibelius,[186] that Acts 27 was not "literary" and that no "fixed account" of a shipwreck existed, Haenchen made chapter 27 a center of his understanding of Acts. On both counts his conclusions are open to challenge. With regard to the notion of a fixed account, this would appear to be an inappropriate extension of form criticism. No one would argue that the category "shipwreck" should be placed alongside "apophthegm" or "miracle story." Such accounts were appropriately framed in the style of the *periplous* (a narrative form for sea journeys), as Eduard Norden showed. This genre, which has its roots in the *Odyssey*, could be employed for everything from navigators' notes to pure fiction. Lucian is representative:

> Well, for a day and a night we sailed before the wind without making very much offing, as land was still dimly in sight; but at sunrise on the second day the wind freshened, the sea rose, darkness came on, and before we knew it, we could no longer get our canvas in. Committing ourselves to the gale and giving up, we drove for seventy-nine days. On the eightieth day, however, the sun came out suddenly and at no great distance we saw a high, wooded island. . . .[187] (Lucian *A True Story* 1.6)

This parody illustrates how well known the genre was, and how open to abuse.[188]

Acts 27 does fall into this stylistic tradition and contains, in addition, a number of recurrent motifs: late departure after the season's end, passengers who know more than the captain, jettisoning cargo, crews who attempt to preempt the ship's boat, encounters with barbarians on strange coasts, as well as an unusually ferocious and long-lived storm and hungry passengers who abandon all hope.[189]

Granting that such things did indeed happen, their occurrence with such regularity in literature suggests that they belonged to a repertory of motifs from which those determined to describe the subject would select. They are thus literary. They are also, needless to say, quite dramatic. Haenchen must be corrected, for Luke does relate a rather typical shipwreck story.

Within Acts 27 are nearly thirty instances of literary allusion and elegant usage, as well as two oblique optatives, twelve genitive absolutes, and ten occurrences of the particle *te*.[190] This is the most sustained passage of good writing in Luke-Acts and thus relatively difficult, as many students of New Testament Greek have discovered. The literary quality of chapter 27 is by no means restricted to those passages identified by Haenchen and others as "interpolations" in a substratum.[191] The rather common comparison with ancient novels and other literature is therefore literarily quite justifiable.

As Ramsay realized, Luke intended in this narrative to glorify his hero and the Christian cult:

> The scene of the voyage and shipwreck in chapter 27 is not directly important in itself for the development of the Church; but it is highly important as illuminating the character of Paul, showing how, even as a prisoner and a landsman at sea, he became the dominating personage in a great ship's company as soon as danger threatened.[192]

Paul the prisoner is the focal point of this action,[193] knowing when to sail, what will happen, how to revive the passengers, and what the crew is up to. His safety seems to be the centurion's concern. For his sake all will live. It is just such characterization that supposedly distinguishes Luke the historian from the fabricators of the Apoc. Acts: "The dominant aretalogical conception of the Apocryphal Acts becomes evident in the tendency of the works to place an individual personality in the focal point."[194] This venerable thesis is worthy of modification, and not only with regard to Acts 27.[195]

"Focal point" is more than biographical or aretalogical. As Ramsay says, "Wherever Paul is, no one present has eyes for any but him."[196] This is the mode of characterization found in most ancient novels. It is aretalogical in the degree to which novels and aretalogies share the same anthropology,[197] but it is popular and often naive. Despite Soeder's denial, Luke also places his central characters in the spotlight. Where they are, they are the cynosure of all eyes.

At no time does this become more revealingly incongruous than in the period following Paul's arrest. His well-being is top priority for the garrison commander; his death is the most pressing issue before the Sanhedrin. Even on shipboard his view is respected and he can rise in the midst of a gale to make a public address, "standing in their midst" (27:21).[198] Haenchen pleads in Luke's behalf, "The author has no real idea of the situation."[199] It is difficult to imagine that this first-century writer understood so little about the conditions of sea travel during his own time. Technique, not idiocy, explains this improbability. By such means Luke demonstrates Paul's aplomb amid chaos and his capacity to attract close attention even in the most distracting conditions.[200] So much does Paul do to save the ship that the centurion's efforts in his behalf will seem quite natural.[201]

If the star is the undivided center of attention, others will be no more than sidekicks and gofers. This is precisely the role assigned in Acts to those who, in Paul's letters, are described as co-senders. Luke provided Peter with such a companion, John, and created an equally meek role for Barnabas, against the tradition.[202] So common is the faithful sidekick in the Apoc. Acts that Soeder opined that their authors may have lifted the idea from the novels. There also a number of Johns and Barnabases may be found, to prop up the hero, prevent his suicide, die in his stead if necessary, and be general nonentities.[203] Such characters might be foils, like Mark, unable to endure the rigors of missionary travel (Acts 15:37), who by contrast allowed the chief characters to glow even more brightly. To a degree they might also represent the reader, the ordinary person for whom feats of heroism are less likely. Acts 27 is an outstanding example of this technique of characterization. The bright light upon Paul pierces even the condition of chains and the presence of a storm, and his companions are so minor as to be anonymous.[204]

The voyage to Rome, of course, is much more than an adventure starring Paul the apostle and Roman gentleman. It is also an aretalogy, for protection of those in peril on the sea was an important responsibility of ancient gods, and the voyage gave Luke a chance to show how the new faith could compete.[205] The entire story is a "miracle," but no less interesting for all that. This is one of Luke's major efforts, as style, structure, and length demonstrate. It is therefore legitimate to look to Acts 27 for an intimation of the writer's intentions. They are glorification of the faith, exaltation of its leading exponent, and narration of high adventure. Formally, chapter 27 is a typical episode from a religious novel. Any diary of these events appears to have been drowned in the shipwreck, as it were.[206] Luke has shaped this material. Once again, there is the dilemma of a historian who fails to behave like one.

Missionary Journeys

Travel has been one of the staple items on the shelf of entertainment literature since the *Epic of Gilgamesh*. Gods, heroes, missionaries, conquerors, and various political and spiritual leaders traveled the known world to spread their message and perform great deeds.[207] Journeys were one of the chief motifs exploited by ancient novelists to expose their characters to dangers and delights and give their readers a secondhand experience of strange lands. For the romantic novels of the Hellenistic and Roman periods, travel was a symbolic expression of the plight of the individual, rootless and left to his or her own devices in quest of private goals.[208] It could thus be used as a metaphor for the "journey of life," a concept not irrelevant to Luke's depiction of Christianity as a Way, symbolized by Jesus' journey to Jerusalem, on which he taught the meaning of that Way.[209]

Externally, missionary journeys form the structure and subject of Acts and most of the Apoc. Acts. Each sees a universal mission as the basic response to the vindication of Jesus. Recognition of this point of contact compelled Soeder to affirm that Luke's work was quite unlike the later Acts, for his itineraries were sternly objective, theirs impossible and arbitrary.[210] Whereas Acts speaks of the expansion of God's kingdom, the Apoc. Acts retail the deeds and experiences of wandering heroes.

In fact, Luke's itineraries follow a plan determined by theology, and he does take note of deeds done by itinerant heroes. Hans Conzelmann describes the mission as radiating out from Jerusalem in concentric circles.[211]

First come the "cities" about Jerusalem (Acts 5:16, Lukan summary), then Samaria. In the latter case Luke has Peter and John dispatched to put the seal of legitimacy upon Philip's mission, bringing the two back with a summary verse that creates a missionary journey (8:25). Philip's work is likewise transformed into a journey with editorial notes (8:26, 40). Acts 9:32, 35, 42 and 11:2 achieve the same result. These are the first three circles, each created by the author of Acts in accordance with an arbitrary plan.[212]

Luke next returns to his sources to narrate the gentile mission at Antioch (Acts 11:19).[213] Subordinating this operation to Jerusalem, against his sources, he then brings in Paul (11:25–26), whose close ties to the mother church are well emphasized by picking up a tidbit inspired by the Collection.[214] From this point on Paul will be the focal point. Luke provided a basis for the modern notion of three journeys, each of which terminated in Jerusalem.

The first narration of these journeys (13:1—14:23) is anything but "sternly objective." A brief foray into Cyprus is followed by the penetration of Asia Minor from the south. From Antioch the missionaries "went to Iconium" (13:51), and then had to flee to the cities of Lystra and Derbe (14:6). Thereafter new work ceases and they return to base along the same route. Problems abound.

For Cyprus there seems to have been little source material. Luke stretched one tale into a preaching tour, albeit with no reported success. The foray into Asia Minor from the south worried Ramsay.[215] This is not an easy avenue, nor does Pisidian Antioch seem the most likely first stop. Iconium was no easy jaunt from Antioch.[216] It is difficult to imagine that Luke is in firm control of the geography here. Fleeing to Lystra and Derbe was awkward, for Derbe was almost twice the distance from Lystra that the latter was from Iconium. Thereafter opportunities to move toward Tarsus, Cappadocia, or the sea presented themselves. Instead the missionaries retraced their way step by step.[217] The final comment, 14:23, creates a neat inclusio with 13:1–3.

Luke has almost certainly created this journey on the basis of several stories.[218] It is a fairly cautious creation, to be sure, but the idea of a missionary journey stems from the author. After the obligatory visit to Jerusalem and a brief sojourn in Antioch, the "second journey" (15:14—18:21) begins with overland movement through earlier sites and a breathless succession of provinces until they reach Troas. Paul is destined for Europe, and all else will be set aside, including such places as Galatia ("passed over"; 16:6). Solemn style and dramatic revelation signal the inception of a major shift.[219] Luke's center of interest is the Aegean region. After three chapters (16—18) on the western side, Paul returns east for a one-night stand at Ephesus and a visit to Jerusalem, after which the missionary dashes back to Ephesus. Once again, a Lukan creation. Whatever does not fit into the pattern of circles radiating out from (and governed by) Jerusalem is excised. The next goal, following yet another stop back at home base, will be Rome, the aspiration of every missionary:

> The lure of Rome, and the knowledge of the great possibilities open there among the cosmopolitan population, were enough to persuade every leader of new movements, either doctrinal or practical, to move his headquarters to Rome and to make of the Roman community the chosen ground of active propaganda.[220]

Paul becomes, in effect, apostle to Rome, for the existence of pre-Pauline Christians has somehow escaped the Jewish leaders,[221] whom Paul can summon for an exposition of a faith that is received by them as something utterly new.[222]

Had the author of Acts wished, as Soeder maintained, to narrate the ex-

pansion of God's Word, such communities as Alexandria and Rome would
have come within this purview regardless of the evangelist involved. In fact,
only certain missionaries qualify. Acts narrates their deeds and experiences
with the object of showing not so much how the message was proclaimed to
the "ends of the earth" (1:8) as how Paul got to the ultimate goal of the
capital.

Soeder's second contention, that Luke's itineraries are "stringently objective," is also questionable. Some journeys were created, others were modi-
fied, and all were brought under the perspective of his fixed theological
model. At the center stands Paul and the Aegean basin. The Apoc. Acts also
tend to stress a particular area and missionary. The *Acts of John*, for instance,
string together a number of "Johannine cities" to form a circuit, as does Luke
in Acts 13—14. According to the *Acts of Paul*, Paul's work was one continuous missionary journey.[223] If this is to be dismissed as a bizarre fantasy, it
must be granted that Paul shared the same fantasy (Rom. 15:19). All of the
Acts engage in some schematization, but none more than Luke. The imposition of schematic models upon one's sources does not, however, imply the
presence of historiography.

The *Alexander Romance* (A-text) provides some useful analogies. Here also
the author lists the "correct" places, but changes the order for tendentious
reasons and adds additional sites.[224] The geographical scope of Acts, from
Damascus to Rome, with Asia Minor and Greece at its heart, is not unlike
that of the romantic novels. Travelogues appealed to their readers' interests,
and the same may be said for Acts.[225] Despite the alleged facility of travel in
Roman times, few people outside certain occupations, especially women,
were ever able to enjoy travel of any significant distance from their birth-
places.[226] Those who heard of the ease with which Paul traversed whole
provinces in a single bound would not be led to reflect upon the blessings of
the Pax Romana so much as to marvel. Luke undoubtedly idealizes the travel
experiences of his missionaries, eliminating drudgery and erasing hardship,
with the exception of the one great shipwreck and rescue (chap. 27).[227]

The novels were about the same. There are grand adventures, pirates,
storms, or bandits, or else painless and rapid travel.[228] Few apparently
wished to hear about the monotonous grind of daily journeys. The glamour
of adventure and the romance of distant places were what were required, as
Luke well knew.

The journeys reported in Acts reflect the author's ideas about the origins of
Christianity. They are neither guesses nor the best that can be pieced together from sketchy sources. To a large degree Luke has created the missionary travels he reports. Contrast with the Gospel indicates that the travels
reported in Acts seek not so much to teach as to describe in an exciting way

the experiences of Paul and his predecessors. Luke had much to say about the early mission, some of it true, some not. He also aspired to present his account in such a way that it would keep the attention of those who read or heard his book. In short, he wished to write in an entertaining fashion. This has been borne out by the survey of his treatment of adventure. Additional evidence for that object will come to light in the following chapter.

EXCURSUS:
THE "ITINERARY STYLE"

Since the earliest times readers have been fascinated with the use of the first person in Acts' accounts of travel, and with the detailed notes on chronology and stopping places. The "we" of Acts and the book's sources presents vexing problems to modern scholars. Before the issue can be resolved it will be necessary to give careful attention to the literary questions. Recent studies present contradictory findings.[229]

Dibelius, who was sensitive to literary issues, proposed that the author of Acts made use of diary material. Good examples of such itinerary journals are available in the (admittedly late) collection of *Itinera hierosolymitana*, produced in connection with tourism of the holy land.[230] These quite unpretentious texts frequently make use of the travel-narrative style, along with descriptions of sites and sights, listings of distances, and notes for travelers. Such texts will please those who cannot make the trip and aid the ones who will come later. The following quotation is representative:

> I left the city of Placentia where I had sojourned. . . . After we had left Constantinople we came to the island of Cyprus, to the city Constantia, where St. Epiphanius rests. A beautiful city, delightful, adorned with date palms. We came to the regions of Syria. . . . We left Byblus . . . then we came to the quite magnificent city of Beirut, in which the study of letters recently flourished. . . . The Bishop of the city told us . . .[231]

In Acts one may observe a similar form for travel narrative, but no useful hints about distance and places to stay, nor local color for its own sake. If Luke did use a diary, one cannot discover it from the present text. As for the style, including "we," details of time, and fluctuations between persons in narration, that was established in the *Odyssey* (e.g., 14.244–58) and hallowed by centuries of imitation. Whether such a mode of narration is natural to travelers or not, it became fixed in Greek for the *periplous*.[232] That style was followed by many writers, including novelists.[233] One cannot infer either source or form from stylistic devices of this nature. One may affirm Luke's literary activity and concern. Study of travel accounts in a variety of settings has led me to espouse a position similar to that of Vernon Robbins, against E. Plümacher and S. M. Praeder.[234] One cannot be too rigid in demanding adherence to a number of fixed rules and conventions. In general, Luke's use of the "itinerary style" is no more remarkable than that of any other writer. This style indicates his concern to relate travel in the conventional manner, to please his audience as well as to inform them.

3. DIVERSIONS LESS ADVENTUROUS

Other Forms of Entertainment in Acts

Miss Prism describes the conclusion of her novel: "The good ended happily, and the bad unhappily. That is what Fiction means."

—Oscar Wilde*

HUMOR AND WIT

For though at times jests may be proper and pleasant, yet they are unsuited to the clerical life. For how can we adopt those things which we do not find in the holy Scriptures? (Ambrose *Duties* 1.23.102)

The New Testament shows no trace of humour. (Rudolf Bultmann)[1]

I disagree, in this instance, with both the great doctor and bishop of the ancient church, Ambrose, and the great exegete and theologian of modern times, Rudolf Bultmann. Luke is far from the humorless and somber writer he was once supposed to be. To establish this, one must attempt to determine the criteria for humor and wit in Luke's culture. This can be a relatively difficult enterprise, as discussion of humor in the writings of Lucian and the ancient novels indicates. Even within groups of the same culture and era, criteria for what is humorous vary widely depending upon education, age, taste, and for that matter, mood of the moment. Republicans may, for example, laugh more heartily at jokes about the late president John Kennedy than Democrats, and four-year-olds can find amusement where adults see none. Ancient and modern[2] discussions of humor agree that incongruity or inconsistency lies at its base, but no one imagines that all incongruity or inconsistency is humorous. Appreciation of just what incongruity is amusing and what is poor taste requires socialization, initiation into the mysteries of the mores and conventions of a particular group.

The translation of Aristophanes exposes the problems. Many westerners find sexual issues amusing, but not all care for jokes about problems relative to the digestive system. Many of Aristophanes' political jokes are bewilder-

---

The Importance of Being Earnest, act 2 (p. 32 of the Bantam ed., New York, 1961).

58

ing. Some may seem to be frivolous treatments of hallowed institutions, such as democracy, or irreverence toward the great, notably Socrates.[3] New Comedy is more readily appreciated, for in it the timeless themes of bourgeois life receive the kind of treatment still found on stage and screen.

Some forms of humor thus do endure from age to age. Among them are burlesque of the most obvious sort, much that has to do with sex, violence, and bodily functions, and some satire, irony, and parody of the less subtle varieties. Tales of rogues and explications of domestic crises likewise appeal to those of nearly every place and era. The parables of Jesus abound with such wit, but readers and interpreters have until recently been loath to see it, searching instead for a moral. Since allegorical exegesis is no longer an acceptable tool, as it was for the late bishop of Milan, the amorality or even immorality of certain parables constitutes an obstacle.[4] Appreciation of humor requires a willingness to admit that it may indeed be present. The search for humor in the NT will do well to begin just where incongruity with approved values is most pronounced.

Not all incongruity of the humorous sort is so readily recognizable. Cicero took note of two types of humor: one being "coarse, rude, vicious and indecent," another "refined, polite, clever and witty" (*De officiis* 1.104—the model for Ambrose). The distinction between them is easily determined, and no gentleman would make use of the first. Writings aimed at the fickle crowds (*mobile vulgus*) do, however, make use of it. These include mime, comedy, comic novels, and the like. This is the kind of humor most likely to appear in popular literature. Acts has a fair amount of it. The other type is elusive, but I believe that Luke does present an occasional whiff of more refined wit within his second volume, Acts. The following summaries seek to evoke some of the humor, wit, and irony still perceptible to modern commentators.

IRONY

Irony exists in manifold forms, ranging from the crude to the sublime. Rather closer to the former is the "poetic justice" that has delighted audiences for millennia. "There is," observed Ovid, "no law more just than that those who contrive at murder should die by their own contrivances" (*Ars amatoria* 1.655–56).

Some people are spiritually blind, such as those cynics in Jerusalem who could not distinguish between enthusiastic inspiration and a holiday binge (Acts 2:12–13). Elymas, who believes that he perceives the truth, finds that he has been blinded. An additional bit of irony here is that blinding is one of the specific talents of a magician. Since he was the spiritual director of a Roman governor, all will draw the proper conclusions. The governor did, and believed (13:6–12). This is the sort of story for which the Apoc. Acts are taken to task, a miracle told "for its own sake." Paul, once blinded for resisting the will of God, has turned the tables.

Punishment miracles no longer enjoy the admiration they once did. The relative absence of such wonders from the Gospels brings relief to many scholars. In Acts and the Apoc. Acts they are common enough.[5] Describing the demise of Ananias, Luke underlined the point by having his wife succumb a short while thereafter. When she collapsed "at the feet of Peter," her life ended at that very place where the faithful had placed *all* their goods.[6] Fans of the punishment miracle well knew that death by worms was a sure clue to a bad life. This fate overcame the wicked king Herod who, determined to slay Peter, found himself slain and thus exchanged his regal dignity for worms. To heighten the irony, Luke describes Peter's release and Herod's downfall with the same term.[7]

Other persecutors have their problems. Paul, who had apparently slept through Gamaliel's lecture on not persecuting new movements (Acts 5:35–39; 22:3), wickedly planned to drag Christians from Damascus to Jerusalem in chains. Instead, he is himself led to Damascus by the hand. "Such is the pitiful state in which the terror of the Christians makes his entry."[8] Sosthenes, seeking to have Paul arraigned before Gallio, found the blows falling on his own back after the astute governor refused to be duped (18:12–17).[9] Acts 23:12–33 relates the pangs of conspiracy. Forty men, whom we may presume to have been "legalistic" and overscrupulous, vowed that Paul's death would precede their next bite or sip. There was no small amount of coarse satisfaction in imagining these poor souls wrestling with their consciences to escape their desperate fate. That once-intrepid band of fanatics would soon crumble into fragments as its members began to debate, waver, rationalize, and finally reach for a drink. As they wrestled internally, the man they tried to slay made, with the aid of Rome, a bold escape. Since he was apprehended while fulfilling a truly pious vow, the humiliation of these oath takers was all the more appropriate. Simon the Magus had once been hailed as "the Great Power of God." We last see him abject before Peter, having been caught in the act of trying to purchase some of that power, about which, it emerged, he knew nothing.

There are also ironies of characterization, the contrast between what people should be like and the way they are. The Sanhedrin probably tops the list, being no better than a mob of bullies. Officials who do not realize the quality of those they abuse also create satisfaction for readers (Acts 16:37–39; 21:37–39; 22:25–29). Demoniacs, as readers of the story of the Gadarene (Mark 5:1–20) would know, often injure themselves and ruin their clothing, if they can be made to wear any at all.[10] How wonderful it was, then, to imagine the sons of Sceva fleeing, wounded and nude, reduced to the state of those they would allegedly aid (Acts 19:13–17)! Some ironies are truly subtle, such as in the use of *ekklesia* in 19:32 for a mob which has no idea why it has assembled; or, perhaps, in Paul's praise of Athenian piety, when all educated people knew that the proliferation of images was a bit on the superstitious side of things.[11]

"Poetic justice" is a universal. The Book of Esther tells of Haman's death on the gallows he had contrived for another. More subtly, Esther, who had been recruited in the interest of finding a royal wife who would serve as a proper role model for uxorial submission, turned the tide by inducing the king to obey her.[12]

The elephants assembled to eradicate Judaism in 3 Maccabees are finally assigned to stamp out the Jews' would-be persecutors, a heavy-footed bit of *lex talionis* but no less piquant for that. Dorcon, bent upon a bestial act of seduction dressed in a wolfskin, was taken for the animal he was and dispatched by a pack of dogs (Longus 1.20). The wicked woman who sought to have Habrocomes crucified for refusing her improper advances was herself to end life on the cross (X. E. 4.4).[13]

The Apoc. Acts have a good sampling of edifying punishment miracles and proper deaths for persecutors and heretics, as well as examples from the animal kingdom, including a lion that can remain chaste and a dog that will not be duped by Simon.[14] Perhaps the neatest touch of such irony is in *Acts of Thomas* 1–2, where the hero, having refused his divinely ordained missionary assignment, was sent to India as a slave.[15]

The novellas contained within Apuleius's *Metamorphoses* edify their readers with a number of condign punishments. Religious polemic is no exception. The priests of the Dea Syria protest against defiling the Holy Lady by placing her image on an ass. Privately, they perform such abominations that the very ass is shamed (8.25–31).[16]

BURLESQUE AND ROWDY EPISODES

Scornful laughter at what is ugly or unusual, at the misfortunes of others, or at raucous violence is a basic form of humor[17] — basic and quite often perceived to be unedifying, Aristophanes, Menander, and Shakespeare notwithstanding. Critics often excuse playwrights by saying that such material had to be inserted to keep the unwashed rabble in line. Luke includes his fair share of such stuff, not having been the first to exploit its value for religious polemic.

Acts 5:17–25: Quis custodiet ipsos custodes? The Sanhedrin sits in solemn dignity, surrounded by the high priest and his entourage, all in all the "full senate of the children of Israel."[18] With bated breath they await the proceedings that will extirpate this pernicious movement. Lackeys are dispatched to have the prisoners fetched, but there is a hitch. The accused are not in their cells. Benches creak. Tempers wear thin. Befuddled and terrified guards frantically seek the apostles, in fear for their lives (with reason: at 12:19 they will die). At last the escapees are located, in the temple, where they were previously seized. While the rulers of the nation sit in pompous arrogance, vexed over the time consumed by this tawdry affair, the followers of Jesus are doing the job of their accusers: teaching the people. Brave apostles make the Sanhedrin look both wicked and foolish.[19]

Acts 12:5–17: Saint Peter and the doors of death. This legend, one of Acts' most delightful stories, artfully combines humor with suspense. Peter, cruelly chained to two guards, sleeps so soundly ("the best pillow is a clear conscience") that the bright epiphanic light does not faze him. He is prepared to face death with equanimity. James has already been done in, and only the Days of Unleavened Bread delay Peter's end. The brief reference to those days evokes a parallel with the fate of Jesus and provides an opportunity for delay. There is irony here, for Passover is the feast of liberation from bondage. Peter, held in bonds, will be freed. When the numinous glow fails to arouse the apostle, the angel tries a kick. Awakened, Peter must be admonished to silence. He stumbles to his feet, stiff from chains and sleep on a dungeon floor. Like a patient parent, the angel must supervise his toilet. First the shoes are laced up, then his belt secured. Do not overlook the cloak. (All this will madden anxious readers. Why spend all this time perfecting the outfit? He is breaking out of jail, not going to a papal reception.) Successive layers of guards must be eluded. After the earlier embarrassment (Acts 5:17–25), nothing is left to chance. There are four shifts of four guards each for this prisoner, often rotated and always alert. Through angelic aid each is eluded. Then comes the final and most awesome barrier, an iron gate. Of its own accord this obstacle opens, and Peter can proceed out into the street. The angel departs (a bit prematurely perhaps), leaving Peter in the chill of reality. Through the gloomy streets he creeps, eager to find safety at Mary's. The gate to her house is the portal of refuge and point of danger. Here again light exposes Peter. Rhoda, a flighty slave girl, answers his knock and foolishly leaves him in the hostile street as she rushes back in with the good news. Peter may be paying for an earlier encounter with a maidservant in the light (Luke 22:56). Those inside, assembled in prayer for Peter, take a realistic approach: he has been executed and Rhoda has seen his guardian angel. The debate is doubtless lively, but Peter is out in the cold and has no choice but to hammer at the door desperately. This will almost certainly arouse sleeping neighbors already suspicious of Christians and ready to investigate the racket from this sectarian nest. Finally, a solution to the argument about Rhoda's crazy vision emerges: send someone to investigate.

What more could there be? Within sixteen verses humor and suspense, drama and miracle, emerge. Passover provides both parallel and delay. Peter is rescued at the last minute, in response to a praying community somewhat skeptical about the power of prayer. An angel opens one gate, but Peter is blocked at another because mistaken for an angel. He believes he is dreaming. The others believe Rhoda is seeing things. She is like a figure from New Comedy. The guards who were to have murdered Peter die themselves, victims of tyrannical pique. Wicked Herod will not escape. By the toe of an angel Peter is brought to safety and Herod to a well-merited death.[20]

Acts 16:16–18: The importunate python. It is best not to vex an apostle. When a missionary becomes irritated at the free advertising offered by his erstwhile competitor, he exorcises the poor woman, inadvertently destroying her owner's business and bringing the law down on his head. If this tale were found in the Apoc. Acts, it would draw waves of critical ire, for it is just such willful use of divine power that makes those works so unlike Luke's. Or so we are told.[21]

Acts 19:14–16: Some fleecers shorn of their clothing and dignity. Sceva's sons are itinerant exorcists, sons of a Jewish high priest who somehow migrated to Ephesus and bore offspring who became religious quacks. Creedal considerations are really secondary to their practice, for, like all good merchants, they keep an eye on their competitors. Discovering that the sacred name of Paul is working wonders, they decide to pirate it for their own operations. Even the demons know better than to allow such shenanigans, and the exorcists end up in need of their own services. The point that Christianity is not just magic is obvious enough (see the following verses), and its humorous character can scarcely be overlooked. Martin Dibelius, who was not amused, would not even call it Christian.[22]

Acts 19:21—20:1: Pagan follies. Admonished by the foregoing, the populace of Ephesus comes forward to pitch their magical papyri onto a bonfire. The followers of John have left the fold, Judaism is on the run, magic has gone up in smoke. Only the great cult of Artemis remains, and it is hurting, or better, those who find superstition good for business are feeling the pinch of this elevated preaching. Demetrius organizes the fabricators of expensive religious souvenirs to foment a "spontaneous demonstration" in behalf of their patron goddess. The mob, sheeplike as ever, pitches in with a public prayer meeting that verges on riot. The only result of such disturbance will be Roman intervention, bad for business and freedom alike, not the kind of epiphany desired. As Ernst Haenchen notes, paganism can do no more against Paul than shout itself hoarse. "Artemis," archly observed Saint John, "should have helped herself."[23] A famous cult loses face.[24]

Acts 23:6–10: Disruption in the Sanhedrin. Few of the Greek mobs criticized by oligarchic Romans were less elegant in their legal procedure than the Sanhedrin of Jerusalem. Paul, who in this book claims still to *be* a Pharisee, pulls from his rhetorical bag of tricks that party's leading slogans (as Acts would have them). The result is pandemonium, including physical violence. The two sides would tear Paul to shreds were the alert tribune not to escort him to safety. Luke is willing to say nearly anything to make the Sanhedrin look like a pack of jackals. His treatment of trials resembles that of the *Acta Alexandrinorum.*[25]

The affinity of such episodes to ancient "lowbrow" taste will become clear to those who survey the Oxyrhynchus mimes, Plautus, and popular biographies like the *Life of Aesop.* The *Satyricon,* the *Ass,* and Apuleius's *Metamorphoses* contain a wealth of such material.[26] Hagiography and the Apoc. Acts do not lag behind.[27]

That Luke had a serious intent in these passages requires no proof. Rather than debate issues, he preferred to ridicule opponents. Instead of narrating unpleasant incidents, he chose to poke fun at the opposition. This is popular theology at its most primitive level.

CLEVERNESS AND WIT

If Luke would often have earned Cicero's disapproval for being "coarse, rude and vicious," he sometimes struck a more refined note.

Acts 14:8–18: A lesson learned—the Lystra episode.[28] The problems of this story appear to require the presumption that Luke has reference to a Hellenistic legend, preserved in Ovid's sentimental and humorous tale of Baucis and Philemon (*Metamorphoses* 8.611–724). Ovid describes a visit to Phrygia by Zeus and Hermes in human form. No one will give them the time of day until they come upon the elderly and impoverished Baucis and Philemon, who share their pitiful resources. The gods then reveal their true nature in a miracle, transform the couple's shack into a temple of Zeus and Hermes, and make the pair its priests. The peculiar features of this account are thus accounted for by regarding it as "transformation of a story familiar in literature, to represent the Lycaonians as in effect saying 'We are not going to make the traditional mistake.'"[29] Appreciation of the humor requires familiarity with the myth. The learned quality of this episode is enhanced by the addition of an elegant little address. When, to be sure, the would-be deifiers are so overconverted as to attempt to stone Paul, this is but one more theme beloved of Greek literature: the fickle and irresponsible nature of barbarians.

Reception of human beings as gods is not unusual in ancient writings.[30] Acts, like the *Alexander Romance*, plays both sides of the street, sometimes taking the educated line, in which divine honors (*isotheoi timai*) are spurned.[31] One can in such passages meditate upon cultural superiority while gathering how awesome the particular heroes appeared to lesser breeds without the law.

Acts 28:1–7: The Malta episode. This episode follows the same course, with the added fillip of dramatic irony. When these equally fickle barbarians see that Paul did not die, they cease to regard him as a murderer or worse and begin to regard him as a very god. Paul, a bedraggled prisoner picking up driftwood, is suddenly bathed in an aura of glory, and this without uttering a word. Dibelius was offended.[32] Once again, Luke has crossed the line that. should firmly separate canonical from apocryphal Acts.

Ancient novelists likewise loved to assume a Hellenic pose and sneer at barbarians. Even the Victorians rarely did better. To the simple, the heroes of the romantic novels seemed to be very gods come down to earth.[33] Luke makes use of the same techniques to glorify his chief characters.

Quite a change of pace from the rather endless round of persecutions and flight came during Paul's interlude at Athens. A. D. Nock concluded that Luke's picture of Athens was literary.[34] Perhaps it would be better to remark that everyone knew of the Athenians' piety and curiosity,[35] about the philosophical schools and the Areopagus, just as even the most uncouth Americans of an earlier day had notions about French cooking and lovemaking, and the Eiffel tower, of course. Luke makes these references, and speaks also of the local love for novelty, another stereotype, the pieces of art, and the agora. Once again, there is the potential for making the traditional mistake, in this case, by treating Paul as their ancestors had Socrates. All of this Luke evokes with great artistry and charm, in but a few words. By means of this droll little episode, and the equally charming oratory it frames, one is allowed to overlook a rather dismal missionary failure.

Acts 20:7–12: The boy who could not stay awake. Who does not smile, even if guiltily, at the delightful little episode of the boy who could not stay awake in church even with the great Paul in the pulpit? The happy ending comes almost before there can be time to lament, despite the interval of potential suspense. The blend of sentimental description with pathos and burlesque is genuinely popular, and appealing enough to be imitated later.[36] For Dibelius this was "as secular as possible."[37] It is in fact quite religious, an edifying account of a cultic miracle with a good moral about staying awake and out of dangerous places. *Profan* here means "entertaining."

Officials other than the Sanhedrin may appear in humorous contexts. Gallio does not want to hear the niceties of halachic dialectic, and Felix can tell when a defense speech is about to become a theological lecture (18:15; 24:22). Followers of the latter's career might smile at his later reaction to Paul's message. "Righteousness" and "self-control" were not his most evident virtues, after all (24:25–26), and a coming judgment was not the sort of thing he wished to ponder, particularly since the judgment of Paul was not as forthcoming as it should have been.

Luke thus uses humor to entertain and distract his audience. Humor is often a weapon with which to bludgeon the opposition. At other times it may serve to divert attention from the real issue, and its pain. Luke does not use humor as a tool to expose the paradoxical nature of human existence, because he does not wish to promote a paradoxical understanding. He sees humor as a way to lift the burden of the world from his readers' shoulders, to give them escape and relaxation, to fasten upon some risible stereotype rather than penetrate the nature of things through insight derived from the detection of irony. This is by no means "mere" entertainment. It is thoroughly consistent with Lukan theology. It is also a bit closer to the world of the Apoc. Acts than some would prefer Acts to be.

PATHOS

Through pathos, writers seek to excite pleasurable feelings of tender sympathy or sadness directed toward the characters of their story. Pathos belongs to the essence of the sentimental style. Rhetorical historians and novelists in antiquity exploited this sentiment to the full. It was one of the qualities of the Asiatic style often derided but more often followed. If literary critics disapproved, popular audiences did not. Early Christian literature mirrors the popular admiration for pathos, including some baroque examples.[38] Luke is one of the first Christian authors to evoke a pathetic response.[39]

Death scenes were an obvious opportunity for pathetic description, including the passion of Jesus and the martyrdom of Stephen (7:54–60; 8:2). In the latter, Luke effectively contrasts Stephen's serenity with the rapacious brutality of his murderers, who are stirred by his piety to redouble their efforts. Stephen's later burial by pious Jews is another pathetic touch, to which Luke adds a sentimental note: young Paul, the coatcheck boy. The blatant inconsistency of that role indicates Luke's fondness for sentimental fiction.[40]

The moving story of Tabitha's resurrection (9:36–42) impressed Dibelius.[41] Luke, doubtless building upon a quality present in his source, effectively describes the sad loss of one so devoted to good works. "Why must such people perish?" asks the sentimental reader. In due course, Peter arrives upon the sad scene, an upper room packed with weeping widows who display for the exfisherman's discerning eye some examples of the good lady's handiwork.[42] Such tears will soon turn to joy, through the intervention of God by the hand of his chosen instrument. Scenes like this are the aretalogical manifestation of the happy ending. In the romantic novels, death is merely apparent, but believed.[43] One could thus have a good cry and revel in funeral and regret for the cruel loss of someone snatched away in the full bloom of youth and beauty. Novel and miracle speak to the same feelings and fill the same void, with a similar lack of realism. Paul will be able to work a similar wonder, also linked to an upper room, with its own sweet blend of pathos and humor (see Acts 20:7–12, discussed above).

In his portrayal of Paul's farewell journey (see Acts 19:21–22; 20:16–35, 36–38; 21:4–6), the author of Acts unveils a new character. Although Luke elects to overlook the fact of Paul's death, he will not deny him the satisfaction of tearful farewells and moving rhetoric. By coloring this last visit with all the shades of pathos, Luke permits his readers to feel its pangs without facing the facts, to be edified by the last words of a dying leader who, within the context of the book, does not die but lives and recounts the deeds of the Lord. At the same time he will develop a rising sense of suspense through dramatic foreshadowing.

The opening *dei* ("I *must* also see Rome"; 19:21) places the coming journey into the framework of Jesus' predictions of his death and Paul's own conversion, with its promises of suffering. What will happen is not due to human wile alone. It is a divinely ordained imitation of the Lord's passion.[44] The drama acquires momentum with the enumeration of the companions and the detailed, coldly factual "itinerary style" clicking off the days and places on the way to destiny.[45]

The speech at Miletus (20:18b–35) is a miniature masterpiece of pathos.[46] With touching modesty Paul relates his faithful mission in the face of plots, a life of "tears and trials." He will go to Jerusalem, come what may (as well it shall), in the face of dire prophecy. He speaks also of his own demise and the heresy that will spring up in the garden he no longer tends, and affirms his innocence, even speaking of his refusal to accept support. Blood, sweat, and tears. By the conclusion all are in tears, and the scene dissolves in a general breakdown.

So gripping is this passage that few will ask why it is that Paul now faces danger in Jerusalem when hitherto he has moved back and forth with perfect ease, why he speaks of blood, sweat, and tears when, one chapter previously, the only blood shed came from Sceva's sons and his sweat served to work miracles? How has the companion of Asiarchs suddenly become a toiler for his daily bread? Apparently making use of other traditions, Luke has made a drastic shift in his characterization of Paul, not for the purposes of historical fullness but merely to reap the literary and theological benefits to be derived.[47]

With such scenes one may profitably compare many an episode from ancient novels. In the following, Dorcon, a reformed luster after children, utters his last:

> In just a little, Chloe, I shall die; those accursed pirates have cut me down; . . . the pipe itself I give you as a present; with it I won many a contest. . . . In return for all this give me but a kiss while I am yet alive, and shed a tear for me when I am dead. And when you see another tending my cows, think of Dorcon. (Longus 1.29–30)[48]

Many soliloquies delivered by the various heroes catalogue their extensive sufferings to date.[49] The apex of presumably unintentional excess was doubtless reached by Xenophon, who assigns a speech to the hero's drowning tutor, too old to be enslaved by the pirates who have taken off his master:

> Meanwhile the Tutor of Habrocomes now an old man of venerable aspect and pitiful because of his age, when he could not endure to see Habrocomes carried off, flung himself into the sea and swam to overtake the galley, crying as he went "Where will you leave me, my child, the old man, your tutor? Where are you off to, Habrocomes? Kill me yourself, wretch that I am, and bury me. How can I live without you?" Thus he said, and at length, despairing of seeing Habrocomes any longer, he gave himself up to the waves and died. (X. E. 1.14)[50]

One may compare the farewell scenes in Acts 20 and 21 with a scene from Chariton:

> And they all wept, and clinging to Paul's neck they kissed him, sorrowing most of all because of the word he had spoken, that they should see his face no more. And they brought him to the ship . . . and they all, with wives and children, brought us on our way till we were outside the city; and kneeling down on the beach we prayed and bade one another farewell. Then we went on board the ship, and they returned home. (Acts 20:36–38; 21:5–6)

> When the designated day of sailing arrived, the crowd ran in a body toward the harbor, not only men but also women and children, and there were mingled together prayers, tears, groans. . . . Ariston, Chaereas' father, was carried down. . . . He put his arms about the neck of his son and clinging there, he wept and said . . . (Chariton 3.5.3)[51]

Pathos has been called a "requisite feature" of the Apoc. Acts.[52] Farewells, martyrdoms, and the loss of youth and beauty gave adequate occasion for such expression. (Thecla's story is representative, as is *Acts of John*

20–21). Nor did Jewish novels lag behind. Ruth is one of the earliest examples of temperate and skilled pathos in literature. Tobit has some choice moments of pathetic despair and appeal, and *3 Maccabees* brings to Jewish writing the kind of extravagant pathos so beloved of melodramatic historians.[53] When Apollonius expressed willingness to die with the citizens of Aspendos if he were not given a chance to end the disorder, he made a pathetic gesture that gained the desired end (*Ap. Ty.* 1.15).

Luke's pathos is often effective, and not by the standards of that day especially overdone. It served him as a useful literary device, foreshadowing danger and thus raising suspense, providing a change of dramatic pace that at the same time firmly wedded his readers to his hero immediately prior to Paul's highly controversial experience in Jerusalem and whatever that meant for the gentile mission.

UTOPIAN, EXOTIC, AND COLORFUL SCENES

Stories of distant places with strange customs and novel terrain have long delighted armchair travelers. Among the earliest Greek novels were accounts of ideal societies in often remarkable faraway lands. What remains of the works of Hecataeus, Theopompus, Iambulus, and Euhemerus is adequate to establish that they had more than entertainment in mind.[54] Political and religious propaganda was their chief object, presented so attractively that even romantic novelists retained vestiges of the utopian tradition.

If Oscar Wilde is correct in maintaining that "a map of the world that does not include Utopia is not worth even looking at,"[55] it will be necessary to add Utopia to the well-known maps of Acts with their lines denoting Paul's travels. Whatever the historical basis or nature of the sources, one object of the so-called communism of Acts 2:44–45 and 4:32–35 is to depict the ideal primitive society, the community of those who live close to the divine and thus do not suffer competition, oppression, or want. Far from trying to make an example of an experiment that failed,[56] the author of Acts wished to portray an eschatological miracle, the return of the Golden Age, awaited by Vergil no less than Jewish prophets.[57]

> Now is come the last age of the song of Cumae;
> The great line of the centuries begins anew.
> Now the Virgin returns, the reign of Saturn returns.
> (Vergil *Eclogue* 4.4–6)

The proverbial character of the early community's renunciation of private property coincided with an equally proverbial political ideal. Both the "researches" of "anthropologists" and the accomplishments of philosophical societies testified to the benefits of communal living.[58] Philo and Josephus took such thinking into account when preparing their descriptions of Essenes and Therapeutae, as did the writer to Aristeas in his account of life in Jerusalem.[59] By portraying early Christian life as he did, Luke thus evoked a utopian tradition that every person with a modicum of education would immediately recognize. Rather than pursuing a foreign superstition lacking either morals or intelligence, this group had achieved that for which philosophers had long been striving and that which religion had long been promising.[60] Since this utopian coloration derives from the summaries (Acts 2:42–47; 4:32–35),[61] credit for it must be placed at the author's feet. Luke was well aware of financial and distributional problems (Acts 6:1–6; 8:40; 11:27–30; and 24:17 reflect the use of money as a weapon in theological conflicts), but he preferred to describe a Utopia, that is, to relate idealistic fiction rather than history. The subsequent appeal of his description[62] testifies to the success of his propaganda.

EXOTICA AND ORIENTALIA

In his last substantial work devoted to Acts, Henry J. Cadbury demonstrated the author's responsiveness to public craving for descriptions of unusual people and places.[63] Theologically this interest is wholly compatible with Luke's well-known "universalism." The catalogue of nations (Acts 2:9–11) foreshadows the subsequent mission, and more. This list intends to symbolize all the nations of the world;[64] it portrays one of the objectives of the Golden Age, the end of barriers created by linguistic diversity.[65] By framing his program in utopian and exotic colors, Luke has achieved a miniature tour de force.[66]

The exotic quality of the tale of a eunuch from Ethiopia, a foreign place much in the news during the latter half of the first century C.E., was considerably enhanced by Luke's additions (Acts 8:26–40).[67] If the source described this person as a Gentile, Luke does not. He rather wished to stress the pathetic quality of this outlandish official, a man of high status who was barred from full participation in the religion of Israel because of his physical condition. The story points not to a basic shift in the mission (Peter will convert the first Gentile) but to the "ends of the earth" in all its glamour. Despite the "barbarian" character, Acts introduces a veneer of education through the use of elevated diction and paranomasia.[68]

Artapanus (432c–433d) also brings Ethiopia into his portrait of Jewish heroes, and the *Alexander Romance* (3.18–24) describes the great Macedonian's encounter with Queen Candace. In the novel of Heliodorus, Ethiopia shines forth as an ideal state (see also *Ap. Ty.* 6.1–27 on the Ethiopians). This was an opportunity Luke clearly did not wish to neglect.

Acts was also willing to smile at the unpredictable nature of barbarians (14:8–18; 28:1–7).[69] Such references to the uncouth and naive character of "native" peoples functioned, then as later, not only to provide the reader with fascinating information but also to reinforce a sense of racial and cultural superiority.

Foreign lands, especially Egypt and Persia, provided at least part of the setting for most romantic novels, the heroes of which frequently found themselves exposed to the lust and injustice of oriental despots and their minions. The combination of national pride and foreign attractions was hard to surpass, as nineteenth-century writers would also discover. The Apoc. Acts include not only Thomas's adventures in distant India but also an encounter with cannibals and a sojourn at the Isles of the Blessed.[70]

Luke's vivid use of local color and details has largely been caught up into the debate over historical worth. This tends to detract from the admiration it would otherwise naturally command. In general, those who point to the presence of good local color in Acts would be hard pressed to explain why this or that detail aids the reader in clarifying the legal entanglement or historical circumstance under discussion. What is beyond debate is that such details make the book vastly more interesting and readable. Hard-nosed examination yields mixed results. In the first place, Luke is able, through his literary artistry, to give the impression of an abundance of local color with a remarkably small number of well-stated details. About the Aegean region—Ephesus Philippi, Athens—he appears rather well informed. For the interior of Asia Minor he is rather less knowledgeable, and his grasp of the geography of Palestine is notoriously debatable. He can delineate the temple by reference to the Beautiful Gate and Solomon's stoa (3:2, 11). David's tomb, Bethany, the Mount of Olives, and the prison and audience chamber of the Sanhedrin also figure, although not without difficulties, particularly with regard to distance between places. It cannot be determined if this is due to poor sources, faulty guesswork, or indifference.[71] What should not be neglected is the contribution such circumstantial data make to the appeal of the narrative. The following discussion by a band of pirates contributes almost nothing to the plot of Chariton's novel:

> One man said, "Athens is nearby, a great and prosperous city. There we shall find a great number of dealers and an abundance of wealthy men. You can see as many whole cities in Athens as there are men in the market place."
> So they all thought it best to sail down to Athens. But Theron [the chief] did not care for the peculiar officiousness of that town. "Is it possible," he said, "that

you have not heard of the meddlesome curiosity of the Athenians? They are a talkative people [and] the Areopagus is near at hand." (Chariton 1.11.6)[72]

The motifs herein mentioned are mainly the same used by Luke: agora, curiosity, love of gossip, the Areopagus. Chariton and Luke apparently wrote for similar audiences. Each presumably had readers who would enjoy such displays of erudition.[73] In both cases the story would change not at all were the Athenian sections omitted. But how much less interesting they would be!

If Luke could not write, as so many ancient historical novelists, including Jewish authors did,[74] about the good old days of the Persian period and evoke the sentiment of nostalgia, he was able to create quite an ideal portrait of the early church, which he can sometimes call *archaios*, "ancient."[75] This was of course edifying, as all admirers of bygone days (*laudatores temporis acti*) know very well, but it was not therefore a whit less entertaining. It is also worth observing that Luke allowed an apparently selective exercise of his famous penchant for local color, applying it most thickly where there was trouble (Jerusalem, Philippi, Ephesus) or failure (Athens). If this is due to sources alone, the coincidence is remarkable.

THE LITERARY AND AESTHETIC FUNCTIONS
OF REVELATION AND PROPHECY,
SPEECHES AND LETTERS

Various modes of revelation play an important role in the theological message of Acts. Through such concrete manifestations, Luke portrays in a vivid way the guiding hand of God. They are also literary devices for motivating action and supplying the audience with information. Both of these functions may be illustrated by reference to ancient popular literature.

The Book of Acts opens with a prediction of the risen Lord that serves as a geographical outline (Acts 1:8) of the work.[76] By this means Luke achieves the summary expected as part of the preface. Rather than "spoil the plot," such advance descriptions[77] whet the readers' curiosity, giving an interpretive framework and assurance that all will end as God happily wills it. Writers of fiction employed similar devices for similar ends. The editor of Greek Esther prefixed to the (presumed) original a dream of Mordecai obliquely summarizing the plot.[78] The attempt to preserve suspense encouraged writers to produce murky oracles, of which Xenophon of Ephesus may have the most inept example.[79] Had they no literary value, it would be difficult to explain their frequent appearance in novels and other works of fiction.[80]

In addition to this initial prophecy, dreams, visions, or promptings by the

Spirit regularly direct the characters toward some course of action.[81] The more difficult or controversial the matter, the more elaborate the apparatus of intervention is likely to be. Luke certainly wishes to prove that God was the initiator of the gentile mission. The instrument selected was a popular one. Since such devices loom large in ancient novels, it is appropriate to conclude that the readers found them no less attractive than did their authors. Even in the romantic novels, the impetus to travel often comes via dream or divination.[82] No author of the Apoc. Acts dared omit a command delivered by way of a nocturnal vision.[83] Two types are worthy of special mention, the climactic decision and the double dream.

The epiphany that compelled Paul to transfer his operations to the European shore of the Aegean was an artistic way to display a major transition in history or the career of a great person.[84] Paul, like Alexander and Caesar, experienced the vision of a personified province or nation. He is therefore at a significant turning point in his own history, which is also that of the world. Apollonius, not surprisingly, had a similar experience:

> While he was reflecting on these things, he had the following dream: a very tall and aged woman appeared, embraced him and beseeched him to visit her before sailing to Italy. (*Ap. Ty.* 4.34)

This is an elegant literary introduction to a climactic moment. Through it Luke indicates the importance of what is about to take place (and raises Paul to the level of Alexander).

"Double dreams," like those recorded in Acts 9:1–19a and 10:1–48, provide unmistakable guarantees of divine guidance. This popular motif[85] played a vital role in a number of religious novels, the sources from which C. Burchard found the most fruitful parallels to Acts 9. In the Cornelius episode Luke has probably made the vision of Peter coincide with the angelophany to Cornelius in a way that achieves the result of a double dream.[86] Since this aretalogical mechanism was all but irresistible for so many religious novelists, it is legitimate to infer that in its literary place in Acts it fulfills a similar function. Achilles Tatius had, at any rate, heard enough double dreams to parody the whole convention.[87]

Revelations also foreshadow, raise suspense by telling the audience that suffering or disaster is on the way or by promising eventual deliverance.[88] The dramatic benefit of such devices is once again illuminated by their repeated appearance in various sorts of ancient fiction.[89] The use of dreams and other modes of divination and revelation in Acts is basically the same as that in the Apoc. Acts and other popular literature. Through these techniques the stories could be enhanced, structure could be provided, and readers could be both given assurance and held in suspense. As "levers through which new activities are set in motion,"[90] the techniques undergird an apparently capricious plot with a providential foundation.

EXCURSUS:
PROVIDENCE AND CHARACTERIZATION IN POPULAR RELIGIOUS WRITINGS

The verifiability of God's "providence" is constitutive for the theology of Luke.[91] All salvation history, all history, including the course of nature, is in God's hands. This providence is not a mystery but may be verified by reference to empirical criteria, as Gamaliel made clear in 5:38–39. Success will distinguish between the human and divine wills. When God is opposed, both individuals and society are punished: witness the fates of Ananias and Jerusalem, the blinding of the magus, and the riot at Ephesus. Miracles may most visibly manifest providence, but they are merely the tip of the iceberg (14:15–17).

Such an unabashedly concrete and unreflective theology fully deserves the label "popular." Culturally, it is thoroughly compatible with the naive idealism that emerges in sentimental fiction.[92] Virtue triumphs over evil because God is on the side of the virtuous. Evil fate only masters those who have not the protection of a benevolent deity. Those who remain true to an ideal will win with the aid of divine providence. In sentimental novels, love is the primary symbol of such fidelity, and marriage the perfect expression of that ideal, but there were other possibilities, including reunion, return to one's home or status, or more pertinently, union with a god rather than a lover.[93] That God is on the side of lovers is a theme not only of Jewish and pagan religious novels[94] but also of the romantic tales of love and adventure.[95]

Cultivated minds can weary of all this. Rohde, winding up his summary of Xenophon of Ephesus, breathed a sigh of relief: "One is glad when . . . the puppets can be put back into their box."[96] He was not alone in laying this charge against one or more ancient novels.[97] Of Acts, Haenchen said that

> here stands revealed a peculiarity of Lucan theology which can scarcely be claimed as a point in its favor. . . . The obedience from faith which Luke would have liked to portray turns into something utterly different: very nearly the twitching of human puppets.[98]

One may regret the melodramatic effect of replacing character with providence, but its cultural and ideological roots require examination. Popular writers did (and do) not replace character with circumstance simply from inability to portray character, as some would have it. Their audiences do not wish to be told that they are responsible for their own troubles. Rather than seeking growth of character through acceptance of responsibility for one's fate, the "immature reader"[99] prefers a beneficent providence, not least a providence partial to youth and beauty. Works that establish causal links through a god rather than by characterization reflect a certain view of life. Examination of popular fiction provides insight into Luke's theology and the sort of audience toward which his work was directed.

ORATORY AND EPISTOLOGRAPHY

Treatment of oratory and epistolography in a chapter dealing with entertainment may strike many readers as ill advised. Survivors of the pews and banquet halls of today, who must daily sift through computer-generated advertising mail, may not be prepared to consider rhetoric entertaining. Whatever the present situation, it was not so in the Greco-Roman world, where public speaking was, among other things, a type of public entertainment. This was even more true when Roman dominion had rendered much political rhetoric obsolete. Even such stern critics of frivolous speaking as Dio of Prusa and Lucian of Samosata produced little orations that were pure entertainments.[100] Since literature was often published through readings and speeches were literary works of intended artistry, the difference would be even smaller than it is now. The people who flocked to hear the apostles in the stoa of Solomon (Acts 3:11; 5:12) or Paul in the Antiochene synagogue (13:34) would be presumed to be drawn not only by a novel message but also by some talented oratory, just as Augustine would later visit the Milanese basilica to hear Ambrose, and learned pagans would drop by to listen to Chrysostom preach.[101] As a skilled speaker, Paul could draw crowds in barbarous Phrygia, cultured Athens, and a host of places in between. In his defense speeches of Acts 24—26, Paul serves as a rhetor who by his wit and elocution can make life in a dreary province just a bit less intolerable. One intent of all these packed halls and jammed forums is to impress the reader with the oratorical skill of the early Christian missionaries. Even unconvinced pagans like Felix and Festus found Paul impressive (24:24–25; 26:24).

One of the most attractive aspects of the speeches in Acts is the great variety of setting, subject, and style that they display. They are, of course, the equivalent of samples: bits and pieces long enough to convey the desired effect. Repetition is relatively rare despite the basic paucity of themes: mission and defense. In addition to availing himself of a variety of settings, Luke makes use of different styles. For the early chapters in particular, he imitates the Septuagint. Although the source is different, the technique is that of the schools, wherein pupils were trained to imitate Thucydides or Demosthenes.[102] Recognition of mimesis was a source of pleasure to readers, as was the identification of rhetorical figures and devices such as assonance or antithesis, and the perception of formal structures, just as hearers today increase their pleasure when they can identify the form of a piece of music, its compositional techniques, or the imitation of an earlier composer or work. Luke evidently expected at least some of his audience to be familiar with the Greek Bible and to be aware of some rhetorical basics.

The speeches of Acts are largely without parallel in the Gospel of Luke and
are presumed to be the writer's composition, even by those who contend that
Luke often reported the gist of what was said on a particular occasion. Comparison with ancient historians has been customary, but this comparison
must not be exaggerated. In the first place, the use of speeches does not establish the genre. One will not find missionary addresses in Thucydides, after all, and defense and kindred orations are to be found in many genres, including novels.[103]

There are also some differences. Dibelius argued long ago that the
speeches in Acts do not resemble those found in the historians.[104] The lack
of stylistic unity, however realistic and interesting, does not conform to historiographical canons.[105] By repeating similar speeches in varied settings,
Luke could show how his heroes responded to different situations. This is
novelistic.[106] So is the "fondness for direct speech"[107] that permits the
audience to hear closed deliberations and overhear private conversations.
Choral addresses are likewise unusual (5:29–32; 14:15–17). Like ancient
novelists, Luke frequently resorted to having speeches interrupted, a dramatic device.[108]

Historians were not supposed to assign speakers positions they had, in ac-
tuality, rejected. Luke did this often.[109] Pseudo-Callisthenes provides, in
this instance, a more apt model than Thucydides.

The *Alexander Romance* gives a verbatim report of the Athenian assembly's
response to Alexander's demand for surrender of their leading rhetors.
Aeschines was willing, but Demades denounced Alexander with vigor. In
this moment of uncertainty the public naturally looked to Demosthenes, who
rose to speak eloquently in Alexander's behalf. Nearly everyone approved the
subsequent resolution, including Plato and Lysias.[110] Is not Luke's Gamaliel a similar figure from the past, whose legendary status made him an ideal
mouthpiece for the author's opinion, never mind how improbably?

Ancient novels will again provide more convincing and useful parallels to
the contents and literary function of the speeches in Acts than will histories.
The courtroom was a favorite place for a rhetorical display, often containing
surprising revelations and leading to unexpected results.[111]

The rhetorical duel of Acts 24:2–21 has many analogues. The two
speeches in Chariton 5.6–8, like those in Acts, begin by currying the audience's favor (*captatio benevolentiae*) and show appropriate stylistic variation.
Hellenic Dionysios uses an Attic style, whereas Mithridates, a "Persian," is
flamboyantly Asiatic.[112] At least some of Chariton's readers would admire
such clever touches. In the same way Luke's audience is treated in 22:1–21
to an "Aramaic" speech and in 26:2–23 to its Greek counterpart. Even the
unsophisticated readers of *Ninus* were regaled with the injection of the

nature-vs.-convention (*nomos-physis*) debate into a speech pleading that the hero be allowed to marry an underage bride.[113]

Letters provided another fascinating subject for those of moderate education. Then, as more recently, handbooks were prepared with sample letters for every circumstance, and letters, real and fictitious, enjoyed literary success. Letters create a warm and personal atmosphere, and they serve as a kind of documentation lending verisimilitude to the situation. The so-called apostolic decree of Acts 15:23–29 is framed in the style of a state letter. This is a fabricated official document, like the royal letters in Esther, *3 Maccabees*, the *Alexander Romance*, and a number of ancient historical novels and tracts.[114] By such means Luke has given the decree more weight and has painted the early church with glowing colors.

The letter of Claudius to Felix is likewise an invention, based upon neither data nor probability but wish (Acts 23:26–30). By this means the tribune stated his conviction of Paul's innocence, testimony needed here because he would never come to court to give it and end the case. Historians did not have such license to concoct letters.[115] The appeal of letters inserted into popular narratives is once again evident from various novels. Missives convey information, arouse feelings, generate action, and create a lifelike narrative world.[116]

The Apoc. Acts contain their full share of speeches and documents, including a variety of intellectual and rhetorical displays.[117] The similarity between them and the speeches in Acts is more on literary than stylistic grounds. Speeches thus work to achieve similar results in narrative literature. Through these addresses Luke no doubt said some important things. He further provided his readers with a kind of stimulation they would find no less pleasing than wholesome. In the speeches Luke helped create for his audience a narrative world that would allow them to become present in the actual world of the apostles and eyewitnesses of the Word. They form an important part of the narrative world Luke sought to create.

LIFE IN HIGH SOCIETY

Acts strongly emphasizes the status of its leaders and converts, through the impression made by its missionaries upon ruling bodies and the ease with which those leaders, in particular Paul, move in the upper level of society. Already at Pentecost, Roman citizens were converted. Paul and Silas enjoyed the Roman franchise. Early converts included Barnabas, a Levite (4:36), hordes of priests (6:7), property owners, an Ethiopian official, a centurion, one of Herod's companions (13:1), the wealthy merchant Lydia,[118] the jailer, an Areopagite, the head of the Corinthian synagogue, wealthy and leading citizens in Thessalonica and Berea, and a Roman proconsul (13:12). The masses are there also, faceless, nameless, deferent, and orderly, but those singled out by Luke are nearly always quite prominent in the social world of their day.

Through display of their erudition, Peter and John (and later all the Twelve) impress the Sanhedrin (Acts 4:13–19; 5:29). Peter must in fact rebuke a centurion who grovels before him. Yet all of this is minor compared with the accomplishments of Paul.

> The Paul of Acts . . . appears . . . in his educated tone of polished courtesy, in his quick vehement temper, in the extraordinary versatility and adaptability which made him at home in every society, moving at ease in all surroundings, and everywhere the centre of interest whether he is the Socratic dialectician in the agora of Athens, or the Rhetorician in its University, or conversing with kings and proconsuls, or advising in the council on shipboard, or cheering a broken-spirited crew to make one more effort for life.[119]

Luke does not, as might be expected, introduce Paul with a summary of his background, as a systematic biographer might do,[120] but he reveals in stages the status of his hero. By pooling data we learn that Paul was born in Tarsus, of which he was a citizen, holding Roman citizenship also, but was reared and educated in Jerusalem, where he became in due course a member of the Sanhedrin.[121] In addition to enjoying this Jewish educational heritage, Paul was also a learned Greek and skilled orator able to impress a governor.[122] Throughout Acts he moved as Ramsay saw, with equal facility among the ruling class of both Jewish and Roman worlds. He could impress the Areopagus, manipulate the Sanhedrin, and fill the leisure time of Festus and Agrippa (Acts 17; 24; 26). His friends included the most wealthy and snobbish inhabitants of the Roman province of Asia (19:31). He was able to convert Sergius Paulus, a senatorial governor, and came near to adding the names of Felix and Agrippa to the baptismal register of the church at Caesarea. His manner of teaching was also dignified. No fees were charged, nor would he resort to use of the streetcorner or marketplace (except in Athens). Magicians despised him. He could stop rioters in their tracks. The style of his life and the circle of his friends qualified Paul as the kind of person one would read about in a letter of the younger Pliny, a sort of Dio of Prusa.[123]

Even in custody he shone. The leaders of Philippi hastened to correct their mistreatment. Felix ascertained that his confinement was not too rigorous. The chief citizen of Malta received him and his colleagues as honored guests, their status notwithstanding. Roman officials kept him in a mild form of house arrest (Acts 28).[124] Lesser types all but abased themselves in his interest. The concern displayed by his jailer at Philippi, by Lysias, the tribune who arrested him, and by Julius, his centurion escort to Rome, is touching.[125]

Just as the assemblies of the church resembled the senate of Rome, so Paul appeared wherever he went before the highest authority available, and never did he fail to acquit himself nobly. Throughout his captivity in Caesarea, Paul functioned like the chief attraction in a fashionable salon.

Historians will enter hosts of appropriate objections. If some early Christians were fairly well-to-do, the vast majority were not.[126] It will be some time before one can begin to jibe about the "Tory party at prayer." Can competent scholars really maintain that all of this is so? Has Paul not obtained just a bit too much of a good thing, in being both a citizen of Tarsus and a Roman gentleman, a member of the Sanhedrin and a learned Hellene? Paul's own letters give no impression of wealth or great education, and there is at least some room for skepticism about his citizenships at Tarsus and Rome.[127] Not even the leading defenders of Acts say much about Paul's sitting in the Sanhedrin casting one vote after another for the death of Christians. Luke has certainly gilded the lily, probably painted a weed to look like a gilded lily. Why? The viewpoint of Acts is snobbish and aristocratic: workers are despised, the crowds of unemployed scorned, and only the well-to-do given prominence.[128]

It simply will not do to claim that Luke was an aristocrat, or writing for a wealthy church. Christians had not yet made such progress on the social ladder, and aristocrats were better educated. The customary procedure has been to minimize these exaggerations and then refer to Luke's "apologetic interest," always a convenient refuge. In reality, what Luke does in the matter of status is better described as propagandistic fiction than apologetic idealizing. The upward mobility of many new religions encourages fictional propaganda about their adherents' social status.[129]

How thrilling it was for Luke's audience to hear of the grace and charm of Paul, of the reception accorded their foundational heroes by their social superiors! The achievements of Paul coincide with the fondest social aspirations of the petite bourgeoisie[130] of that time, of the very people to whom Luke was making his primary pitch. Success like this was a pleasant subject for meditation. Implicit within the story of Paul is the message that worldly recognition and success are possible and desirable for Christians. They are an incentive to good Christian citizenship[131] as well as a consolation for those who find their faith an obstacle to social advancement, to participation in civic cult and life. Luke did not achieve this aim in the manner of the deutero-Pauline Epistles or *1 Clement*. He narrated instead a story of "Christian virtue rewarded."[132]

Similar aspirations shine forth in the pre-Sophistic and other novels, wherein status is a pressing question. The leading characters are, whether they know it or not, persons of quality.[133] Through one calamity or another, usually several, they often lose their status and must face life as persons of menial or even servile rank. By providence and persistence they are able to regain their place in society and live happily ever after. The status into which they fall is at or below that of their intended readers (and their ancestors), people who aspire to rise to wealth and comfort. The audience may thus identify in fantasy with the principal characters and move up the social ladder with them.

In those novels, as in Acts, the leading actors move in the presence of powerful officials and kings, outwitting tyrants and their minions. These heroes, too, can shine in the exotic atmosphere of regal splendor and survive the pitfalls of palace intrigue. There was much attraction in the great pomp (*pollē phantasia*) of a trial before the royal throne (Acts 25:23).[134]

Romantic leads loved to stress their descent from the leading families of the older Greek cities,[135] their Hellenic standing,[136] their education,[137] and their class.[138] The fascination with prominent citizens detectable in Acts has no lack of parallels in novels of the period.[139] From the viewpoint of the primary readers, such persons belonged to the quality. They were their "betters," the kind of people they longed to be.

One could no more use these novels to discover the mores and values of the royalty and aristocracy of their time than use 1 Corinthians to learn what was of interest to the Asiarchs. The actions of the characters are motivated not by the dictates of their class and breeding but by the naive idealism of their readers. The outlook of these people is bourgeois, their attitude sentimental.[140]

Through such popular writings one can strengthen the interpretive profile for Luke-Acts. The writer was not appealing so much to the Roman rulers as to the aspirations of his readers. He has created, in Paul and others, the kind of heroes admired by upwardly inclined persons of modest education and resources.

Status also serves other literary goals. Paul's eloquence enables him to evade difficult situations (Acts 14:14–18; 23:6–10). His *paideia* is a powerful weapon, as even an embattled tribune could recognize (21:38). His civic privileges are hidden trumps, revealed only when needed to take the final trick.[141] Luke uses Paul's citizenship as a literary device, as a deus ex machina. This is novelistic. Through it Luke excites and surprises his readers, most of whom would like to imagine that they also might be wealthy and prominent, always ready with the right phrase and able to put troublemakers in their place with an offhand reference to their own background or position.

Thus Lucius, just restored to human state, naked in the middle of an arena, and about to be lynched as a witch, is befriended by the governor, an old friend of his parents, after revealing his ancestry, homeland, occupation, and status (*The Ass* 54–55). Of Apollonius we also discover a good background, from an old and wealthy family, and a good education. He too was the friend of philosophers and impressive in the presence of rulers. Like Paul, the sage from Tyana met with deference from his military escort and had to endure but a light form of confinement.[142] Philostratus made Apollonius respectable for purely apologetic purposes. In the case of Paul, the portrait was also a source of enjoyment.

Silence about one's status is a common device in popular fiction. Had Esther advised the king at an earlier point that she was Jewish, the story would have been quite different. When Callirhoe first met Dionysios, she reluctantly told him all but one crucial fact: she was already married. Her husband, Chaireas, was crucified for refusing to speak. Leucippe used a false name. Xenophon several times kept the pot boiling by having his characters withhold information, sometimes agonizingly.[143] That Paul would not unveil his Roman citizenship until after a beating or night in jail or until stretched out upon the rack exceeds probability. Whether the data are true or false, Luke's use of them accords with the practice of novelists. The amount of space in Acts 16—28 devoted to describing Paul's status and friends among the elite, the high character of his teaching and practice, the quality of his followers, and the baseness of his opposition is truly remarkable and must be appreciated if the nature of Acts is to be understood. Luke affirms, in a most engaging way, that one can be a Christian and still have social aspirations.

EXCURSUS:
TO WHOM WERE ANCIENT
POPULAR NOVELS ADDRESSED?

The surviving body of ancient novels, even when narrowly defined (see further, chap. 4 of this book), is far too disparate to be attributed to a single readership group.[144] With specific regard to those works he classified as pre-Sophistic, namely, *Ninus*, Chariton, X. E., and the Greek prototype presumed to underlie the *Pseudo-Clementines*, the opinion of B.E. Perry long prevailed. Following the suggestions of J. Ludvikovsky and Bruno Lavagnini, Perry proposed that such novels were destined for the edification of naive (possibly juvenile) readers of a middle-class, pagan society.[145] In recent years this theory has been challenged.[146]

More or less intuitive judgments tend to flourish in this area because of the difficulty of identifying and applying specific criteria. Most important would be exact profiles of the groups who read such works, but little information of this sort is available, except for the Christian literature, and even in this case there is no definite consensus about social conditions.[147] Indirect testimony emerges in the almost absolute silence of aristocratically oriented authors toward the novel, punctuated by only a few contemptuous references and an occasional parody.[148] The novel was a genre lacking status, as nameless and voiceless as the myriads of slaves who tilled the fields and waited upon the tables of the wealthy.

Material remains tell a similar tale. Of the group Perry designated pre-Sophistic, only Chariton survives in more or less complete condition. Xenophon of Ephesus may be an abridgment, and the others are fragmentary, pieces and fascicles of papyrus recovered from the dustbins of Egypt. Being deemed unworthy of preservation by sophisticated critics, these works largely disappeared from human memory. Other material criteria, including quality of paper, type of script, and employment of the codex format rather than the roll, lend additional support to this understanding of a large portion of the ancient novels about which anything is known. The majority were despised by those with the refined taste developed by wealth and education.

Style and cultural level are more difficult to evaluate. Chariton, Xenophon, and the authors of many fragmentary novels used a relatively unadorned *koinē* Greek without elaborate periods.[149] They can also be much more sensitive to such matters as avoidance of hiatus than the writers of the NT, for example, and do not neglect literary allusions and quotations from recognized classics. Observation of such amenities has led Graham Anderson and D. Levin to express reservations about the degree of "popularity" of any romantic novel.[150]

The most employed yet least controllable of all measuring sticks depends upon inferences from the content: the groups represented and the manner of their depiction, the values and attitudes communicated by the texts, as well as the type of material presented. It is beyond dispute that the readers of ancient novels, whoever they were, found great pleasure in appeals to basic emotion and sentiment, in action and excitement, in heartbreak and tension, in demonstrations of unfailing fidelity and safe delivery from the most varied and horrifying dangers imaginable. Kindred material was to be found in mime and novella, folk tale, and New Comedy. A similar spirit nurtured the games and spectacles of Hellenistic and imperial times. These productions were pitched toward the bottom of the social ladder, and if they were often popular with those of higher standing (and they were), those enthusiasts were frequent targets of critical disdain. From the thematic perspective, the early novels were unabashedly "popular."

Their values are bourgeois. Genuine love can find its fulfillment only in marriage, one result of which will be children. These paeans to the nuclear family are quite different from the notions of love presented by the Latin elegiac poets and the writers preserved in the Greek Anthology, for instance. Other values that come to light are civic and national pride, respect for wealth, admiration of education, ambivalence toward the "gentry," and nostalgia for the good old days. In the more "popular" novels these standards are proclaimed with neither reservation nor nuance. So that such ideals are made perfectly clear, the readers are treated to readily recognizable collections of good and bad characters, the former of which embody those ideals even at the expense of what we call characterization. Fondness for domestic virtues is particularly noticeable when applied to such figures as Ninus, Alexander, and any number of oriental monarchs who appear with the trappings of royalty and the hearts of shopkeepers. Historians like Thucydides and his emulators wrote for the education of future statesmen (*Histories* 1.22). Those who dipped into *Ninus* in pursuit of such edification would be gravely disappointed. If, however, a reader craved painless and pleasurable reading that nurtured traditional bourgeois values, a popular novel describing how observance of such principles restored the great Ninus to his throne and brought him a fine bride would be of obvious utility.

Although these romantic novels paid at least lip service to the merits of fidelity and tenacity, they did not really attribute fate to character. The attitudes communicated are rather like those implicit in many of the miracle stories of the Christian gospels. They do not portray much growth of character nor recommend it, for the attitude implicit in most ancient romances looks rather to a mighty god or kindly providence[151] to bestow upon one the power needed to overcome fate. Twentieth-century experience assigns such sentiments to those who perceive themselves as victims, as sufferers from bad luck and the machinations of others. Adolescents frequently attribute their maladies to others and see themselves as victims of undeserved ill treatment, just as they are likely to rely upon beauty and charm to achieve their goals. Gilbert Highet's description is memorable:

[The Greek novels] are meant for the young, or for those who wish they were still young. All the leading characters in them are about eighteen years old, and think almost exclusively about their emotions. No one plans his life, or works toward a distant end, or follows out a long-term career. The hero and heroine are buffeted about by events without deserving it—as young people always feel that they themselves are buffeted—and yet no irremediable damage happens to them, they are united while they are still fair and young and ardent and chaste. In these, as in modern romantic stories, the Cinderella myth is one of the chief fantasies: a typical wish-fulfilment pattern, in which one does not have to work for success or wealth, but is miraculously endowed with it by a fairy godmother and the sudden passion of a prince. . . . Even the style reflects youth: for the commonest devices are antithesis and oxymoron. Everything is black or white, and these devices represent violent contrast and paradoxical combination of opposites.[152]

Intuitive perception of this "immature" view of life—no less common in modern romance than ancient—presumably led Perry toward his definition of the audience of the early romantic novel of antiquity. His intuition (if intuition it was) will stand the test of time and more rigorous examination. More recent critics, especially Schmeling and Hägg,[153] have raised doubts regarding the validity of composing too distinct a social profile from the foregoing observations and seeing this as the literature of adolescents. Immaturity is not a quality restricted to the young, and even mature adults may draw occasional pleasure from writings based upon rather immature premises. G. Schmeling and Tomas Hägg thus prefer to speak of a sentimental group as the implied audience of the early novels.

The values of the works in question are thus conventional, staunch virtues of bygone Golden Ages. Their attitudes are adolescent, beauty being the most important quality one can possess, and a true love the chief aim of life. One is not encouraged to accept responsibility for one's life; rather, troubles are assigned to cruel fate and jealous adversaries. The universe depicted operates according to the laws of a naive idealism in which virtue has its reward and the Golden Rule is written into the molecules. Egoism flourishes.[154]

A substantial portion of the intended and actual readership were women. Facile comparisons with "ladies' magazine fiction" and soap operas may be in order, but such observations are not decisive. Nonetheless, the prominent role of female characters cannot be ignored. As often as not, the heroines are more resolute, clever, and effective than their mates.[155] Chariton's novel was probably entitled *Callirhoe*, and female nomenclature may have been employed in other cases.[156]

C. Miralles has noted that the depiction of love as a disease for which matrimony is the preferred antidote was suitable to the circumstances of many women. Recommendation of marriage as a kind of golden mean between the excesses of free love and celibacy supports both popular morality and the position of women, who had in general little protection outside marriage.[157] Women had even less opportunity than men for adventure and excitement, and there was a dearth of heroic literature pertaining to their sex. Thus, as Hägg says, this may have been one of the first genres to receive its main support from women. The Apoc. Acts lend additional weight to this possibility. Were women perhaps among the composers of romantic novels? Hägg is quite sympathetic to this suggestion, although he shrewdly observes that the idea of a beautiful yet faithfully chaste woman is perhaps a typically male fantasy.[158]

The major question outstanding is that of cultural level and the corresponding demands upon readers. Levin and Anderson have questioned the notion of a middle-class readership of limited education. The argument from style is inadequate. Even if these writers eschewed hiatus like marital infidelity, no one will mistake their products for works of high stylistic attainment. Greater weight must be attached to the use of literary citation and allusion, the imitation of classic scenes, and the employment of learned motifs.

Chariton presents the strongest case. There are a number of quotes, the vast majority from Homer, two-thirds from the *Iliad*.[159] In addition, a number of scenes are based upon Homeric models.[160] Chariton also imitates the historians, especially Xenophon.[161] There is little doubt that readers who recognize his mimesis and allusions will have their pleasure enhanced. Since Homer was the standard and basic school text, Chariton has given his readers every opportunity of doing just that. Citations from Homer will be recognized by all those with a basic education, the kind of training without which one could not attempt to read this or any novel.

Moreover, those who miss these allusions or discover them only in commentaries (like some readers of modern versions) will not thereby have their enjoyment reduced to such an extent that the novel will lose its appeal. Unlike some of the recherché works of the Second Sophistic, which cannot be appreciated without knowledge of the model being imitated, it is quite possible to read Chariton without recognizing his limited literary allusions.[162] Nor is it valid to presume that the literary culture of an author is the same as that of his or her readers. Those who found Chariton a bit above their heads in places would be well assured that reading this book was an improving accomplishment. Not even the "best" of the pre-Sophistic novels thus appears to require a highly cultured audience.[163] These works were evidently composed to meet the leisure needs of citizen groups in the cities of the Hellenistic and imperial east. These persons were the beneficiaries of general education, open in many cases to women. The local pride and nostalgia for the days of ancient glory which so frequently infuse the novels would be congenial to such persons, and the values expressed in most novels reflect the themes of sepulchral and honorific inscriptions. They may thus be appealed to for information about the social life and thought of this important but largely silent segment of the ancient world. It was among people of this condition and background that early Greek Christianity found much of its leadership and from which it drew substantial support.[164] Roman society in the west lacked this kind of broad literate base, and therefore popular novels failed to emerge until late antiquity.[165] The two major Latin novels, those of Petronius and Apuleius, were directed toward cultivated readerships.

The most culturally acceptable form of light reading for the highly educated was provided by dramatic historiography, including many of the monographs, and gossipy biography. Those who looked for romance could also find a good deal to satisfy them in epic. The *Argonautica* of Apollonius of Rhodes can be described as a novel in verse, and the *Aeneid* contains numerous romantic features and motifs.[166] The very wealthy and well educated did, of course, turn to romantic novels also, as standard complaints and disparagements of "trashy" reading confirm.[167] In due course some of them took a hand in the composition of novels, and works like those of Apuleius, Longus, and Heliodorus began to emerge. Novels had moved from the bedside tables of the elite to their salons. Literary genres can display the same zest for upward mobility as new religious cults. By the early third century c.e., Origen could speak in fashionable settings and no less a Sophist than Philostratus could seek to do for Apollonius of Tyana what Luke had earlier done for Paul. To write the history of the ancient novel one must take social history into account.

The question would probably be beyond dispute had more truly "popular" pieces of fiction survived. Fragments like the *Phoinikaka* and the *Iolaus* novel suggest the existence of a literature as racy and crude as anything performed in spectacle and mime. *Joseph and Asenath* and the *Acts of Paul and Thecla* indicate what some Jews and Christians read. It is difficult to imagine that pagans of similar educational and social levels lacked comparable writings. In circles like these the novel developed and acquired many of its basic characteristics.

4.   THE ANCIENT NOVEL

Its Origins and Nature

The reign of God is also like a dragnet thrown into the lake, which collected all
sorts of things.

—Matt. 13:47 NAB

In the preceding chapters I have attempted to demonstrate that preconceptions about genre have discouraged critics from appreciating Luke's interest in providing readers with a pleasurable account of Christian origins. Although clearly a theological book and a presentation of history, Acts also seeks to entertain.[1] This conclusion challenges one of the traditional criteria used to distinguish canonical from apocryphal Acts.

To leap from this conclusion to the further inference that all Acts should be lumped together and then analyzed for generic characteristics would be premature. In the first place, the Apoc. Acts are too disparate a group to constitute an easily definable literary type.[2] Differences in form, structure, and style are substantial, not to mention in theology and theme.[3] Arrangement of books by titles does not exhaust the resources of form criticism.[4] There is not one, unified (sub)genre of Christian Acts with which Luke's book may be compared.

Methodologically, such a body of texts would be too small. One cannot account for the Apoc. Acts as internal developments within the group. Their diversity suggests responses to a variety of literary, cultural, and religious stimuli over a significant expanse of time and space. There has been an implicit recognition of the need for a broader formal sample. Traditionally, Lukan scholars have sorted the fish scooped up by the net of historiography, whereas investigators of the Apoc. Acts have tended to look toward the ancient novel, albeit with reservations. Both groups have made occasional appeals to sui generis solutions.[5]

Thematic, structural, and stylistic affinities with various novels should at the very least provoke further reflection upon the ancient novel and upon the usefulness of the genre for enhancing present-day appreciation of early Christian narrative. The aim should not be such sensationalistic oversimplifications as, Acts is a novel, concocted by Luke. My study intends to be more subtle. There is more at stake here than a label to pin upon Acts or an against-the-grain proposal to embrace or despise.

Hitherto, numerous parallels to a number of ancient novels have been introduced. This procedure was justified by the reasonable certainty that romantic novels and works of adventure were intended to entertain, however dull or didactic we may find them today. Definition of a genre requires more than a listing of similar motifs. To determine the degree to which the term "historical novel" will give profile to Acts it is necessary to arrive at some understanding of what that phrase means and, most important, what works it may comprehend. The object of this chapter is not to devise a definition of "novel" into which works like Acts may be squeezed but to determine whether comparison with a body of texts so defined may shed more light upon the form and function of this book than will comparison with learned pieces of historiography. I shall begin with a review of scholarly discussion.

THE ANCIENT NOVEL: FROM ROHDE TO REARDON AND BEYOND

In the summer of 1976 an international group of scholars gathered at the University College of North Wales, in Bangor, to commemorate the centenary of Erwin Rohde's *Der Griechische Roman und seine Vorläufer*. The presentations made there, as summarized in the proceedings edited by B. P. Reardon under the title *Erotica Antiqua,* and in the publications deriving therefrom, constitute incontrovertible evidence of the end of Rohde's sway over this field. So erudite and persuasive was his monograph that one hundred years were required to shift discussion beyond the boundaries established by Rohde. The object of his investigation was first and foremost to explain the origins of the Greek novel, specifically the romantic novels of the imperial age, collectively known as the *scriptores erotici.*

Rohde's focus upon this narrow corpus was not due to his admiration of it, for he dissected these novels with all the disdain expected in an academic examination of popular fiction. For Rohde the novels were really a problem, a blemish on the fair complexion of Greek culture, even in its imperial decrepitude. They were an aberration for which accounts had to be rendered. Since his intent was to describe the genesis of the novel, Rodhe's major insights and energy were expended upon the precursors (*Vorläufer*) he identified. That aspect of his work has not yet been superseded. Much of this material, Hellenistic love poetry in particular, is rather generally esteemed; it conformed to the contents of nineteenth-century classical syllabuses. Rohde's literary taste is no longer of particular concern, but this taste distorted his understanding of the material and dictated his focus. Since the novelists de-

rived neither standards of taste nor canons of excellence from their forerun-
ners, what they did take was theme, and Rohde's logic thus led him to understand his subject in terms of theme and motif. The novel was a degenerate
imitation of good literature.

One of Rohde's own predecessors was A. Chassang, whose somewhat dif-
fuse and largely summarizing survey of a wide variety of ancient fiction, or alleged fiction, he found inadequate. Chassang identified two types of fiction,
"poetic" and "novelistic," the latter derived from historiography. Rohde's
program took shape by establishing a similarity between the romantic view of
love found in the novels and the spirit of Hellenistic love poetry. This de-
stroyed the basis of Chassang's distinction. It further enhanced Rohde's inclination to limit his survey to romantic works and to disregard the potential role of historiography. By current standards such reasoning may be
defective in that it explains all literary phenomena by genetic literary
theories. Rohde did not, for instance, describe the romantic notion of het-
erosexual love as a phenomenon of the Hellenistic and imperial eras revealed
in different ways by elegists and novelists among others. The idea of romantic love came to novelists from books rather than life. Hellenistic poets were
resources for later writers rather than representatives of a new spirit.

Despite what now seems a fairly mechanical approach to the material and
decades of new discoveries and ongoing scholarly comment, Rohde's work
has endured.[6] This is in large part due to his masterly description of the material and his comprehension of a vast body of writings. Although far from
unaware of popular tales, oriental stories, local sagas, and travel books (material that has furnished his critics with the bases of their counterproposals),
Rohde steered a straight course toward his explanation of the romantic novels
and evaded all such murky distractions.

The corpus of romantic novels was undeniably Greek and generally bore
the stamp of the movement called the Second Sophistic.[7] Rohde therefore located the origins of the corpus in that movement. To claim something as a
product of that phenomenon was less than high praise: the Second Sophistic
was then in low repute. "Artificial," "dead," "bookish," and "derivative"
are typical epithets used to describe that era and literature. Having observed,
like the good patriarch Photius (whose summaries of several novels are both
invaluable and frustrating), that love and travel were the two major motifs in
the novels, Rohde posited a concoction blended from these two disparate
themes in the kitchen of the Second Sophistic.[8] He sensed a lack of necessary
or internal connection between the themes and subjected each to a lengthy
survey.[9]

Rohde's instinct that love does not require travel and vice versa was sound,
but his solution—that the prominence of the two themes is due to an artificial synthesis—is questionable.[10]

Artificial syntheses are by definition not natural developments and require an intentional act by a synthesizer. Rohde's candidate was Antonius Diogenes, author of *The Marvels beyond Thule.*[11] Rohde thereby answered the question of origins. Ancient Greek novels were superficial creations with highly improbable plots. Rhetorical training did include no little exposure to superficiality, and compared with a number of rhetorical topics for exercise, the plots of those novels seem routine. Since subsequent discoveries have shipwrecked Rohde's chronology, it is easy to overlook the value and force of this thesis.[12] By describing the novel as an artificial creation Rohde did not have to account for its failure to correspond to the normal history of genres, from simple to complex, "pure" to decadent. Others found such development and attributed to Rohde's theory a bit of his own artificial synthesizing.

W. Heintze and K. Bürger fastened upon the apparent insignificance of love in Antonius Diogenes, and the latter rejected Rohde in detail.[13] For E. Schwartz restriction of the genre to love stories was question begging. He found Rohde too narrow in focus and unwilling to recognize the role of historiography in shaping the genre. Challenging Rohde's use of Hellenistic poetry as a primary and direct source, Schwartz refuted the notion that "free invention" of material was the leading technique of ancient novelists.[14]

Criticism continued, and papyrus discoveries soon revealed that Rohde had placed their emergence too late, incorrectly ordered their sequence, and thus overlooked the composition of non-Sophistic novels.[15] Nonetheless, his definition of the novel by reference to the twin motifs of love and travel has long dominated discussion. Several weaknesses may now be identified in this theory:

1. It is not true, unless one wishes to subtract *Daphnis and Chloe* (generally regarded as the best of Greek novels) from the genre because it lacks travel, and to overlook Apuleius' novel, which is not a love story (nor was its Greek prototype).[16]

2. Rohde did not deal adequately with a number of the elements that have contributed to the development of ancient novels, including historiography, folk tale and literature, "oriental" writings, and important changes in society, culture, and religion.

3. As Reardon succinctly notes, even a complete list of materials from which novels could be constructed does not constitute a reason for producing them.[17] Rohde identified a valley of dry bones and left them there, assuming, apparently, that Sophists could not breathe life into anything and that no one of that age would particularly care or be able to notice.

In various metamorphoses, however, the dogma that ancient novels can be identified by the presence of certain (in fact, two) motifs has persisted.[18] Such arguments are conveniently self-justifying and happily circular. Any genre that can be described by a list of motifs is unworthy of serious evaluation, and the repeated insistence upon such requisite elements constitutes a form of ritualized ridicule. Even when applied to so minuscule a collection of texts as the Greek romantic novel of antiquity it is inadequate in regard to both content and function. One will not be able to understand any literary form so complex as the ancient novel by appeal to the presence or absence of any motif or motifs, however useful such catalogues may be as guides to similarity and diversity. The apparent similarity of the romantic novels to one another is often exaggerated, and much of it stems from literary dependence and imitation. Similarity and imitation in popular literature are not due to limited imagination and the desire to pirate a source. Writers for popular markets give people what they like and plenty of it.[19] Where nondevotees see wearying repetition, admirers detect subtle differences or the joy of repeated pleasures. If you like chocolate, why switch? From the marketing perspective, success is a more important factor than originality. The recurrence of plots, motifs, and incidents is an indication of their appeal and thus helps establish what was popular. Imitation was, moreover, a leading feature of the literary culture of the imperial age. Recognition of the model was a source of pleasure to the reader or hearer, and elicited appreciation for the variations introduced by the author.[20]

EXCURSUS:
THE ALLEGED SIMILARITY BETWEEN
ANCIENT NOVELS

Of Greek novels only Chariton, Achilles Tatius, Longus, and Heliodorus survive intact. Xenophon of Ephesus may be an epitome.[21] Others are known by fragments, summary reports by Photius, or as mere titles. Of the four fully extant, no two are quite similar. Chariton is simple in style, sentimental in tone, historical in form, and restrained in the use of coincidence and bizarre plotting. The couple marry at the outset, but Callirhoe must remarry and thus be unfaithful. Her husband apparently remained chaste. Achilles Tatius is quite sophisticated in viewpoint, often comic and prepared to poke fun at the conventions. This work uses the classical convention by appearing to be exegesis/ecphrasis of a painting. Achilles ridicules chastity, and his plot is baroque. Longus is also based, in theory, upon a painting, but the tone is religious or at least symbolic. The couple do not travel and their "separation" is ignorance of sex. The hero loses his virginity, but no more innocent and naive characters have ever been devised. Both style and content are at once simple and sophisticated. Pastoral poetry provides much of the literary inspiration. Heliodorus develops a very complex plot with nonsequential narration. Separation is not constant, and the goal is not a return to the original home but a new destination. The plot is very complex, the style difficult, and dramatic and epic conventions prevail. The *Odyssey* was a major model.

Xenophon *did* apparently imitate the structure of Chariton, but the effect is cruder and the theme more religious. Both of his characters preserve their chastity against strenuous assaults, but the evaluation of chastity is not so high as in Heliodorus.

Among the others, Antonius Diogenes appears atypical. In Iamblichus's novel the couple were often physically united but estranged by jealousy and anger. There is a great deal of violence. Parthenope, heroine of another novel, apparently searched for her male mate, rather than the opposite.[22] And so on. No two of the complete examples can be called twins. The evidence thus indicates far greater variety in plot, structure, tone, and style within the group of Greek romantic novels alone than some surveys would suggest.

Many popular motifs belong to no one genre or era. The *Odyssey* also portrays the reunion of a separated couple after years of absence filled with travel, adventure, and intrigue. There are rival lovers, powerful opponents, shipwreck, and visits to exotic places. Should this be called a novel? Only at the expense of ignoring the cultural environment in which romantic prose fiction flourished.[23] Motifs do aid in the delineation of subgenres, such as "romantic novels" or "travel novels," but they alone cannot define the genre. The supposition that they can has been one of the least fortunate inheritances from Rohde.[24]

Schwartz took a different tack. This historian contended that the novel came into being through the gradual decomposition of historical writing. His thesis gained impetus from the newly discovered fragments of *Ninus.*[25] Schwartz appealed to style and structure rather than content and theme, and invoked the presumed deterioration of historiography in the Hellenistic period. This perspective allowed space for historical and biographical novels (such as the *Cyropaideia* and *Apollonius of Tyana*), categories ignored by Rohde. At the basis of such evolutionary models is a typology that, in this case, would show history becoming "worse and worse," with a bit of sex added here, a dash of vivid adventure there, subplots and love stories slipped in until, lo and behold, a novel had emerged.[26] Schwartz would not, of course, have endorsed such reductions to absurdity, but his attempt did imply that novels are "bad" history, perhaps the result of bad faith, if not ignorance and barbarism. The process would, moreover, have to be continuous, since historical novels were written in classical times and historiography did not disappear from the scene. Would Xenophon have been "degenerate" while writing the *Cyropaideia* but in good form for the *Hellenica?* Schwartz was able to account for a good deal, but not the origin of the novel. He has found many supporters, including R. Rattenbury and F. Zimmermann, and he has found appreciation from others, including the often difficult to please B. E. Perry, despite that scholar's aversion to evolutionary theories of literature.[27] Identification of *Parthenope* as historical in quality adds another jewel to this theory's crown. Schwartz would have found the contributions to the 1976 International Conference on the Ancient Novel much more congenial than Rohde would have.

Schwartz further pointed to the role of popular traditions in various genres and thus grasped that novels tended to *transform* the substance of older myth, legend, and saga.[28] Bruno Lavagnini and K. Kerenyi would later advance this insight in very different ways. Schwartz did not turn toward the cultural background, for like Rohde he was concerned with the origin of a genre that was at bottom degenerate. His focus on history was, however, a major contribution to subsequent research.

G. Thiele looked to the outline definitions of narrative genres found in rhetorical handbooks.[29] This proposal could only be of indirect benefit, since those definitions were too general and too rhetorical, and because the novel was not a recognized genre. He did stimulate R. Reitzenstein to note the relationship between novels and historical monographs.[30] The findings of Thiele and Reitzenstein established that the use of a format devised by historians does not determine genre. This is true even if there are specific claims to accuracy and detailed chronology, and even if there are the insertion of documents and references to actual persons and events. Popular Greek novels tended to present themselves as works of history, even if romance was their major concern.

In 1913, O. Schissel von Fleschenberg essayed a developmental history of the Greek novel. He was more sympathetic to the subject matter, seeking to describe the various narrative techniques the novelists employed. Thus sensitized to the differences in structure and content, he rejected Rohde's approach. Schissel also took issue with Rohde's dictum that novellas were realistic but novels ideal, a distinction that prevented interaction between the two and any development from novellas to novels. Later scholars endorsed this refutation, and one of them, Lavagnini, argued that novels did arise from novellas, thus adding another theory to the field.[31]

Lavagnini's 1921 monograph on the origins of the Greek novel picked up one of Rohde's insights, the presence of local legend and saga in Hellenistic poetry. Rather than see legend>poetry>novel, Lavagnini regarded both as developments of folk traditions and in this way turned from a mechanical explanation of the novel to an understanding of the genre as the results of literary transformation in response to cultural and social changes.[32] Instead of showing dismay at such signs of literary decay, he spoke of individualism in the wake of the decline of the autonomous polis and the collapse of traditional morality. Individual concern nurtured the humanization of older stories and the introduction of sentiment, together with a decline of religious and patriotic emphasis. What had once enlightened local histories as entertaining episodes could become the nuclei for full-length books, as interest shifted toward the individual. When in response to changed conditions local tales were developed into romantic books intended for individual consumption, "the novel was born."[33] Lavagnini recognized a similar process operative in the

Egyptian and oriental sphere, a line followed later by M. Braun.[34] Lavagnini thus broke decisively with the tradition by insisting that novels must be understood as phenomena of their times rather than as literary abortions. To this insight Perry and Reardon would be greatly indebted.[35]

Lavagnini underscored the essentially popular quality of the early novels in contrast to the complexity of Alexandrian elegy. As an editor of fragmentary novels he was well aware of their simple prose style, and he recognized the social significance of that quality. In criticism of his work it should be noted that local legends are too narrow a base for explanation of the entire genre. The legends examined were, moreover, love stories, and his theory thus required him to regard love as primary, with adventure merely a device to create problems for the lovers. But of the novels known, only Longus (which is not derived from a local saga) gives love priority over adventure. The other Greek novels, as Reardon says, present a relatively simple love story amid complex adventures.

J. Ludvikovsky's 1925 Czech thesis on the Greek adventure novel followed Schwartz in seeing the novel as degenerate history but made a new contribution in providing popular adventure writing with a social profile.[36] Ludvikovsky regarded adventure as primary and described the novel as a broad phenomenon, the epic of half-educated people of the Hellenistic-Roman age. He further offered a series of stimulating ideas about the entertainment value and function of these works. Following H. Weil, he stressed the importance of the *Cyropaideia* as a model for later writers.[37] Ludvikovsky also discouraged the application of ancient professional theory to the novels, which as popular documents were less inclined to obey such rules. Ludvikovsky's insights have been widely disseminated by Perry, and quite deservedly so.

In 1927, Kerenyi looked to the transformation of concepts from the history of religions rather than local stories.[38] In line with current notions about oriental mystery religions, Kerenyi looked to the east and to mysteries as key phenomena of the age. He suggested that the archetype of the romantic novel was Isis propaganda in entertaining, fictional form. Novels were "secularized aretalogy." In ancient terms, they represented the metamorphosis of *pseudos/mythos* into *plasma*. He supported this theory by appealing to the presence of aretalogical style and materials in the surviving novels.[39]

Kerenyi had a profound understanding of the reflection of myth in life, of its "deep structure." He sensed the religious and cultural spirit of the age and sought to comprehend the novel within it. For that reason he looked less to direct prototypes and genetic connections than to the predominance of oriental and mystery ideas in the world of the novelists. He also sensed the link between aretalogy and entertainment and the nature of some ancient religious propaganda. His theory has not gained much approval, however, and the author must share some of the responsibility. His method lacks consistency, some of his claims appear extravagant or arbitrary, his references are difficult to manage, and his thesis far too refined to be encased in so cloudy a style. Cross-disciplinary efforts rarely meet with approval from any side, and this work is no exception. A. D. Nock's critical review is frequently cited as decisive. Nock listed a number of errors, postulated the need for some missing links, and deplored some generalizations, but one may question the extent to which Nock really grappled with Kerenyi's thesis.[40] In retrospect one can observe that by the end of the productive 1920s the question had shifted from the *how* to the *why* of the ancient novel. But Kerenyi was not done.

In 1937 Kerenyi made a brilliant contribution to a papyrological conference on the significance of book culture, the "transference" to papyrus of spiritual life in the Greco-Roman world after Alexander, and the focus upon the individual reflected in and facilitated by a culture of books (rather than, I presume, the oral world of the epic and the civic world of the drama).[41] In 1971 Kerenyi's slender *Der antike Roman* avoided the specificities of his major work and focused upon the novel as a phenomenon. In it he speaks of the cultural needs satisfied by initiation and novels. Novels, like mystery religions, provided a wider world and an intensification of existence. Kerenyi has thus come of age, for a number of scholars have come to agree that Christianity, mysteries, and novels appealed to similar groups and met related needs.[42] Escape from drudgery and fate, experience of transcendence and transfiguration, liberation, and new identity are some of the wishes and fantasies expressed by a broad spectrum of the ancient public. Those who wish to understand something of the desires and aspirations of common people in antiquity will be well advised to peruse these novels with care.

F. Altheim worked from similar premises in his treatment of the novel within the context of literature and society in late antiquity, first issued in 1948. Altheim aligned the genre to its age, which he characterized as syncretistic, ecumenical, open, and expansive. Religions of salvation and narrative fiction were responses to kindred spiritual needs. Religious emphasis aside, Altheim's analysis would seem to share with Perry's an understanding of the novel as comprehensive and open.[43] Altheim was not concerned with developments prior to the second century, and much of his focus was upon the novel of Heliodorus. If that work is finally assigned to the fourth century, his insights will have to be sifted with care.[44]

Several philologists have prepared brief essays for the general public. O. Weinreich's essay of 1932, first issued as an introduction to Heliodorus, is a delightful and stimulating survey, with emphasis upon epic and romantic history and analogies to contemporary cinema. P. Grimal's preface to his versions of Greek and Latin novels (1958) is quite suggestive. Grimal understands the historical and cultural setting of Greek novels as expressions of "spiritual milieus." One target of the oft-expressed Hellenic pride may be the Romans, to whom novelists could refer in coded language. R. Helm's 1948 survey was largely descriptive, avoiding the presentation of general theory. Helm took a broad approach and surveyed a range of novels. A strength of his work is his sensitivity to the literary background of various novels.

In 1962, R. Merkelbach proposed specific links between ancient novels and the mysteries. Despite obvious connections to the earlier work of Kerenyi (whose lack of specificity Merkelbach intended to rectify), the two writers had different objectives.[45] With no lack of clarity and methodological rigor he contended that the ancient novels were romans à clef, coded presentations of cultic practice and belief. Episodes and details refer to cultic activity. Merkelbach forthrightly claimed that novels provide some of the best evidence for ancient mystery religions. He has subsequently become everybody's whipping boy. Methodological limitations aside, Merkelbach's work is not without merit. His studies of Apuleius and Longus, in particular, deserve thoughtful attention.[46]

Merkelbach's theory is perhaps the final effort to account for ancient novels by a single description of origins. As such it fails. Symptomatic of its failure is his contention that Chariton is a derivative and secondary work —whereas it is almost certainly the earliest surviving complete novel and a model rather than an epigonid.[47] Panaretalogy will not succeed. Is not the refusal to allow the possibility of a religious novel equally narrow and open to criticism? That attitude pervades the most substantial modern discussion of the ancient novel, *The Ancient Romances* by Perry.

Perry's 1967 monograph, the published version of the Sather Lectures given in 1951, is the mature form and detailed justification of a theory that first appeared in 1930.[48] Refutation of Rohde and many others endows this book with a polemical tone. Perry's own research and the work of others during the 1920s led him to the view that *why* novels arose is much more important than *how*.[49] Thus, although the subtitle of his work spoke of accounting for origins, he was rejecting not only Rohde's answer but also his intent. Perry flayed the notion of generic development and the idea of a (quasi-Platonic) form with fixed rules and prescriptions.[50] Ancient novels neither possessed a definable form nor were the product of literary evolution. The novel was born through an individual act of will, "on a Tuesday afternoon in July."[51]

What did develop was culture. Novels came to be when there was a view of life congenial to their genesis. With assistance from analogies in the history of later European literature Perry sketched a convincing portrait of the conditions under which novels might take root and flourish. Others, including

Lavagnini and Ludvikovsky, whom he admired, and Kerenyi and Altheim, whom he did not, had urged the importance of Zeitgeist, but none with such rigor. Perry determined that intention alone—as observed by the reader (i.e., Perry)—was the criterion for genre. There is no sure correlation between form and function, and literature, unlike natural species, does not develop.[52]

Readers may be surprised to encounter after these assertions Perry's own history of the development of the novel, with particular reference to historiography! For Perry, historical stages were of value as bench marks of cultural change, and a historical format was merely the (essentially irrelevant) outer shell. In the last resort every piece of literature is sui generis.[53] This probably improves upon the notion of degeneracy lurking beneath earlier theories, according to which the first creator of a novel simply did not know or care. Discovery of intention does, however, require reading the author's mind. Perry defines *Ninus* as a novel but not the *Alexander Romance*, because "Pseudo-Callisthenes thought that he was doing the same kind of thing as the real Callisthenes,"[54] that is, composing history. Many would find that quite unlikely. Perry's remarks on Pseudo-Callisthenes resemble some of E. Haenchen's claims about Luke the historian.

Like Rohde, Perry accepted entertainment as the single purpose of the novel, which was written "for its own sake."[55] Historical and utopian novels need not apply, let alone the Apoc. Acts, "propaganda for a fanatical, antihumane creed."[56] Perry's subjectivity again emerges, for although willing to grant the edifying quality and historical content of some romantic novels, he invokes his sui generis clause to cope with message-oriented fiction and relies upon his own taste to determine what was entertaining in antiquity.[57]

Religion is a case in point. Whether because of his own attitude toward religion or through his desire to gain for the ancient novel a measure of literary respectability, Perry tends to project upon the ancient novels an anachronistic secular view of life. There is much room for debate about the religious message of this or that ancient novel, but no accurate picture of the Hellenistic and Roman eras can fail to take into account the significance of belief. Composers of the type of novel Perry regarded as normative—Chariton is his model—did not pitch their products toward the likes of Lucian, or even the Epicureans, whose views probably bore the closest resemblance to post-Enlightenment secularism.[58]

"Pure entertainment" and "for its own sake" are quite slippery terms with little real value in the history of literature. Their major strength may be in revealing what a particular critic finds unworthy.[59] In this instance they underline the subjective quality of some of Perry's judgments. There is a bit of irony here, for few have done more than Perry to stress the open and agglutinative nature of the ancient novel, qualities which would seem to militate against the assignment of a single criterion for its identification. Nor did he seek to delineate criteria for entertainment.

To be sure, Perry intended to describe only one type of ancient novel, the romantic. By claiming to define all novels he did not strengthen his case. Yet, if his "literary-historical" account of the origins of the ancient romance tended to become a phenomenological study of a particular group of works, it was anything but a failure. One of the first to risk the ridicule of defying Rohde's disdain for the genre, Perry was also the first to take the revision of Rohde's chronology to detailed and logical conclusions.

Reardon devoted a major section of his 1971 study of Greek literature in the second and third centuries to the ancient (especially the romantic) novel. Deeply influenced by the early work of Perry,[60] Reardon also reflected attentively upon the ideas advanced by Kerenyi and others. Perry led Reardon to see that the question is not the origins of the novel but its "essential nature."[61] Appreciation of the spirit of the age requires awareness not only of social and technical change but also of religious feelings and developments. For Reardon every epoch has a characteristic "myth," a deep structure of belief manifested in many forms, including religion and literature. A description of characteristic features will illuminate the contours of the appropriate "myth," and conversely, literary motifs and conventions will reflect elements of the myth.

Central in his estimation is the emergence of the individual. When social change led to a distance between individual and community, introduced a wider geographical horizon, brought forth a broad stratum of somewhat educated but not highly cultured individuals who saw themselves as isolated and largely without power, the climate for creation of romantic novels was ripe. Travel reflects both the immensity and accessibility of the world and the sense of rootlessness of its disenfranchised and culturally pluralized inhabitants. Love is the quest for identity. Neither is "essential," but each exercises a powerful fascination. Novels need not have love, but there must be a problem to resolve, a goal or object to attain, an identity to find. In religious novels one finds the true god. In romantic works the couple discover themselves in each other.[62] Adventures serve as challenges to test the characters' commitment and to educate them for the trials of life. Phenomenologically they correspond to the trials and tests of the mystery initiations.[63] Reardon may indeed be one of the few principal students of the ancient novel to have grasped what Kerenyi intended to suggest. Reardon's understanding of the importance of religious values and beliefs and his willingness to permit religious interpretations of individual novels constitute an important corrective to Perry. Even more important is the nuanced and balanced way in which he portrays various novels' evocations of spiritual and philosophical ideas.

Reardon also reflects the emergent resolution of the old conflict about the "oriental" or "Greek" origin and essence of the novel. Working with a broader definition of the genre and unconvinced by Perry's strictures against "development," Reardon sides with the "orientalists." Hellenistic culture was, after all, a hybrid one, and a likely milieu for hybrid forms. The papyri reveal the popularity of historical novels starring Nectanebo, Sesonchosis, and possibly, Amenophis.[64] It is regrettable that Reardon and others pay relatively little attention to the Jewish novels, which are less fragmentary and offer examples from Persian through Hellenistic to Roman times. Like Lavagnini, Reardon sees popular history overtaken by social forces and transformed into a vehicle for the expression of individual sentiment. Unlike Lavagnini, he looks to Egypt (Alexandria) and the east as likely sources for this impulse.

Although individuals will continue to refine and refute Reardon's understanding of the novel's essential nature, few will disagree with the appropriateness of his question. He has also provided what is certainly the best composite description and analysis of the individual writings, together with a full discussion of secondary literature. His subsequent contributions suggest no imminent recantation. In a 1976 article Reardon even came to ask the heretical question "Why love?" Since the combination of love and adventure presented romantic novelists with problems they could only master with difficulty, why did they not just compose novels of adventure? His answer is that whereas adventure is perennial, love (or, one may add, whatever the "goal" is) imposes itself as the essential expression of the current "myth." In one sense,[65] then, all novels have a message. In response to Perry's argument, one way of providing entertainment is through statement and restatement of the current message or messages.

In 1977 A. Heiserman's study of ancient fiction appeared (posthumously). Heiserman, who had planned a comprehensive treatment of the history of fiction, differed from many modern literary critics in recognition of the value of the ancient novel and its influence upon later literature. His approach was broad and independent of many common prejudices and convictions. As such, his approach is refreshing. Lack of specialized training was, however, also a detriment, for Heiserman's view of ancient culture was somewhat superficial and he sometimes misunderstood the texts, which he appears to have known mainly through translation. Nonetheless, Heiserman's knowledge of literary theories and his probes into critical labels have had a healthy and stimulating effect upon students of the ancient novel, most of whom have had little training in formal literary criticism.

Graham Anderson's *Eros Sophistes* (1982) both runs against the grain and pursues older goals. Anderson is among those who are reasserting the significance of the Second Sophistic for ancient novels. His approach is classically oriented, with many references to literary allusion and imitation, and considerably less attention to the currents of the time. Anderson finds much more humor in the novels than has traditionally been recognized. In many cases his arguments are very persuasive. As a comprehensive theory his view will not stand. Anderson does not propose it as a new theory of origins and purpose, but he does extend it to such works as Chariton and Heliodorus, where he is, in my view, much less convincing. Anderson is disinclined to find serious purpose in Longus and is at least skeptical about Apuleius. At points he seems to contend that a novel cannot be serious and contain humor at the same time.[66] Anderson has continued his analysis of the novel in *Ancient Fiction* (1984).[67] This compact, ably written volume testifies to an emerging consensus of perspective on the ancient novel. Anderson aligns himself with those who regard the genre as quite diverse. Rather than restrict his study to the romantic novels, he examines a number of religious, historical, and other types. Even the romantic works reflect a number of interests and authorial abilities.

Anderson has made a number of important observations and suggestions about plot, structure, character, and theme. He also claims to have found a solution to the problem of origins that has dominated study of the genre since Rohde. His solution lies in the orient. To demonstrate that the basic plots of ancient novels derive from oriental tales the author advances evidence ranging from Sumerian myths to Islamic short stories. Among the prototypes he discusses are myths and legends, novellas and hymns. It would be unjust to suggest that Anderson proposes these parallels as direct sources for the novelists, but it is correct to note that he does not often attempt to establish any links in the chain of tradition. Although familiar with folkloristic studies and methods, he does not employ them. There is thus no clarity about the nature of this "solution." The reader must sift among archetypes, prototypes, derivations, and parallels in search of connecting threads.

One source of the elusiveness of Anderson's solution may be that, however fascinating these discoveries appear to him, his own real interests are not in the origins of a rather despicable literary genre, as Rohde's were. Anderson sees much that is admirable in a number of the writings, and therefore advances his theory as a means of viewing the novels in their own right rather than as "degenerate" history, epic, and the like. He is prepared to view the novels as reflections of the social and cultural life of the Hellenistic and Roman eras and adduces many interesting literary and documentary parallels from writings of these periods. Unlike Hägg or Reardon, however, he does not follow these through.

Though willing to recognize the existence of popular novels, Anderson is primarily a literary critic who finds such vulgar writings unappealing, particularly when they are religious.[68] He can find nothing good to say about Xenophon of Ephesus, *Joseph and Asenath*, the *Life of Aesop*, and the Apoc.

Acts, for example. Anderson wishes to win respect for the aesthetic merits of
the major novels. Aware of the value of each of the theories advanced to explain the genre, he endorses none, because he prefers to let the genre speak
for itself through the mouths of its finest representatives. More ably than
Perry, Anderson defends the ancient novel against the charges of its cultured
despisers among modern classicists. For this project the lack of a unified
method and viewpoint is not a major flaw.

The Novel in Antiquity by Tomas Hägg (1983)[69] is modestly described as a
popular work for general consumption. Succinct and readable as it is, the
work far surpasses its predecessors of similar format. Hägg, who had previously written an important dissertation on narrative technique and a substantial challenge to the view of X. E. as an epitome, has a thorough grasp of both
primary texts and secondary discussion, as well as balanced and sound judgment. Hägg maintains that understanding of the genre requires attention to
the earlier, more popular, novels. He presents an excellent discussion of the
social milieu and readership of the works, and surveys a wide range of literature, including Christian products. Hägg's understanding has much in common with that of Reardon and may suggest an emergent consensus or domi-
nation of the field by that theory. As a bridge to later times Hägg offers a
discussion of later popularity and influence, together with many illustrations.
The author well satisfies the need for classicists to communicate in clear language to specialists in the European novel the significance of ancient writings. He has further provided a fine survey for those who wish to become ac-
quainted with the subject, as well as a useful bibliography.

The 1976 conference to mark the centennial of Rohde appears not to have
mentioned his name.[70] The proceedings of that assembly mark several turning points. The entire subject of origins was ignored. Anderson summarized
the situation by saying, "We are all eclectics now."[71] The novel has come of
age. Rather than seek to trace its development or apologize for its existence,
present-day scholars are beginning to produce a series of sophisticated studies of individual works. The effort to account for novels by the kind of uni-
tary hypothesis offered by Rohde, or even as described by Perry, has reached
a stage of dissolution. Nearly all theories have something to say about one or
more works. Only Professor Merkelbach was a consistent target of criticism,
and he was not present. Oriental influence is widely accepted, and the evidence of the papyrus fragments is being given careful attention. The one form-
ative critic and theorist who may have viewed this meeting as vindication
was Schwartz. Greek and Latin novels are now being studied in conjunction,
witness the title "Ancient Novel" to commemorate a work on the "Greek
novel." Rohde was mainly interested in antecedents, which received equal
billing in his title. Conference papers had much more to say about the ongoing tradition, especially Byzantine.

In accordance with this trend are the flurry of new editions of various texts, burying forever the old corpus of *scriptores erotici*, translations into modern languages to replace the old standards of the sixteenth through eighteenth centuries, and commentaries upon the various works. One outstanding need is for new editions of papyrus texts, the earlier works being both incomplete and inadequate. Other needs are for serious attention to the corpus of Jewish novels and new research on the place of Christian writings within the tradition. Investigators of Christian origins have yet to play their role.[72]

Conclusion

Expert opinion would now seem to support the conclusion that although each of the theories advanced to explain the origins of the ancient novel has contributed to its understanding, no one of them is fully convincing. The novel is too complex a phenomenon to be reduced to a single impetus. Greek novels arose in a popular context, with oriental influence.[73] Hellenistic Greeks did not invent the genre independently, nor did they borrow it. Approaches based, like Rohde's, upon typical features fail. Cultural explanations, such as Perry's, are very useful but cannot be used to eliminate the need for tracing literary development. Novels are not a unified phenomenon with a single *lex operis* (generic formula).[74] They cannot be dealt with by reference to a single theory.

Novels cannot be described in conventional terms, because they took shape in circles that paid no heed to the canons devised and noted by cultured literary critics. Those whose major interest is the Sophistic romances and their immediate predecessors describe processes of adaptation of earlier genres and transformation of literary and cultural values. They are doubtless often correct, but this concentration upon a particular body overlooks the continued production of older types, most notably historical novels. If the leading indicators for success are translation, international diffusion, and continual reproduction, the most successful of all ancient novels was the *Alexander Romance*, and not by a slim margin. Yet typologically this is the most "primitive" of all! One question not yet resolved is the breadth with which the genre will be usefully defined. Ancient terminology will not provide a remedy, for ancients gave novels neither "official" recognition nor title. Writers resorted to a variety of known terms in their quest for acceptance.[75]

The efforts to establish various theories of origins have unearthed a variety of remains: love poetry, travel writings, local and national saga and legend, myth, collections of heroic exploits, and others. Transformational interpretations, like those of Lavagnini and Kerenyi, have selected a single predominant type of material. Granted that one should view "all shall have prizes" solutions with extreme suspicion, the plurality of novel types and developments warrants recognition that it is not a case of "secularized aretalogy" or bourgeoisified history or sentimentalized legend so much as a case of a variety of degrees of transformation of numerous literary and cultural phenomena. The link between Hellenistic poetry exploring the psychology of love, and romantic novels, is not immediate, but it is scarcely accidental. The resemblance of novels to mysteries is not one of cause and effect, but it is far from fortuitous.[76] Since the attempt to comprehend the ancient novels within a single theory has given way to eclecticism and respect for the diversity of different works, it should be possible to acknowledge that even Merkelbach may, in one or more cases, be illuminating.[77]

Comparisons from other genres and artistic forms are in order. Ovid's *Heroides* retells older stories with greatly changed emphases, including psychological depiction. Within the *Metamorphoses* there are a number of older legends and aretalogies subjected to sentimental treatment. Horace, let alone Petronius, can write a Priapus aretalogy as a piece of humor (satire). Such actions are far from unconscious recastings of traditional forms and material. Traditionalists take offense at this flippant handling of material that has lost its earlier function. R. Seaford, writing about the artistic decor found in Pompeian homes, speaks of "degradation into amusing, erotic or sadistic art which bears no resemblance to the solemn origin of the subject."[78] Seaford offers parallels from Ovid. His judgment bears a striking resemblance to Rohde's or Schwartz's strictures about the novels.[79] At quite another level is the use of initiatory language by philosophers to describe intellectual enlightenment. The significance of such terminology varies from case to case, but it would be unwise to write off all this usage as meaningless metaphor, just as it would be foolish to see propaganda for particular cults lurking behind such savants.

The standard Greek novel thus came into being as a result of the changes wrought by Hellenism. Non-Greek prototypes probably played an important role. The environment was most likely Hellenized, rather than Hellenic. Varieties of older sources were transformed, translated, or simply incorporated in accordance with the spirit and taste of the age and the goals and audience of a particular novelist. No one theory serves to account for so diverse and productive a phenomenon.

THE ANCIENT NOVEL: THE QUEST FOR
DEFINITION AND COMPREHENSION[80]

Since the ancients lacked a name for this genre, moderns are free to make use of whatever term or terms provide the most value. The classification of literature is a tool for comparative study, and the terms selected or devised ought to meet the needs of the classifiers.[81] "Novel" appears preferable to the once-fashionable "romance," since the latter is more narrow in range and pejorative in connotation.[82] If "novel" is used as it is in English there is little reason to employ terms like "prenovel" or "near-novel."[83] The terminological question is closely related to the understanding of the genre: will the genre be broadly or narrowly conceived? Two leading reasons for wishing to restrict application of the word "novel" to the small body of romantic tales (to which one may wish to add the Latin novels of Petronius and Apuleius) lie in the notions of "pure fiction" and "mere entertainment."

"Mere entertainment" is a traditional epithet for denouncing writings that do not conform to the idea that the potential for producing unadulterated improvement is the criterion of literary value. Subjectivity abounds, both in the definition of entertainment and the measure of its dominance. Human beings find pleasure in a host of literary experiences. The elder Pliny advertised his *Natural History* as leisure-time matter for the learned[84] but would resist any who attempted to dismiss him as a "mere entertainer." Conversely, if conceiving the novel as pure entertainment means that the desire to communicate serious ideas must be subordinate to an interest in giving pleasure, then it is questionable whether the novels of Longus, Apuleius, and perhaps, Heliodorus can be so characterized. What in fact disturbs critics is not so much that certain novels lack a "message" as it is the kind of message present or implicit in their products. The decision that this or that writer intended entertainment to be primary is likely to differ from reader to reader and may be reached concerning nonfiction no less than fiction.

"Pure fiction" is equally unrewarding. Few ancient novelists pulled their plots and characters out of thin air. Various sources, written and folkloristic, legendary and historical, were normally used. "Poetic license" was in antiquity more nearly just that. S. Praeder thus says that fictionality cannot be a criterion for the ancient novel, but a "tendency toward fictionality."[85] Since these two categories of entertainment and fiction are so elusive and the application of them to ancient novels is questionable, there is a prima facie case for a more open approach to definition of the genre,[86] one prepared to encompass more overtly historical and didactic works.

In pursuit of such a comprehensive understanding I am about to examine three different but complementary approaches to defining ancient novels, with a brief glance toward a fourth. The first seeks to be a concise and prescriptive definition of the textbook sort. The second probes the benefits of constructing a list of typical features. The third and most adventurous attempts evocation of the novel's essence by way of its cultural function and setting.[87] The fourth turns to the question of structure. I do not claim adequacy for any one of these approaches and would be hesitant to say that the four will cumulatively achieve perfection. Each seeks to illuminate the problem and to illustrate the complexity of the issue.

Prescriptive Definition

Although prescriptive definitions tend to be circular, they do reveal some prerequisites. Novels are relatively lengthy pieces of prose fiction. "Prose" may be taken for granted in an age when poetry has become somewhat specialized and restricted, but the use of prose for Greek novels constituted a decisive break with the tradition of verse as the medium for entertaining fiction, a break that had significant social and cultural ramifications. To write in prose, initially in simple, unpretentious prose, was to reject the heroic tradition and the literary conventions, often antiquated, associated with it.

"Relative length" is not only quantitative. There is no point at which the addition of a word will transform a short story or novella into a novel. Novels may be rather short, but the scope and complexity of their plot will distinguish them from short stories proper. Most of the early ancient novels were by our standards extremely short, witness the Jewish examples.[88] Of the Greek romantic novels only that of Heliodorus approaches the length modern readers would find customary for a work of such complexity. On the Latin side, Petronius's original work was apparently substantial. Apuleius's length derives from his inserted stories and tales. The historical and biographical works that achieve some length do so at the expense of what present-day readers find interesting.[89]

Fiction has been defined as a tendency toward fictionality. In ancient terms the concept *plasma* did not imply total concoction so much as a creative shaping of material. It is rarely possible to ascertain which authors (particularly those of less literary accomplishment) believed that they were composing truth and which fiction. Historians duped by a legend or misled by a lie do not thereby become novelists. With regard to ancient novelists it is perhaps safest to refer to the creation of fictional sequences of events, that is, arrangement to suit the writer's purpose or pleasure, and the composition of fictional episodes, together with a generous use of fictional details. Such fiction derives not so much from malice or ignorance as from the desire to tell a pleasing story that conforms to some standard of realism yet also sets forth the author's ideals or world view. The conventions of realism governing ancient novels have little in common with those of the present time.[90]

Fictional structuring and arrangement are fundamental for understanding the genre, since novels communicated their ideas primarily through the depiction of events and description of action. Characters embody ideals or vices. Edification therefore emerges in an entertaining garb, in the age-old fashion of popular literature.[91]

These descriptions focused upon the life and experiences of one or more characters, as the tendency toward biographical titles indicates.[92] The heroes of ideal novels exceed the limits of ordinary life. Various novels record and promulgate new standards of heroism.[93] Among the standards will be love and fidelity, and the novel will enshrine these accomplishments by portraying new types of heroes and old types in new ways.

Prescriptively defined, the ancient novel was a relatively lengthy work of prose fiction depicting or deriding certain ideals through an entertaining presentation of the lives and experiences of a person or persons whose activity transcends the limits of ordinary living as known to its implied readers.[94]

Typical Features

As mainly formulaic works intended for an unsophisticated public, novels employed a number of conventions. By surveying these one can gain a general notion of the limits within which the surviving examples tended to operate. Rather than restrict this survey to motifs, I shall also take into account the themes or ideals portrayed and attempt to delineate the various modes utilized. These lists are not exhaustive. They do intend, however, to stress variation no less than repetition.

THEMES

Politics. In this category fall novels about social or political life, including utopian schemes, portraits of the ideal ruler, social criticism, and concerns of minorities oppressed by the ruling power. Examples would include Euhemerus, Iambulus, the *Cyropaideia*, the *Alexander Romance*, Esther, *Aristeas*, and Artapanus.

Patriotism. Group consciousness distinguishes this from the preceding. Foci include the support of ethnic cultural heritage (including orientals against Greeks and the latter vis-à-vis "barbarians"), local pride, and nobility of lineage. Extant Jewish novels exemplify what was once a much larger body, as may be inferred from fragmentary remains of Egyptian works and the Alexander tradition. Although this type appeared rather early and on the cultural fringes of Hellenism, its power may still be seen in the romantic novels. What apparently took shape to assert the claims of older cultures against Hellenism endured to maintain a sense of pride in Greek institutions and culture against later, presumably Roman, claims.

Religion. The role of religion in novels varies greatly, but it is perhaps the most extensive single theme. At times it seems little more than epic mechanism, with a nod to local pride, which would seem to be a minimum interpretation of the role of Aphrodite in a novel written by a resident of Aphrodisias (Chariton). Other works, like the *Metamorphoses* of Apuleius and the *Ephesi-aca* of Xenophon, are fundamentally religious.

Wisdom. The oldest of oriental novels, *Ahikar*, appears to be an entertaining vehicle for communicating proverbial wisdom. Chion of Heraclea wrote a Greek philosophical tract in novel form. The nature of the wisdom may vary greatly, and its presentation ranges from the marvelous subtlety of Apuleius and Longus to the heavy-handedness of the earlier sapiential writings. Even the most romantic of books display a fondness for sententious utterances and conventional proverbs.

Fidelity. Love and chastity receive the most attention here, but loyalty to family and friends, not to mention various gods and nationalities, is far from lacking. Most of the romantic novels of the ideal type had as their object reinforcement of traditional models of married life and domestic virtue.

Status. There is in many novels a near-obsession with questions of wealth, rank, education, birth, and social standing. The treatment of status questions is probably the most convincing indicator of the social circle to which early novels were directed.[95]

Most novels speak to several of these ideals. When one is predominant, it often forms the basis for descriptive classifications, such as of the "romantic" or "utopian" novel. Such themes were more than incidental decor. Whether or not these ideals belonged to the writers' specific intentions, however those are to be discovered, is not essential. Implicit ideals are no less real or significant than intentional ones. The "messages" of written texts need not be innovations, nor must one seek for overt propaganda. The reinforcement of accepted values and ideals is an important form of communication, and one source of pleasure, not least in popular publications, is the reaffirmation of social mores and conventional beliefs.

MOTIFS

No catalogue of recurrent typical motifs would be both complete and useful. The following list aims at a compromise between economy and comprehensiveness. The fact of recurrence is a strong indication that ancient readers found pleasure in these features, however unlikely that may seem to us. Readers of popular literature seek originality only to the extent than it enhances the experience they already seek without altering its essential nature.[96] Even the most sophisticated reader reaching for a mystery at night will be disappointed if the work contains more philosophy than detection. Criticizing such works for their lack of originality fails to appreciate their form.

Travel. Whether as a means to an end, a source of adventure, a voyage of discovery, a device for motivating a plot or delaying resolution, travel of all kinds for many reasons was the most general motif employed by ancient novelists. It is the most concrete means of escape, of "getting away from" whatever is dull or oppressive in the present. Travel, especially the sea voyage, was a powerful metaphor and symbol in antiquity, and many writers exploited the potentials of travel as a symbol for one's quest of or search for reality and identity.[97]

Adventure and excitement. The fairly limited and predictable, yet often fantastic and incredible, adventures undergone by the characters of ancient novels tend to disappoint modern readers, but there can be little doubt of their popularity and appeal. Trials, shipwreck, piracy, banditry, threatened rape, kidnapping, seduction, imprisonment, riots, execution, intended suicide, and apparent death appear to have been perpetual favorites of which readers simply could not get too much.

Warfare. This is a specialized type of adventure with political ramifications. In some of the earlier, more epic and nationalistic, works, warfare predominated, but even Heliodorus, the last of the romantic novelists, relied upon military campaigning both to advance and to retard his plot. Battles with pirates and thieves are another form of combat, handled with great amusement by Longus and with less skill by Xenophon of Ephesus, to single out two ends of the spectrum.

Aretalogy. The plots of nearly every ancient novel are "aretalogical" in that the resolution redounds to the glory of the god who effected the final victory of the heroes and the vindication of their ideals. Specific aretalogical topics include miracles of various kinds, deliverance by divine intervention, dreams and other revelatory media, and every denouement attributed to providence. It is the structural and incidental quality here designated as "aretalogical" that makes even romantic novels highly illuminating texts for those whose primary concern is the world of Christian origins.[98]

Miscellany. This is a catch-all including the interest in what is exotic and bizarre and *faits divers*[99] relating to natural history, science, geography, anthropology, and ethnography. The Second Sophistic stimulated dissimulation of such encyclopedic data in excursuses (frequently presented as entertainment while traveling), but they are as old as the *Odyssey* in the Greek world and were a staple of utopian and travel narratives.

Court life and intrigue. Ruthless tyrants with unlimited powers make formidable adversaries. They give scope for splendid descriptions of regal pomp and magnificence, opportunity for Hellenic sneers at eastern despotism and oriental pride in an imperial past, and occasion to shed light on the leading characters. Those whom kings pursue are beautiful indeed, and eluding such powerful creatures will not be easy. Court life exercised a fascination upon many, not least those of relatively low status.

Rhetoric. The rhetorical education that dominated society exercised a profound influence upon the novel (as Rohde maintained and Reardon and Anderson have lately reiterated).[100] Chariton, author of the standard pre-Sophistic novel, was secretary to a rhetor. On the level of content, rhetorical training did nothing to minimize interest in the sensational. Complaints about rhetorical *Controversariae* resemble those about novels, and for good reason. Formally, rhetoric contributed to the interest in speeches, sermons, monologues, apostrophes, descriptions, and other flourishes. Even those with a modest education could appreciate differences in style or references to classic battles in the history of thought. Rhetoric gave pleasure not only through the aesthetic merits of particular passages but also by allowing readers to sense and applaud their own erudition.

Most ancient works normally described as novels have most of these motif groupings, however differently they might be organized for more precise or particular analysis.

MODES

By "mode" I mean what some literary critics call "genre," as in the sense of "genre pieces," like "western," "mystery," and "gothic." Mode encompasses features of tone, style, setting, and manner. For my purposes lack of precision and rigor will not be fatal. Modes are subgenres, which may be defined by different criteria, often quite adequately even when one is an apple and another an orange.

The marvelous. This mode refers to worlds where things take place by magic and all disbelief must be suspended if enjoyment is to be found. Antonius Diogenes' novel was of this sort, as were many utopian and travel tales. Apuleius plays upon the marvelous to create the atmosphere of the tales within his *Metamorphoses*, as well as his basic plot.

The historical. Real personages in important roles, description of historical events, and the use of historiographical style and techniques mark this genre. Biographical novels may be considered under this heading also. To one degree or another, the vast majority of ancient novels were historical.

The sentimental. Sentimentality is essentially a tone or point of view in narration which evokes personal sympathy and identification. Sentimental novels describe a world as "it should be" rather than as it is, a world where love conquers all and virtue brings happiness.[101]

The comic and satiric. Comedy was a permissible outlet for social criticism and the depiction of ordinary life in realistic detail. The ancient comic novels that have come down to us exhibit a wide range of viewpoints and tones.[102] Some claim, for example, that Petronius has a serious message, and others that Apuleius is not serious. Achilles Tatius has been read in several ways, as serious, comic, or satiric. Noncomic works may, of course, contain some humorous material.

The realistic. In addition to the realistic content of the Latin comic novels there is, according to a growing body of fragmentary evidence, the use of realistic and graphic episodes in novels that may not have been comic.[103]

The didactic. Some novels were mainly concerned to convey information or teach fundamental truths. The term "didactic" is not flattering, usually being applied to books in which the instructional material interferes with pleasure, which is at most a sugarcoating. Not all novels with an important message should be described as didactic. But the sapiential writings certainly are, to which biographies like the lives of Pythagoras, Aesop, and Apollonius may well be added.[104]

The missionary. This is a particular type of didactic novel. Missionary novels are those in which propagation of a religious or philosophical message is the primary objective. The Apoc. Acts are missionary novels. This may be a more appropriate designation for the religio-philosophical biographies of figures like Apollonius and Pythagoras.

The pastoral. Only Longus and, to a degree, the *Euboicus* of Dio Chrysostom *Oration* 7 fit this traditional mode. Perhaps others were written.

The tragic. The category is striking by its absence, pointing to one of the reasons that ancient novels are considered to have produced no "great" literature. Can the human condition be portrayed without reference to tragedy?

What about the tragedies of individual persons and ideas? Recent study of ancient novels may indicate some new answers to issues long regarded as settled.

Probably not one of the themes, motifs, or modes listed in this section does not have numerous attestations in other genres. One cannot define literary categories by typical features alone. They are helpful aids to subclassification and comparison. Reference to them enables appreciation of both the diversity and the sameness of the prose fiction produced by ancients, revealing the potential of the genre for absorption and development. The sheer number of elements refutes any suggestion that ancient novels were written to a single formula. What is fundamental, however, is the manner in which these themes, motifs, and modes were put to use in the creation of novels. I now turn toward an examination of these works in terms of their social settings, their functions, and the characteristic understandings of life displayed in them.

Cultural Function and Setting

Chronologically and geographically novels occupied the center of the Hellenistic and Greco-Roman worlds. They flourished during the most stable and prosperous periods of those eras for the Hellenistic east, that is, before the appearance of Rome and after eastern recovery from the ravages of early Roman imperialism. Forms like the novel required the existence of a literate public with some leisure time and a moderate or better economic situation. They further required a culture in which public performance and recitation were no longer available or able to satisfy the leisure needs of all its inhabitants. In short, novels needed a cosmopolitan society. When the diffusion of Greek culture had led to a literate public in towns like Oxyrhynchus, cosmopolitanism had arrived. The composition of literary epic, drama, and lyric testifies to the existence of a book culture after Alexander.[105] Under Hellenism the classics became classics, the property of highly trained experts imposed upon students to their joy or sorrow but otherwise detached from daily life.[106]

"Primary" epic flourishes in feudal societies with heroic ideals. Ancient drama flourished in the Athenian polis, as it later would in the comparable culture of Elizabethan London. The careful definition and formal conventions of those two genres reflect the structured and discreet natures of the societies in which they thrived. Open and cosmopolitan societies, with their lack of shared social conventions, clear social definition, and restraint upon individual ambition apart from communal needs, are likely to develop less structured, more flexible, adaptable, and individualistic literary forms. The novel is well suited to an age of general education, cultural diffusion, and turbulent change.[107]

Novels thus began to flourish when the parochialism of the polis was no longer dominant, when the community of citizens had been replaced by a distant and powerful monarch, and when the shattering of political boundaries had opened the world to a barrage of change and opportunity, bringing about the weakening or destruction of social, economic, religious, and moral limits in the wake of new boundaries and new rulers.[108] Insecurity increased no less than opportunity, and the question of the relationship of the individual to the cosmos became prominent for centuries. Power and authority became issues of concern and for debate, penetrating even into the world of the NT.[109]

Loss of world and the creation of new worlds by power and daring stirred people to despair and to dream. The creation of an ideal world without the disorder, ambiguity, and limitations of the known world belongs to the realm of the novel no less than to that of apocalyptic. "Escapist" is often the term applied to both. The worlds evoked by both apocalypticists and novelists transcended the limits and frustrations their readers experienced in daily life. Both Revelation and the utopias pilloried by Lucian deal with the solution of typical urban problems, including food, water, streets, and light.[110] One group expresses its hopes by reference to exorcism. Expulsion of demons restores the Gadarene to full humanity (Mark 5:1–20). Others refer to status, the discovery that the shepherdess is of noble lineage, or to fidelity, or to discovery of one's true and eternal mate, each with much the same results. In these ideal worlds the virtuous and faithful overcome the powers of Satan or the caprices of fate. Salvation and the happy ending are in their object one and the same.

Hellenism and the later diffusion of Roman privilege and power muddied many traditional distinctions based upon race, sex, social standing, and religion—and established others. Proud old cultures were despised as defeated and inferior. Acculturation did not mean rejection of the old. Mythical figures like Ninus became conquerors comparable to Alexander. National heroes like Moses became ecumenical benefactors and givers of culture. Women could leave their homes and experience no end of excitement and adventure, outwitting (even killing) men and eluding both disgrace and passive mediocrity. Apparently ordinary people proved their mettle in encounters with fiendish tyrants, rapacious pirates, and ruthless rivals—or at least in novels, where all of this was sure to take place.

The newness of novelistic worlds could be illusory in several senses. In response to upwardly mobile audiences endued with all the old-fashioned virtues, novelists tended to reinforce existing values. Characters, even regal or historic persons, were repainted to reflect the values of novel readers, and life was repainted to reflect their wishes. When marital fidelity became the only heroic virtue worthy of note, the triumph of bourgeois values was complete.

But not all novels were this sentimental. Utopian writings and the Apoc. Acts often rejected all conventional approaches to sex and marriage, and even the most orthodox novels exhibit traces of ambivalence.[111] Still, the goal is usually to get back where you were in the beginning—*Endzeit wird Urzeit*—and stay there "happily ever after."[112]

With such conventional values went unremarkable prose, the language of commerce and domesticity. Early novels were *koine* both culturally and linguistically. Just as that Greek dialect blended various elements, so novels reflected the various and sometimes contradictory features of cosmopolitanism. One is portraying the deeds of non-Hellenic heroes in Greek language and Greek categories. Cosmopolitan pride and competition promoted the assimilation of rival heroes' attributes and accomplishments, the ultimate result of which was a cultural syncretism regularly updated to meet current needs, producing a batch of relatively colorless characters subject to casual manipulation.[113] The day might even come when many would prefer Ninus the boy adventurer, with suitable depiction of his efforts to win the cute little girl next door (Semiramis!), to legendary exploits. So too the figures of apostle, savior, and saint would undergo periodic revision to keep them abreast of current orthodoxy and taste.

Individualism is an expected concomitant of cosmopolitanism, as family and community sanctions recede. Individuals unrestrained by normal barriers could achieve almost anything. Most dramatic were the rise of obscure families, including the Ptolemies, the Maccabees, the Augustan and other dynasties, and the awesome power acquired by present and former slaves.[114] Hazards increased at a similar pace, leaving a general perception of helplessness in the face of fate. Novels addressed individuals longing for secure community, at least as much as they spoke to people in their private capacities. At the very least, the individual, apparently friendless, frustrated, and bored in a vast and hostile world, could experience in the private (or intimate) act of reading novels both escape from the drudgery and horror of routine and a suggestion about how things might be better, even if it just meant "let's pretend for a little while."

The symbolic world of apocalyptic reflects the desperation of those most oppressed by absolute or relative deprivation. With glee this world view seeks complete destruction of the present order. Most of the novels are more optimistic, viewing the world as requiring reform rather than re-creation. A microcosmic parallel to this is the Gospel miracles that see healing as salvation. Mark and John are more pessimistic and view the expectations created by such wonders with suspicion. Paul would agree. Luke would not. During the period when Rome was absorbing the east, the only novels known to have been produced were nationalistic in tone, presumably anti-Roman, even if in code. As the east revived, novels reappeared in quantity, and began their climb up the social and literary ladder.

The "escapist" label is probably misleading, for even the romantic novels deal with serious moral problems, and all seek either to promote change or repress it.[115] Novels expanded culturally in every direction, attracting educated readers and then authors, appealing to proponents of new religions and audiences far beyond the Greek (and Latin) linguistic frontiers.[116] The novels had something for everyone and something for every movement and ideal. This genre had more potential for universal appeal than any other of the imperial period. It spoke to the common denominator of educated people in the eastern provinces of the empire. Because the empire ultimately became Christian, verification of this statement must be sought in popular Christian writings, especially those about apostles, saints, and martyrs.[117]

Structure

The structural approach is equally complex and has only begun to yield fruitful suggestions. On the level of surface structure—"skeletal form"—a number of options appealed to ancient novelists, including evocation of historiography, epic, and the interpretation of art. Each of these is derived from a traditional genre or genres. Two recent approaches from more recently constructed models are those of E. Cizek and Praeder. Cizek follows the structuralists who operate from the model of generative grammar.[118] He begins from a relatively small group of Greek and Latin novels and seeks to elucidate a "generative grammar" of each type. In so doing he makes a number of observations more or less corresponding to those adduced from the several categories treated above. His concerns are the intellectual or psychological factors that serve as motive springs for the novels. Greek works take shape from the opposition of *erōs* and *tychē*, whereas the Latin examples are more philosophical in origin. He has proposed, in effect, a new theory of "origins."

Praeder's "narrative paradigm" contains a number of observations about structure.[119] She finds a biographical sequence more or less essential, demonstrating the difference between novels and most biographies in this regard. General as this criterion is, it is open to some objection.[120] She further speaks of the ways in which novels use allusion and citation, and tend to alternate scene with summary and interpolate stories within the major story. To this one may add the episodic character of most novels, the communication of ideas or ideals through representative characters, their penchant for sententious asides or comments, and a number of structural devices, some of which will be discussed below.[121] The structural approach is no more self-sufficient than others.

In conclusion, a novel, specifically the Greco-Roman novel, is not just content, style, or structure but the presentation of certain themes, motifs, and modes in culturally shaped ways. Expressed as a formula,

$$\text{the novel} = \text{material} + \text{manner} + \text{style} + \text{structure.}^{122}$$

My investigation has attempted to grapple with each of these elements in their complexity. As a supplement, I append in table 2 a list of works that appear to fall within this definition. The list does not claim to be complete, but it is meant to comprehend examples illustrating the full range of Greco-Roman prose fiction.

TABLE 2
THE GRECO-ROMAN NOVEL

§*Ahikar*	*Petronius	*§*Acts of Paul*
Cyropaideia	§*Life of Aesop*	§*Acts of Thecla*
*Theopompus	Chariton	**Monica*
*Hecataeus	**Chione*	Achilles Tatius
*Euhemerus	*Joseph and Asenath*	*Life of Secundus*
*Iambulos	+ Xenophon of Ephesus	**Herpyllis*
§Tobit	¶*Iamblichus	**Parthenope*
§*Alexander Romance*	**Iolaus*	**Calligone*
§*Tobiad Romance*	*Acts of Peter*	*Lollianus
Artapanus	§Lucius of Patrae's	Longus
§Judith	*Metamorphoses*	Chion of Heraclea
Aristeas	¶(?*)Antonius Diogenes	§*Pseudo-Clementines*
Sesonchosis	*Onos*	*Apollonius of Tyana*
*Nectanebus	*True Story*	§*Acts of Thomas*
*Amenophis (?)	*Acts of John*	various later Acts
Ninus	§Apollonius of Tyre	Lives of Pythagoras
3 Maccabees	*Acts of Andrew*	and others
(Greek) Esther	Apuleius	Heliodorus

SYMBOLS

*Only fragments exist.	§ Survives only in later edition or version.
**Hypothetical work.	+ Extant edition may be an epitome.
¶Extant only in later résumé.	

5. HISTORICAL NOVELS

Pagan, Jewish, and Christian

C. S. Lewis observed that he never fully understood the widespread disdain for "escapist" literature ". . . till my friend Professor Tolkien asked me the very simple question, 'What class of men would you expect to be most preoccupied with, and most hostile to, the idea of escape?' and gave the obvious answer: jailers."*

NATIONAL ROMANCES

In the light of the preceding attempt to give a literary and cultural description of the phenomenon of the novel in antiquity I now turn toward those examples most likely to illumine the genre of Acts. Both highly literate and crudely popular historical novels were written in Greek. These varied works experienced some reciprocal influence, and oriental historical novels, which had undergone their own development, also made contributions to the Greek tradition. The popular sphere, in particular, proved fruitful soil for this literary syncretism. Although my focus will be upon the popular works, I shall begin with the highly influential *Cyropaideia* of Xenophon.

Ancients were quite aware that the *Cyropaideia* was a piece of fiction.[1] They did not, for that reason, describe it as degenerate. Its author, Xenophon of Athens, not only knew how to write history but did. One means for describing the ideal form of government was by composing a fictional biography of an ideal ruler, and Xenophon's book is the outstanding surviving example.[2] Its narrative structure is often inundated by philosophic discourse, but there are entertaining sections, most of which have a moral.[3] A thin veneer of local color does not mask what is an unabashedly Greek production, the presentation of political theory in an attractive form to an educated public. The structure and format of Xenophon's book were evidently admired, and they apparently spawned a number of imitations, including histories of Alexander.[4] When the Persian king would no longer do for a model and

---

*"On Science Fiction," in *Of Other Worlds: Essays and Stories*, ed. Walker Hooper (New York: Harcourt Brace Jovanovich, 1966), 67

115

Alexander was not quite suitable, the utopian form emerged as a medium for sharing political and philosophical ideas.

At the margins of Hellenism there soon appeared national romances, so-called—fictionalized portraits of great rulers, including Alexander, Nectanebo, Sesonchosis, Ninus and Semiramis, and Moses.[5] The fragmentary nature of the material makes all conclusions somewhat speculative.[6] M. Braun drew attention to this phenomenon. He contrasted the oriental novels of the Persian period, which he found relatively colorless and didactic, to the nationalist nature of the fragments surviving or descending from Hellenistic times. These works asserted the claims of older cultures, probably more in an attempt to prevent total assimilation than in an effort to educate Greeks. However effective in that regard, they were enjoyable books to read, and evidently began to find a wider audience.[7] Successive revisions kept them up to date with changing taste and changing cultural threats.

There is one broken thread that permits the hypothesis that continued evolution of national romances could lead to the creation of another type of novel. That is *Ninus*. The author of that work was no stranger to Greek culture and made direct or indirect use of the *Cyropaideia*. Because one of the surviving fragments of *Ninus* is a tender romantic scene, the work is often considered an "erotic novel." This may not be a valid inference, but *Ninus* focuses upon personality rather than politics, as the presence of a shipwreck indicates. By the time of the Hellenistic work known to us,[8] it is possible that the Babylonian background was little more than an exotic decor and even the military career of Ninus highly personalized. He is, at any rate, an adolescent figure. The legendary eastern potentate has somehow been transformed into a bourgeois individual with feelings rather like those of more ordinary young men. This characterization, so typical of ancient novels, reflects a decisive shift toward personal edification and entertainment. *Ninus* was a historical novel in which the historical element was possibly on the verge of becoming a secondary appendage.

Egyptian and Jewish patriotic novels continued to circulate into Roman times. Within the A-text of the *Alexander Romance* can be detected earlier anti-Macedonian and later anti-Roman jibes. So long as there remained a group consciousness and resentment of the ruling power, nationalistic novels could endure.[9] Christians ultimately preserved a number of intensely nationalistic Jewish writings more or less abandoned by Jews.

These works appear to have been biographical in plan, centered upon the lives and deeds of one or more figures. Their style was that of unaffected *koine*. Religious concerns were prominent. Often the narrative must have included a list of marvelous accomplishments, including miracles. The sources of the works included history and legend, oral and written material, as well as some activities drawn from the repertories of competing heroes. The works intended to be appealing, and were. Most of their entertainment was linked to the several morals and messages. In the course of time most such books would undergo numerous revisions. Their object was the propagation of minority culture in a syncretistic and assimilationist environment.

Oriental apologetic and propaganda took different forms in addressing different groups. Three of these forms can be presented schematically, with a view to providing "national romances" with a cultural context:

	Iranians	*Egyptians*	*Jews*
Historiography:	Beros(s)us	Manetho	Josephus (*Against Apion*)
National Romance:	*Proto-Ninus*	*Nectanebus*	*Artapanus*
Apocalyptic Prophecy:	*Oracle of Hystaspes*	*Potter's Oracle*	Daniel 7—13

The histories conformed to Greek conventions and were written in polished prose for educated readers. National romances were most likely anonymous or pseudonymous and written in popular style for a general audience with basic Greek. The prophetic texts were nearly always attributed to some ancient figure and could circulate in native languages as well as Greek. Only the histories could even pretend to be aimed at the ruling elite; they merit the label "apologetic."

If the national romances had any resemblance to formal literature or any pretense to apologetic, it was more to enhance their appeal to their readers than to entice a foreign governor or monarch. By such means they could heighten their appearance of authenticity and aspire to pass as "highbrow." This tactic would also account for Chariton's historical pose.

Similar observations are germane to the techniques found in Esther, Judith, and *Joseph and Asenath*, which imitate biblical history. Other devices developed to nurture verisimilitude included spurious dedications, lists of sources, letters and documents, inscriptions, accounts of archaeological discoveries, descriptions of translations of foreign writings, and the use of the first person.[10] These methods excite stern disapproval from those who find them dishonest. As conventions of realism, however, they were (and are) standard items in the novelist's toolbox.

In addition, such devices helped create for their readers the illusion that they were people of culture. By our lights such persons would have been Trimalchios, the sort who would commission frescoes depicting scenes from "the Iliad and the Odyssey . . . and the gladiatorial games given by Laenas."[11] The appearance of culture was all they required—or could perceive.

These groups found assimilation very tempting, and the national romances attempted to appreciate their traditional culture in the context of the new. Dual loyalty is thus not out of the question.[12]

Why call such works novels? Why is Artapanus most often called a novel but Demetrius, Eupolemus, Cleodemus, and 2 Maccabees described as history?[13] Of the fragmentary writings of Jewish writers transmitted through Eusebius's report of Alexander Polyhistor's universal history only Eupolemus and Artapanus present questions of genre. Eupolemus is laudatory and apologetic. He does not shrink from invention, especially of letters. His narrative style must have been exuberant. This is no Thucydides *redivivus*, but he is a historian of sorts. In the case of Artapanus, however, a different spirit is at work.[14]

Artapanus was aware of the LXX and other sources. He knew the conventions of historiography and employed them to give his work credibility and "tone." Artapanus composed no unpretentious collection of legends on the order of Pseudo-Philo. The additions to the biblical narrative consistently exploit the possibilities for exciting story, most apparently in the longest fragment, treating Moses. Whether Artapanus, like others,[15] exploited the dramatic potential of the Joseph story is no longer ascertainable, since his work has been quarried by at least two authorities. Polyhistor molded the text into a euhemeristic list of accomplishments. Artapanus's original may have revealed different qualities.

Artapanus supplied Moses with an Egyptian military career—conveniently, if nastily, cribbing the business from a novel written to extol Sesonchosis![16] The advent of Hellenism had made such careers of conquest de rigueur. The exploits narrated in Artapanus supply this deficiency and further serve to rebut Egyptian boasts and anti-Semitic slanders. Intrigue dogs Moses' every step. Pharaoh Chenephres (who was, of course, jealous) organized a covenant against him, sealed by oath, and attempted an ambush.[17] The flight to Arabia thus became a bold escape from ceaseless treachery! Shades of Acts 9:23–31.

Arabia then became the base for Moses' war of liberation, Chenephres having gone the way of persecutors.[18] A new Pharaoh attempted to imprison the Jewish hero, with predictable results. After a series of wonders and a duel with the magicians of Egypt, Moses was able to liberate the people.[19] The devices used by Artapanus to enliven and enhance his account remind one of the methods employed by novelists and writers of the Acts, but they do little to commend him as a historian, nor does his handling of the major sources.[20] The biblical portrait of Moses as a religious leader summoned and directed by God has given place to a fictional creation: the typical international conqueror, national hero, and ecumenical benefactor. Whatever seemed questionable in his character has fallen away.[21] There is no basis for claiming that Artapanus believed that he was writing history but was too stupid to know better, or that he was a sound historian given to an occasional dash of exaggeration. His mind cannot be read, but his writing speaks of an intention to refute Egyptian and anti-Semitic propaganda.[22] This goal shaped Artapanus's work and resulted in fiction rather than truth, romance instead of history.

The extant fragments point to a biographical plan, more pronounced than that of the biblical source. This is most apparent in narrating the Exodus, for more attention is devoted to Moses' accomplishments than to the deliverance of the people. Persecution is likewise personal, aimed at Moses.[23] The career of the liberator, rather than the event of liberation, remains at center stage. Artapanus's intent, as revealed in his plan and emphases, is that of a historical novelist.[24]

JEWISH NOVELS

The importance of Artapanus as a close parallel to Acts warrants its examination in some detail. Other pieces of Jewish narrative writing also deserve attention, including those generally regarded as novels. Luke's ability to imitate the LXX in the way that other writers imitated Greek classics indicates that Scripture may have provided him with formal models and a repertory of literary techniques and motifs "sanctified" by tradition. Daniel 1—6, with its Greek additions, Tobit, Judith, and Esther, were almost certainly known to the author of Acts. These works achieved popularity among Christians, despite scholarly reservations.[25] Versions and editions proliferated.[26]

Jonah was almost certainly influential in the shaping of one NT passage and was not neglected by Luke in the composition of Acts 27.[27] A full survey of Jewish fiction and kindred material would make a substantial addition to available sources for understanding the ancient novel. The traditional division of labor has excluded most of this from consideration.[28] *Third Maccabees* and *Aristeas* are works of considerable stylistic accomplishment. *Joseph and Asenath* is quite similar to Acts in style and more like the romantic novels than any other Jewish work. The fragments of Artapanus and traces of novelistic sources in Josephus indicate that a substantial body of writings has been lost.[29] What endures presents a substantial variety of forms and themes.

Ahikar and Tobit reflect an older Aramaic category of "sapiential novels," the continuation of which may be seen in *Aristeas* and perhaps, to a degree, in *Joseph and Asenath*.[30] Judith and Esther are historical novels each with a single major character. An entire community is the historical subject of *3 Maccabees*. Jonah and various prophetic lives are missionary novels. Love

takes a part in Tobit and is central to *Joseph and Asenath*. Sex is not neglected, witness Judith, Esther, and the novella about Susanna, which contains a tightly structured narrative about a woman of high status victimized
by wicked clergy who plot to destroy her, only to be exposed at a trial witnessed by the assembled *ekklesia*. Judith and *Joseph and Asenath* supply military action; Esther and *3 Maccabees* deal with large-scale persecutions and
governmental decree. Jonah has one of the most famous accounts of nautical
adventure of all times. *Aristeas* incorporates both travel and utopian romance.
Even Tobit, a prosaic piece of transparently didactic writing, includes persecution, pathos, travel, love, sex, miracle, reunion, and a perfectly satisfying
happy conclusion. Within the corpus of surviving Jewish fiction there exists
about the same range and variation of quality that characterize pagan novels.

The entertainment value of the Jewish novels is beyond dispute. If one has
to argue it will be for edification, in some cases at least. No less than pagan
works, the Jewish novels stress national and religious pride and extol their
culture's superiority and glorious past. Christian readers have not always
been amused, especially since the Renaissance and Reformation introduced
different understandings of religious value.[31] Indeed, the debate about the
religious content of Jewish fiction is not unlike the discussions about the religious significance of pagan novels. In both cases the issue is blurred by
anachronistic views of religion. From these works comes a full range of interpretations of Judaism, including "ecumenical wisdom" (Tobit), preservation
of cultic identity (Daniel, *3 Maccabees*), syncretistic speculation (*Joseph and
Asenath*), and differing assessments of the ruling power (Artapanus, *Aristeas*).

Jewish novelists did not invent their characters. They elaborated figures
and events from myth, legend, Scripture, and history.[32] The writers of historical fiction took pains to emulate both their own and Greek historians.[33]
As in the case of Luke, it is not valid to insist that the authors were either telling the truth or engaging in deceit. Comparative analysis leads to the conclusion that their devices were employed, as by Chariton, for example, to create
verisimilitude.[34]

The authors of Jewish novels sought to communicate desirable ideas and
behavior patterns through the medium of an interesting story. Moral tales
had from time immemorial featured the rewards available to those who opted
for virtue. The plots of sapiential novels enlarged on this theme, and the novels often included a batch of proverbs for good measure.[35] Novels could help
the public deal with such perennial problems as liturgical change and new
translations of Scripture.[36] Characterization was a major instrument for edification. The leading figures are outstanding models of Jewish piety. They
win because of, not in spite of, their fidelity to traditional observances and

beliefs. God is on the side of the faithful, providence aids the righteous while punishing the wicked, and all ends well for those who follow the true path.

Jewish novels, which stood on the literary boundaries separating their own culture from the Greek and oriental worlds, addressed problems raised by those same boundaries. Within a context marked by acculturation and assimilation and the questions of the proper limits to each, they addressed men and women tempted to abandon Jewish observance in pursuit of wealth and status or redraw the traditional limits to facilitate participation in the macrosociety. The value of the novel for communicating various views on these questions was enhanced by its similarity to pagan writings. Most of the novels sought to maintain Jewish boundaries. One way in which they did this was by providing Jewish alternatives to pagan writings. Luke-Acts also wrestled with the boundaries between Judaism, emergent Christianity, and paganism. One of its objectives was to provide a mainly gentile audience with a firm sense of identity through creation of a Christian "story."

Although probably originating in the Persian period, Jewish novels came under Greek influence and tended to evolve in the direction favored by Greek novels. Increasing attention to romantic love is a leading indicator of this change. Comparison of Greek to Hebrew Esther is revelatory in this regard. *Joseph and Asenath*, probably the last of the extant Jewish novels written in Greek, contains the largest number of parallels to the romantic novel.[17]

Since Jewish novels did not develop in isolation from others, and were composed, copied, and revised during the Hellenistic and Roman eras, they may properly be considered within the framework of Greco-Roman novels. Portions of some apocalyptic books and narratives like the *Genesis Apocryphon* indicate that Jewish novels were not limited to Greek. Aramaic works were still read and even translated into Hebrew. Novels constituted part of the literary background of Palestinian no less than Hellenistic Christianity. Their existence is certain. The availability of many of them to NT writers is beyond question. Jewish novels are thus one element of the "background" of early Christianity.

CHRISTIAN NOVELS

Would Christians produce novels of their own or choose to abandon this genre? Jewish precedent had given ample evidence of the genre's value as an instrument for religious communication. The majority of those who acknowledge the existence of early Christian novels appear to say that they did not emerge until well into the second century, during the ancient novel's Golden Age, and that Christians wrote in response to secular and pagan literature rather than in continuity with their Jewish heritage.[38] Behind this theory lurk notions about the uniqueness of canonical genres and a vision of church history as decline and fall. I maintain, on the contrary, that revelation does not deprive writings of their human features and that human beings ought not dictate what God may or may not choose to inspire. My thesis is that the canonical Acts are best explained as an example of one type of historical novel. Genealogically stated, there is no clear continuity from Luke to Eusebius through Hegisippus,[39] but one can trace developments from the type of writing exhibited by Artapanus to Acts, to the Apoc. Acts, and into later hagiography. I hope that it is by now clear that relating Acts to ancient novels is hardly a means for writing the book off for being fiction, least of all, pure fiction. This classification seeks rather to account more satisfactorily for Acts' literary character and its content than does association with formal historiography. To accomplish this goal it will be necessary to reconsider the traditional critical evaluation of the nature and genre of the Apoc. Acts.

Apocryphal Acts

Within the framework of the definition proposed above, the Apoc. Acts are historical novels, extensive narrative prose works of historical fiction centered upon the actions of one or more characters, which seek to entertain as well as edify. Alternative terms, such as "aretalogies" and "praxeis,"[40] are not really genre-specific. Just as romantic novels derive some of their substance from erotic poetry, and philosophical novels make use of philosophy, the Acts have sources of particular types and certain subgeneric features. In general, however, "historical novel" is an adequate characterization.

Christians produced other novels than Acts. The infancy gospels, the *Pseudo-Clementines*, and the adventures of Xanthippe and Polyxena illustrate the general range. When, in addition, the disparity between the various Apoc. Acts is taken into account, it is clear that there was no more a fixed pattern for Christian novels than for any other. Tendencies to lump the Apoc. Acts into one bag reflect the kinds of prejudices that motivated Erwin Rohde. In the specific case of the Apoc. Acts, this penchant is a residue (probably unintentional) of Rosa Soeder's research.[41]

Soeder did not intend to define the Apoc. Acts so much as to profile them by comparison with romantic novels. For this purpose she analyzed a number of literary components, the five most striking of which were the motifs of travel, aretalogy, teratology, teaching, and love/sex. For those trained in classical NT form criticism, this list appeared to be a formal definition. All such comparisons stress similarity against variation and can lead to the view that any representative of the category is about the same as the rest. Yet the Apoc. Acts do differ from one another, in content, style, and technique, as well as in theology.[42] These differences prevent the Apoc. Acts from being understood solely by reference to one another. They must be studied in conjunction with other works, among which ancient novels have yielded the most fruitful results. As this investigation reaches out to examine more closely contacts and parallels with fictionalized biographies of heroes like Moses and Alexander and characters like Secundus and Aesop, it will shed even more light upon the problems. Consideration of the Apoc. Acts within the realm of ancient novels has already been justified by its results.

Despite important differences, the Apoc. Acts do resemble one another in obvious ways. Among these are focus upon the missionary careers of one or more apostles. Birth stories do not occur, presumably because the interest is not upon the apostles' lives in their entirety but upon their missions. The missionary perspective further colors the sermons, adventures, miracles, and even martyrdoms. It is the missionary focus that distinguishes Acts from the lives of holy men and women, such as Antony, Apollonius, or Pachomius. Those concentrate upon the great character revealed from the moment of birth, at the very latest. The Acts are also biographical in that they regard the history of early mission and the account of apostolic labors as one and the same. When W. Schneemelcher and K. Schäferdiek find the Apoc. Acts inadequate witnesses to early church history as the "wonderful advance of the Word of God,"[43] they are voicing a criticism that few early Christians would have found intelligible.

The Apoc. Acts reflect missionary thrust in another way: in their unrestrained enthusiasm for nearly every type of religious propaganda then in vogue. When tyrants were reproached, crowds awed, the prominent converted, opposing cults humiliated, great sermons offered, astonishing feats of self-denial performed, and the entire enterprise topped with nearly as many miracles as one could ever demand, the faithful were entertained, encouraged in their own faith and life, and stimulated toward missions of their own.

All this makes the learned nervous. Scholars have read A. D. Nock's *Conversion* and found that the only good analogies to Christian conversion are pagan conversions to a philosophical school. For intellectuals that is all well and good. What of those "ordinary" persons? They, R. MacMullen says, looked chiefly toward miracle.[44]

Cultural disappointment may have led Schneemelcher and Schäferdiek to claim that the Apoc. Acts were practical rather than theological in their intentions, lacking, in contrast to the canonical book, an explicit theological program. "Not primarily theological" is their judgment.[45] But popular theology, however abominable, remains theology. Even if the Apoc. Acts said no more than that Christianity is superior because it produces more miracles, they would still be determined by a way of speaking about God (*theologoumenon*). They are popular works and may be expected to exhibit popular theologies.[46] Before sustaining these generalizations it will behoove researchers to determine whether the Apoc. Acts are exclusively popular and nonreflective in theology, the extent to which their narratives carry out their theological intentions, and finally, whether the canonical book is so vastly superior in contrast to them.

In truth, the extant Apoc. Acts are a theological smorgasbord. The *Acts of Thomas* cannot be said to sustain Schneemelcher and Schäferdiek's claim. It presents a highly complex theology fully integrated into the content. Few ancient religious works achieved so felicitous an interpenetration of structure and content with theology. Few early Christian writings were more determined by theological reflection. Perhaps, however, this is a rare exception.[47]

The *Acts of Andrew*, poorly preserved as they are, contain at least enough intellectual pretension to spark a debate on their relation to second-century philosophy.[48] Whatever the final outcome of this debate may be, the *Acts of Andrew* will not easily be relegated to that corner of hell reserved for writers of nontheological Acts. Content and theology coincide. Continence has a metaphysical basis, and crucifixion provides an ideal "text" for demonstrating the illusory nature of matter. Andrew thus joins the ranks of such famous figures as Calanus and Peregrinus.[49] These Acts are a second exception to the strictures proposed.

What of the *Acts of John?* Do they exhibit theological reflection and does this shape the text? Reconstruction of this fragmentary and oft-rewritten book is difficult, but it certainly represents the most advanced and radical type of Johannine speculation known. Theological considerations have invaded the content. Nearly all the miracles are resurrections, symbols of the rebirth experienced by those who accept the apostle's message. Askesis is a natural concomitant of that belief. Popular the *Acts of John* may be, but the book is far from unreflective, and both contents and structure undergird its theological premises.[50] Three of the five major Apoc. Acts have not supported the thesis of Schneemelcher and Schäferdiek.

The *Acts of Paul* (including the Thecla portion) and the *Acts of Peter* may offer them some consolation. Although the *Acts of Peter* (I refer to the *Actus Vercellenses*) are without doubt inclined toward the nonreflective, they have no lack of theological ideas, however disappointing these may appear to some.[51] There is the amusing notion that heresy could not bloom while the apostles tended the field,[52] as well as the quaint idea that Peter and Paul worked in perfect harmony. These are theologically derived ideas, and in any event, Luke agreed with them. When, as in *Acts of Peter*, divine power rather than theological discourse is the medium for the refutation of Simonian gnosis, "popular" theology is speaking quite clearly. Those who wish to trump the Apoc. Acts on this trick had better look to their cards, for Luke did much the same.[53] When Peter bests Simon without condescending to a debate, the readers are being advised about how to handle heretics. The *contestatio* is one means by which theology and content become one. Even Schneemelcher allows that the work has a Christology appropriate to its character.[54] The *Acts of Peter* have theological intentions and are able to carry them out in the narrative.

Last come the *Acts of Paul.* In these, we are sadly advised, the apostle emerges as but the "herald of a very simple faith," reducible to a few formulas, mostly polemic against gnostic speculation, rejection of the OT, denial of the resurrection, and relaxation of ethical standards.[55] Readers of Acts and the Pastorals will find this familiar ground. In effect Schneemelcher says that "popular theology is no theology at all." This is both elitist and historically erroneous. A revival of W. Bousset is in order.[56] In reality the *Acts of Paul* do have a coherent theology and the writer was capable of expressing his or her intentions. Tertullian found no lack of theology in the work.[57] Most would agree that the *Acts of Thecla* cogently express their position. How can it be, moreover, that absence of polemic condemns *Acts of Peter* while its presence in *Acts of Paul* demonstrates lack of theological content and interest?[58]

Speeches, hymns, and prayers are major sources for specific *theologoumena*. Schneemelcher wishes to disregard their bearing upon his thesis.[59] Application of the same criterion to Luke's work would create a kindred poverty of theological data. In both canonical and apocryphal Acts theology is presented mainly through speeches. They are not theological treatises.[60] Comparison of Luke's speeches to those in the *Acts of Paul* does little to humiliate the latter. Luke's speeches, as is well known, reproduce but a minimum of Pauline theology. They are the author's own edifying compositions. Their theology is nonspeculative and quite popular in content.[61]

The speeches in *Acts of Paul* are similarly edifying compositions of the author. They too are of value as a source for the theological climate in which they were written.[62] Unlike those of Luke, they are rather dependent upon Paul's letters.[63] This is scarcely a flaw. The chief distinction is their moralism. For many second-century Christians they may have had more relevance than the set pieces by which Luke displayed his skill. Luke's are more Lukan and entertaining. The speeches in *Acts of Paul* are more Pauline and edifying. The sweeping condemnations of the Apoc. Acts so succinctly propounded by Schneemelcher and Schäferdiek do not appear justified. That the Apoc. Acts are not concerned with some of the "distinct axioms" of Lukan theology[64] may come as a painful disappointment to those for whom Luke is normative,[65] but that does not exclude the possibility that they have distinctive theologies of their own.

Because apostolic travel and adventure serve as the common framework of these books, they are frequently regarded as works of entertainment rather than fantastic pieces of church history. For Schneemelcher and Schäferdiek this characteristic technique is symptomatic of the genre:

> The interest of the apocryphal Acts depends upon the personal fortunes and deeds of the apostles, and not on the history of the church. . . . The intention [is to use] these stories to glorify the apostles as miracle workers. Hence one can hardly speak of an "edificatory" trend: their intention is better described as entertainment.[66]

I question whether this description might not also apply to the canonical Acts. First, some qualifications must be made. It is not correct to claim that miracles in the Apoc. Acts glorify the apostles rather than God. Their performers sometimes appear as beings of divine potency, but their power comes from on high. Since the forms used in the Apoc. Acts are basically those found in the NT, claims made about one apply also to the other. In fact, the apostles appear as servants of Christ, and his power becomes manifest through them. They work miracles to evoke faith in Christ, not themselves.[67]

If the apostles were the sole interest, there would be little about the mission and life of the Christian communities. But there is. Local traditions appear in them.[68] Some biographical legends may reflect local interests. Even if the *Acts of Peter* did not stem from Rome, as the book seems not to, Roman Christians would still find it of value. The Apoc. Acts abound with names of local converts, not all of which are fictitious,[69] and even imaginary names glorify the community no less than the founder. The vigorous moralism of these works, with frequent support from edifying miracles, is not apostolic glorification but spiritual and pastoral education. When sinners meet wretched ends and those in peril of losing their virginity are delivered by divine aid, one cannot speak of wonders "retailed for their own sake."[70]

One of the most castigated features of the Apoc. Acts is their use of animal fables and stories. Concession of their improbability should not lead to denial of their utility. Does not the example of a continent lion speak volumes to mere humans with much lesser sexual interest and capacity? John concludes the notorious incident of the bedbugs with a sage observation about obedience to the voice of God.[71] Critics should, in any case, exaggerate neither their readers' lack of humor nor their credulousness.

Heresy also involves the entire community threatened. *Acts of Peter* 1–11 is, as it were, a "history" of the Roman church during the time when Simon gained the upper hand. This is a more sustained treatment of community problems than any supplied by Luke. Had the "greater glory" of Peter been the single concern, this situation could have been summarized in a few sentences. The *Acts of Paul*, on their part, devote substantial space to the apostle's conflict with gnosis in Corinth.[72] Polemic against magic is another example of pastoral concern.[73]

Worship and church order are also more prominent than they should be in novels devoted to nothing but apostolic miracles. Local leaders and patrons often emerge. The material devoted to descriptions of worship is an invaluable aid to historians of liturgy. The Apoc. Acts devote more space to the description of preaching and liturgy than to the narration of miracles.[74] One reason for this is their desire to give their readers wholesome edification.[75]

Dissatisfaction with the nature of moral and theological teaching in the Apoc. Acts does not justify denying its existence. The Apoc. Acts also seek to entertain. Those who compare the Apoc. Acts with Luke are first impressed by the differences. Are those differences features of the genre, or do they belong to matters pertinent to changes in date, theology, and audience? One characteristic solution has been wholesale denunciation and revulsion at the bizarre and utterly uncontrolled exaggeration evident in the Apoc. Acts.[76] Those who dare bring up Peter's therapeutic shadow and Paul's healing handkerchiefs are rebuked with the admonition that these have been subordinated to Luke's theological program.[77] That such considerations may also be operative in the Apoc. Acts is not worthy of consideration. The defects of such arguments are obvious. There is no indication that even the most culturally disappointing passages of the Apoc. Acts do not serve their theological programs, just as there is no warrant for denying that Luke's program contained as one of its features glorification of the apostles.

Then there is sex, about which most of the Apoc. Acts have a great deal to say, little of it favorable. Talking beasts and balking wives have led many to seek to put as much distance between the canonical and apocryphal Acts as possible.[78] Luke appears to be in general agreement with the Apoc. Acts on the question of celibacy, but he chose not to exploit it for propaganda.[79] Still, his apostles do not have wives, and those who follow him leave spouse behind.

Frequently in the Apoc. Acts the apostle converts a leading woman whose subsequent refusal of conjugal rights motivates the authorities to launch a persecution.[80] Soeder and others see in this the manifestation of a different genre. Since one may not deny that Luke's Paul often finds women converts and sometimes gets in trouble over them,[81] the only generic distinction that may be claimed is celibacy. The Apoc. Acts are "erotic," therefore entertaining, therefore novels, since all who know their Rohde (*Griech. Roman*) are aware that this element is indispensable. Love and sex are not the same, however, and ancient novels treat one, both, or neither in quite varying ways. The sentimental novels exalt love and marriage, but can be quite delicate about sex. The Apoc. Acts, which often oppose both, often contain more prurience than the modest Heliodorus.[82]

The subject does underline some differences between Luke and many of the Apoc. Acts. The canonical author did not wish to portray Christianity as a destabilizing factor in social life. Had he known of such tales as may decorate the Apoc. Acts, he would have kept his silence.[83] When the Book of Acts was written, Christians were the target of charges of sexual impropriety. When the Apoc. Acts emerged, the climate had changed; most of the extant works are indifferent to worldly criticism and standards. The culture as a whole was beginning to admire chastity, as can be seen in the evolution of views from early novels to late.[84] The posture of the Apoc. Acts at least attempts to preserve the radical otherworldliness of primitive Christianity, whereas Luke seeks a dialogue with society.

Sex receives no less varied a treatment in the Apoc. Acts than in other novels. *The Acts of Peter* exploit it but little. It is mainly Thecla episodes that deal with sexual themes in the Pauline tradition. Lurid scenes can be found, as in *Acts of John* 70–74 and *Acts of Thomas* 82ff., but most of the sexually oriented scenes refer to domestic strife.[85] In addition to the value for generating persecution and thus motivating the plot, such episodes speak directly to the concerns and life styles of ordinary believers, particularly women, who are thereby encouraged to assert their freedom and independence from male rule. Finally, sex is not a form-critical category, a criterion for classifying literary types.

Despite biblical precedent,[86] the appearance of talking animals would seem to be, in the eyes of many, ample reason for placing the Apoc. Acts beyond the pale. Yet animal fables were time-honored modes for the pleasant expression of didactic wisdom. In the second and third centuries c.e. such material gained currency in learned and philosophical circles.[87] With reference to specifics, it is questionable whether one can justifiably swallow Jesus' cursing of a fig tree while straining out the story of the bedbugs.[88] The articulate asses whom Thomas meets are, after all, modeled upon the Balaam narrative and are no less symbolic than Apuleius's ass-man.[89] Most of the remarkable material comes from a section of the *Acts of Peter* devoted to rather extraordinary miracles.[90] Many readers would recognize that Paul's adventures with a lion played upon a well-known tale.[91] Andrew and Matthias encounter cannibals in a Christian parallel to the fabulous travel story. In no case would it be fair to portray such episodes as typical of the Apoc. Acts and essential to the genre.[92]

Equally unacceptable is the contention that such erotic and fantastic passages make the Apoc. Acts unedifying, for it is in just these episodes that the uplifting and instructional intentions of these works are most clearly proclaimed. Before grasping at such data as a basis for relegating the Apoc. Acts to an inferior place, attention must be given to their specific functions, the trends of contemporary taste, and the requirements of dualistic theology with its proclivities for myth, allegory, and symbol, as well as the Apoc. Acts' intense interest in asceticism.

The Apoc. Acts have, in general, fewer literary pretensions than do Luke's, having been directed, apparently, toward a somewhat less sophisticated market. Readers of the *Life of Aesop* and the *Alexander Romance* would probably have found the Apoc. Acts to their taste. Christian literature had diversified. By the middle of the second century C.E. apologies for the learned and unselfconscious writings for the more average were available. Luke stands at the dividing point. One component of his work will be taken up by the Apologists: the effort to present Christianity as intellectually acceptable and socially unthreatening. The Apoc. Acts leave most of this to others and continue Luke's major thrust. The literary disparity that exists among the various Apoc. Acts and between Acts and the Apoc. Acts is not so great as that among the romantic novels, nor may style and literary quality serve as distinguishing criteria.[93]

Formal structure is the last touchstone invoked by Schneemelcher and Schäferdiek to distinguish the canonical from the apocryphal Acts. Luke composed the history of the "march of the Gospel from Jerusalem to Rome," whereas the Apoc. Acts are "primarily interested in the journeyings of the messengers, their miracles, etc."[94] Since the writers of the Apoc. Acts do not derive their structure from salvation history, apostolic actions are substantive for them, incidental for Luke.[95] They go on to note lack of concern in the Apoc. Acts for the "expectation of an immediate end, and the mission to the Gentiles unimpeded by the Jewish Law," matters requiring Luke's attention.[96] Why, one may ask, should they have shaped their works to conform to questions of a bygone age? In all of the Acts theological questions are answered by describing how apostles dealt with similar issues.

Luke does not focus upon a single apostle but, as is often claimed (with reference to 1:8), focuses on the story of the gospel's progress from Jerusalem to the ends of the earth. So it is said.

Acts does not, however, actually tell how the gospel got to Rome but tells how Paul got there, other Christians being already in place. In fact, none of the audience of Acts 1:8 came any closer to Rome than Caesarea Maritima. "Paul is the author's hero."[97] Where he is not at center stage, groundwork is being laid for the gentile mission he will lead but not found (Acts 1—8; 10—12). Acts 1—5 explains the persecution that led to external mission. Luke moves expeditiously from that point to Paul, as quickly as can be done without giving the idea that Paul invented the idea of converting Gentiles.

With a typically brilliant touch, he slips Paul's name into the Stephen story, not as supporter but as persecutor of this unorthodox evangelist.[98] Stephen's work is then finished, and Philip can retire from Acts after gathering in the Ethiopian, just as Peter's missionary labor ends with the conversion of Cornelius. Acts is in content an Acts of Paul with an extended introduction.

Luke also has a geographical focal point: the Aegean region.[99] The relative complexity of his work is not due to his passion for completeness. It arises rather because of the elaborate defense and justification Luke has erected for Paul, including close ties to Jerusalem and engagement in mission to Gentiles only after, and in conformity with, Peter. Since this is essentially inaccurate, it cannot be used to prove that Luke is a better historian than the authors of the Apoc. Acts, nor will the pre-Pauline chapters 1—5 enhance that standing.[100]

The fragmentary and oft-reedited Apoc. Acts are difficult to evaluate for structure, but Schneemelcher and Schäferdiek have seen enough: they find them haphazard, one miracle following another until the apostle dies.[101] Soeder's appendix on narrative structure and technique reveals the shortcomings of this generalization.[102] She observed such techniques as parallelism and interlacement (see p. 134 below), subplots containing contrasts and parallel themes, retardation, and insertions to disrupt consecutive narration. All of these were in use by contemporary novelists and can be found in Acts. She further took note of descriptions, catalogues, letters, speech contests, dreams, and visions, all of which relieve monotonous focus upon a single person's words and deeds. Again, the correspondences with other novels and Acts are abundant.[103]

Luke also likes to use a character as focal point. The loose sequence of scenes which arouses critical ire is due to fondness for episodic narration, another trait shared by novelists, Luke, and others.[104] The literary and structural criticisms raised by the editors of the Apoc. Acts in Hennecke-Schneemelcher (*NTA*) do not apply to the works under their perusal, nor are there the contrasts they wish to establish to Acts. There is more variety, even sophistication, to the Apoc. Acts than a rapid scan of their contents may suggest. When surveys also take into account some of the "minor" Acts not included within the principal five, the richness of theme and structure will become even more apparent.

The Apoc. Acts give every appearance of being contemporary works written by apostles or their contemporaries. There is no dearth of faked documentation and other devices used in ancient fiction to create an atmosphere of verisimilitude.[105] The first person is used with great freedom. If Luke's claims, or apparent claims, are to be accepted at face value, then so must those of the Apoc. Acts.

In conclusion, none of the attempts to distinguish these Acts into canonical and apocryphal types of substantially different genres is compelling. Criticism of the Apoc. Acts does not stand up under scrutiny. What remains is to subject the canonical book to similar tests.

The Book of Acts

If it is accurate to claim that Luke intended to describe the history of the Christian mission rather than apostolic deeds, then his narrative must be shown to have done this. Church life should be given detailed coverage. Yet only Acts 1—5 reflects such concerns, and few historians are comfortable with its accounts of converts by the thousands, utopian life, perfect harmony, and spiritual growth continually nurtured by apostolic deeds and speeches. Worship is all but ignored.[106] Outside the summaries the apostles receive full attention and the faithful are mere anonymous automatons.[107] Luke says little about mission apart from that of the principal characters.[108] The barest minimum is devoted to Antioch (Luke's traditional home!), and nothing comes to light about the evangelization of Alexandria and Rome. These were not unimportant sites. The places visited by Peter receive slim coverage, as do many (but not all) Pauline centers. Other data were certainly available, but Luke chose to overlook numerous sites and give others short shrift.

Very little is said about the communities once the founder moves on. There is the briefest mention of a visitation, pastoral activity being restricted mainly to Paul's last journey to Jerusalem.[109] Key decisions emerge without conflict among the leaders, in settings of great harmony. Regarding church order there is only a reference to the appointment of the Seven (a fictional description unfriendly to deacons and masking a more substantial conflict) and the emergence of presbyters, whose role is unclear except for their identity with bishops.[110] Only Peter, and his faithful companion John, among the Twelve do mission work. The apostles stay mainly in Jerusalem and fade away. Luke has little to share regarding church life, worship, order, and history, let alone doctrinal conflict.

What Luke does relate in great detail is what happened to the missionaries, to Paul and a few others. Without the accounts of their trials and travels, Acts would consist of a few disconnected snippets. These famous summaries cannot establish Luke as a historian. They serve only to provide a framework for his scenes and remind the readers of the successes wrought by the apostles. Luke's writing reveals that his primary interest was the deeds of apostles, particularly those of Paul. This is fundamentally the same as the viewpoint of the Apoc. Acts.[111]

Luke's theological program is not without its popular characteristics. There does not appear to be a consistent Christology, and even eschatology is not worked out in detail.[112] Speculative formulations have no place in the Lukan scheme. The religion he proclaims has a clear continuity with Judaism, is supported by common-sense understanding, and steers clear of any potentially troublesome approaches. The popular quality of this work is most apparent in method: Luke expresses theology by telling stories. Miracle is the convincing point in theological debate and the essential mode of religious verification.

The Lukan works are committed to the use of miracle for propaganda and apologetic. This uncritical stance is not typical of the NT.[113] It is a quality Luke shares with the Apoc. Acts. Another is polemical method. Luke, who is closer to the world of magical thought and practice than the other evangelists,[114] is therefore especially sensitive to charges of magic. When "genuine" magicians confront the apostles, they are lucky to escape with damaged reputations and serious health problems.[115] The Apoc. Acts treat similar problems with kindred means.[116]

The showcase of all such apocryphal confrontations, still successful in print and on screen during the 1950s,[117] pitted Peter against Simon Magus. Schneemelcher regrets Peter's failure to deal with the theological issues at stake.

> Peter . . . achieves decisive success through his miracles, and through frustrating or outdoing Simon's miracles. . . . The popular character of the *Acts of Peter*, as of all the apocryphal Acts, is also shown in the fact that it is not extensive theological discussions that occupy the central place but miraculous acts.[118]

The same must be said of Acts. In the grandparent of all duels between Simon and Peter, Acts 8:5–25, almost nothing can be learned about Simon's theology.[119] Simon is routed in a "beauty contest," the winner of which will gain the whole population as adherents. This exhibition consists entirely of miracles (8:6–12). The discriminating public opts for the Christians, who in this case do not even need their first string. By the time Peter arrives, Simon has been converted. The *Acts of Peter* narrate miracles in much greater detail, but then they also include some theology. When Paul meets a magus, the latter is blinded without further ado, and the offspring of Sceva can even be routed by reasonably intelligent demons (13:6–12; 19:13–17). Internal Christian conflict is also resolved by miracles (10:44–45; 15:8–12). Dissent, other than that over the observance of Torah, is attributed to jealousy or personal issues.[120]

Next to this the *Acts of Paul* will receive good marks. There Paul's Corinthian flock is seduced by false teachers whom the apostle refutes by sending a letter.[121] The setting is fictitious, but it reflects Pauline practice more faithfully than does Luke. All of the Acts use miracle for propaganda and vindication, as an instrument for clarifying just which side God has selected. The function of miracle does not therefore constitute a criterion for drawing a line between canonical and apocryphal Acts. The one outstanding question is literary structure and its theological basis.

According to Schneemelcher and Schäferdiek, this is decisive. Luke's structure is determined by his concern to present the history of Christianity's emergence from Judaism.[122] In truth, Luke does pursue this project, but the means by which it is accomplished is the construction of a fictionalized plot that employs as its building blocks stereotyped scenes of missionary aretalogy: Jewish rejection, persecution, and vindication. This "plot device by which the movement of the narrative as a whole is motivated"[123] has been carefully orchestrated to sustain maximum suspense with a minimum of troublesome fact. Stephen's death, Peter's acceptance of gentile converts, Jerusalem's endorsement, Paul's arrest, and his journey to Rome were all crucial events in early Christian history. Luke gives them careful attention, but since they are presented as exciting tableaux stripped of their actual content and constitute within the structure of Acts major literary turning points, it is possible to say that Luke sees amid all that conflict and pain the opportunity to communicate his intent by reducing a fundamental struggle to a literary device.

Like many popular writers, Luke makes his points by repetition and basic parallelism. No one is surprised at the Jewish delegation's reaction to Paul's message at Rome, nor at Paul's response. It has been driven home by repetition. The detailed parallelisms between the careers of Peter and Paul and Paul and Jesus are generally regarded as intentional components of Luke's structure. Through this artistic means the author propagates a particular image of master and apostle and their relationships to each other. Peter and Paul both say and do the same things.[124] Through simple sermons and pleasing stories the reader is assured that Peter and Paul stand in succession to Jesus (and Moses and Elijah) and that there is no conflict between them. The message takes its shape in the narrative and requires no intervention or authorial aside. For this technique there are abundant precedents in ancient pagan, Jewish, and Christian novels.[125]

Three standard narrative devices exploited by ancient novelists are *duplication* (repetition of a similar event), *parallelism* (matching the experience of one character to that of another), and *interlacement* (shifting focus from one person to another and then back). Table 3 is a conspectus comparing Acts and Xenophon of Ephesus in their use of these techniques.[126]

Appreciation of Luke's characterization requires some comparison with writers of popular fiction. Most episodes revolve around one character who is the focal point against which action occurs and from which interpretation evolves. Motivation is primitive. Good characters act from noble motives;

TABLE 3
Three Techniques

Acts	*Xenophon*
DUPLICATIONS	
Imprisonments: 4:1–22; 5:17–42; 12:3–17; 16:24–40; 21:27—26:32	Robbers, pirates: 1.13, 2.11, 3.8, 4.4
Blindings: 9:8–18; 13:6–12	Rescue by Isis/Nile: 3.11, 4.2, 4.3 (cf. 5.15)
Stonings: 7:55–60; 14:19–20	Rival lovers: 1.5, 2.3, 2.11, 2.13, 3.11, et al.
PARALLELISM	
Peter (with companion) heals cripple: 3:1–10	Anthia crucified: 2.13
Paul (with companion) heals cripple 14:8–10	Habrocomes crucified: 4.2
Peter's prison miracle: 12:3–17	Anthia shipwrecked: 2.11
Paul's prison miracle: 16:23–35	Habrocomes shipwrecked 3.12
Peter curses rival: 8:18–24	Anthia jailed: 4.6
Paul curses rival: 13:6–12	Habrocomes jailed: 4.2–3. [127]
INTERLACEMENT	
8:4–12. Philip	2.3–8. Habrocomes
8:14–25. Peter	2.9–11. Anthia
8:26–40. Philip	2.12. Habrocomes
9:1–30. Paul	2.13. Anthia
9:32—11:18. Peter	2.14–3.3. Habrocomes
13:1—14:31. Paul	3.3–9. Anthia
	3.9–10. Habrocomes
	3.11. Anthia (etc.) [128]

wicked ones from evil inclinations. People represent ideas and concepts to such a degree that they may lack genuinely human qualities. Upholders of the good hold out against impossible odds and receive good rewards. Representatives of the bad come to bad ends. Character is not so much evoked as described. Readers learn what people are like from the reactions of others. In Acts that means respect and admiration from the better sort, envy and malice from the wicked. Officials are either tyrants or statesmen.

The various Acts and the romantic novels tend to reflect a similar anthropology and a means for expressing it. When the heroes appear on the scene they seem to resemble the very gods, and the masses hail them as such. Just as Paul can raise a hand and quiet a crowd or Peter's shadow expel illness, so the male and female stars of the romantic works need only be seen to cause others to fall in love with them. They have magical erotic power. Apostles have magical healing power. Each type is the epiphany of a transfigured being. Their audiences longed for just such transfigurations that would lift them from the constraints of present life.[129]

Through his own kind of magic Luke transformed Peter and Paul into stereotypes, representatives of the ideal missionary. In the case of Paul nothing could fall shorter of the actual mark. The biography of Paul created by Luke is the very sort Paul subjected to ferocious ridicule in 2 Cor. 11:22—12:10. The same arbitrary creation of a character who would appeal to popular taste had earlier taken place with Ninus, Alexander, and Moses. Luke did for Paul what Artapanus had done for Moses. He is thereby revealed as a writer of historical fiction. Since he used the methods of novelists, he may also have shared their intention.

Further observations confirm this view. As a dramatic writer Luke devoted great care to the creation of excitement and the generation of suspense. He used the means of other dramatic authors, including withheld identity, retardation of the plot, interruptions, and last-minute reversals of fortune. His considerable literary skill and ingenuity were employed to lend variation to a potentially wearisome narrative. Few authors have been able to repeat essentially the same story so often without becoming monotonous or to evoke so much with such economy of detail, as Ernst Haenchen's somewhat grudging admiration makes so brilliantly clear.

Luke's freedom permitted him to function as an omniscient author, able to leap from one time or place to another and enter closed chambers to listen in on private conversations and overhear in-camera proceedings. His license extended to the composition of entire episodes and the invention of events. Justification of these procedures by reference to this piece from one ancient historian and that incident from another is not nearly so convincing as the assembly of stylistic, structural, narrative, characterizational, and incidental data from ancient popular novels.[130]

The arguments synthesized by Schneemelcher and Schäferdiek for regarding Acts and the Apoc. Acts as representatives of different genres are ultimately unconvincing. The canonical and apocryphal Acts treat similar material in similar ways. Generically, they are representatives of a subgroup within the broad category of the ancient novel. Luke's work was an inspiration for many Acts, but there is no reason to presume that the genre would not have taken root in Christian soil had Acts never been written.

CONCLUSION

This has been an exercise in form criticism. Biblical form criticism, as classically practiced, attempts to identify ideal social, cultural, or religious settings for various types of oral expression—not as an end but as a means for grasping the function of particular texts and the presence of changed circumstances. The discipline reveals the limits of various forms and clarifies what is or is not typical in particular situations. Similar methods may be applied to the study of written literary forms, with the recognition that variations from formal norms (many of which norms were elaborately defined in ancient introductions and handbooks) are more likely to reveal individual creativity (or its opposite) than direct social changes. With the emergence of redaction criticism older notions about "community products" and "collective compositions" have come to seem obsolete. NT scholars today subject both oral, popular, and written, learned forms to very similar analysis. Despite the volume of controversy surrounding the discipline, this shift has not always been formally acknowledged. From this perspective of form criticism as practiced in an era of redaction criticism, I began to study the genre of Acts. Had I not been so naive I would probably never have made the attempt.

As a comparative discipline, form criticism seeks to uncover the earliest discernible shape of a text or tradition so that its original intent may come to light. Historical linguists and historians of religion use similar methods. Like other scientific enterprises, form criticism seeks the construction of ideal models. The procedure is valid so long as it is recognized that ideal models are tools that may never appear in pure form.

Traditionally the canonical Book of Acts has been regarded as a unique text with close analogies to historiography. But comparison with historiography has been carried out on a piecemeal basis, with little general discussion of the genre in relation to Acts as a whole. There is no doubt that this comparison has been fruitful, but it has also raised questions. In an effort to widen the comparative basis I have sought to introduce a body of literature known as the ancient novel. The nature of this genre excludes the construction of a "pure" type or of "pure" types. Attempts at definition, however multivalent and evocative, yield a series of models, or pieces of models.[1] The essence of the novel resists rigid classification. Ancient historical novels did exist, how-

ever, and it is possible to make observations leading toward the construction
of ideal models regarding them. By reference to novels in general and historical novels in particular I have attempted to provide detailed evidence for the
ancient novel's relevance to the understanding of Acts. My intent is that such
comparison proceed alongside, as well as in competition with, investigations
using historiographical models.

If the question of content may for a moment be placed to one side, it
should become apparent that the data base for comparison of Acts to works of
history that are similar in shape, scope, style, and purpose is rather limited.
Historical monographs with convincing affinities to Acts are difficult to identify. Novels that bear likenesses to Acts are, on the other hand, relatively
abundant. For the type of audience Luke apparently addressed, the edifying
historical novel was then the genre most appropriate to his purposes and most
available. Those who would defend the greater relevance of the historical
monograph must not only engage in painstakingly detailed definition and description of the genre but also explain why Luke should have preferred a
model remote from both his goal and his environment. When the content of
Acts, with its high proportion of exciting episodes, legendary presentations,
and brief speeches, is taken into account, the scale tilts even more sharply toward the historical novel.

The contention that all good writings are sui generis is at best a half-truth
that cannot be used to justify the neglect of comparative study.[2] Whatever
validity this aphorism possesses emerges in novels and works of the Romantic
and later periods. It is doubtful that Luke's would qualify as "good" writing
in this sense, anyway. It is, I believe, equally doubtful that he would have
wished readers to view Acts as unlike anything else they had ever seen. Few
have labored more diligently to absolve Christianity of the charge of novelty.

Description of Acts as a historical novel does not imply that the author
concocted it from thin air. Reconsideration of the question of genre does not
eliminate the possibility of sources. Even the clearly fictional *Metamorphoses*
of Apuleius used sources. Indeed, my proposals about the genre of Acts may
shed some light upon the perplexing source question concerning the book.[3]
Nor do the proposals seek a shortcut to the "truth question"—as if calling
Acts a historical novel consigned it to oblivion. Few works have suffered
more at the hands of friends who have taken it upon themselves to defend the
accuracy of Luke's account regardless of the cost. At the risk of sounding like
the Asian presbyter who perished for publishing the *Acts of Paul*,[4] I have
come to praise Luke, not to bury him.

This praise is not without reservations. Animosity toward Lukan theology,
however overdrawn, has some warrant in this era. Neither church nor society
will benefit from triumphalism, grandiosity, and the excitement of unrealis-

tic expectations. Luke is guilty on these, and other, counts. Moreover, if he composed what we should call a historical novel, he was engaged in activity at least partly frivolous and he did not always tell the truth. In his defense I mention Jesus, who was also sometimes frivolous and who told parables, fictional, sometimes entertaining, stories that crystallized the essence of his message.[5]

Granted the limitations of Luke's long "parable" for the present day, when he composed that parable it was as bold a notion as had ever been conceived. Instead of alternatives advocating resistance or withdrawal,[6] Luke proposed that the world be Christianized. In hindsight his proposal is easily denounced as a sellout. At the time of its origin it certainly seemed mad. Appealing to all that was progressive and idealistic in the church's structures, Luke offered, so to speak, its services to the imperial society of his day. Christianity, which Luke viewed as a renewed form of Judaism stripped of its limitations, had both the interest in and the means for elevating the rude and unwashed masses, for promoting urbanity and ethics, community and loyalty.[7] Luke was something of a prophet who wished to share a vision. For that purpose dispassionate analysis of the often unpromising Christian past was of limited value. What he needed was a form in which to cast his vision of a Utopia. The historical novel was just such a form.

In due course the offer by church was accepted by society. Despite the reservation of both parties, what first emerged as the wild dream of the writer of Luke-Acts and those who had contributed to that dream became one of the pillars of modern civilization.[8] Our debt to the dream represented by Luke is considerable. Because of that dream later believers did seek to Christianize the world. They failed, but the teachings of Jesus and the writings of Paul still exist to stir up subsequent generations, Christian and other. The preservation of those teachings and ideas may ultimately have more to do with people like Luke than with the historical Jesus or the controversial Paul. Be that as it may, the shape of the world religion that Christianity became has more in common with the vision of Luke than with much that is in the theologies of Matthew, Mark, John, or Paul.

Had Luke pursued different ideals we might have a far clearer grasp of primitive Christian history. Chroniclers and annalists do have their value, as do historians of scrupulous accuracy and penetrating acumen. Luke had little in common with such. As a historian he leaves much to be desired. What he did have were vision and the means to express it. Without vision the people will perish.

ABBREVIATIONS

1. ANCIENT NOVELS

Achilles Tatius	Achilles Tatius, *Leucippe and Cleitophon*
Ap. Ty.	Philostratus, *Apollonius of Tyana*
Ap. Tyre	*Apollonius of Tyre*
Apuleius	Apuleius of Madaura, *Metamorphoses*
Chariton	Chariton of Aphrodisias, *Chaireas and Callirhoe*
Cyropaideia	Xenophon of Athens, *Cyropaideia*
Heliodorus	Heliodorus of Emesa, *Ethiopica*
Longus	Longus, *Daphnis and Chloe*
Petron.	Petronius (?), *Satyricon*
A True Story	Lucian of Samosata, *A True Story*
X. E.	Xenophon of Ephesus, *Ephesiaca*

2. SECONDARY WORKS, COLLECTIONS, JOURNALS, AND SERIES

AAA	*Acta Apostolorum Apocrypha*, ed. Lipsius and Bonnet
ACS	American Classical Studies
ACW	Ancient Christian Writers
AJP	*American Journal of Philology*
ANF	*The Ante-Nicene Fathers*
Ann Litt Univ Nantes	Annales littéraires de l'Université de Nantes
APA Mon	American Philosophical Association Monographs
ARW	*Archiv für Religionswissenschaft*
ATR	*Anglican Theological Review*
BAGD	*A Greek-English Lexicon of the New Testament,* ed. Bauer, Arndt, Gingrich, and Danker
BEG CHR	*The Beginnings of Christianity*, ed. Foakes-Jackson and Lake
BETL	Bibliotheca ephemeridum theologicarum lovaniensium
BGL	Bibliothek der griechischen Literatur

BHT	Beiträge zur historischen Theologie
BJRL	Bulletin of the John Rylands University Library of Manchester
BRUCE	Bruce, The Acts of the Apostles
BZ	Biblische Zeitschrift
CADBURY	Cadbury, The Making of Luke-Acts
CBQ	Catholic Biblical Quarterly
CBQMS	Catholic Biblical Quarterly Monograph Series
CLAnt	Classical Antiquity
Class. et Med.	Classica et Medievalia
ClassJ	Classical Journal
ClassPhil	Classical Philology
Coll. Lat.	Collections Latomus
CONZELMANN	Conzelmann, Die Apostelgeschichte
CQ	Classical Quarterly
CREED	Creed, The Gospel according to St. Luke
CRINT	Compendia rerum iudaicarum ad novum testamentum
CSEL	Corpus scriptorum ecclesiasticorum latinorum
CW	Classical World
DIBELIUS	Dibelius, Studies in the Acts of the Apostles
EA	Erotica Antiqua, ed. Reardon
EncJud	Encyclopaedia Judaica
ExpTim	Expository Times
FITZMYER	Fitzmyer, The Gospel according to Luke
FRLANT	Forschungen zur Religion und Literatur des Alten und Neuen Testaments
FRSKA	Frankfurter Studien zur Religion und Kultur der Antike
GASQUE	Gasque, A History of the Criticism of the Acts of the Apostles
GGM	C. Mueller, Geographici Graeci Minores
HAENCHEN	Haenchen, The Acts of the Apostles
HDR	Harvard Dissertations in Religion
HJP	Schürer, History of the Jewish People
HNT	Handbuch zum Neuen Testament
HOMEYER	Lucian, Wie man Geschichte schreiben soll, trans. and ed. Homeyer
HTR	Harvard Theological Review
HTS	Harvard Theological Studies
IDB	Interpreter's Dictionary of the Bible, ed. G. A. Buttrick

IDBSup	Supplementary volume to *IDB*
JAAR	*Journal of the American Academy of Religion*
JAC	Jahrbuch für Antike und Christentum
JBL	*Journal of Biblical Literature*
JHS	*Journal of Hellenic Studies*
JRelHist	*Journal of Religious History*
JRS	*Journal of Roman Studies*
JTS	*Journal of Theological Studies*
KzAT	Kommentar zum Alten Testament
LAaa	Bovon et al., *Les Actes apocryphes des apôtres*
LCL	Loeb Classical Library
MARSHALL	Marshall, *The Acts of the Apostles*
MPER	*Mitteilungen aus der Papyrussammlung der oesterreich. Nationalbibliothek*
MusHelv	*Museum Helveticum*
NewDoc	*New Documents Illustrating Early Christianity*
NovT	*Novum Testamentum*
NTA	*New Testament Apocrypha*, ed. Hennecke and Schneemelcher
NTAbh	Neutestamentliche Abhandlungen
NTD	Das Neues Testament deutsch
NTM	New Testament Message
NTS	New Testament Studies (London)
PERVO	Pervo, "The Literary Genre of the Acts of the Apostles"
PhilWoch	*Philologische Wochenschrift*
RAC	*Reallexicon für Antike und Christentum*
RE	*Realencyklopädie der classischen Altertumswissenschaft*
REL	*Revue des études latines*
RESup	Supplement to *RE*
Rev. and Exp.	*Review and Expositor*
RevBib	*Revue biblique*
RevTheolPhil	*Revue de théologie et philosophie*
RHPR	*Revue d'histoire et de philosophie religieuses*
RHR	*Revue de l'histoire des religions*
RivStudClass	*Rivista studios classicos*
RSR	*Recherches de science religieuse*
SBLDS	SBL Dissertation Series
SBLMS	SBL Monograph Series
SBLSBS	SBL Sources for Biblical Study
SBLSP	SBL Seminar Papers

SBT	Studies in Biblical Theology
SC	Sources chrétiennes
SCHNEIDER	Schneider, *Die Apostelgeschichte*
SecCent	*Second Century*
SJLA	Studies in Judaism in Late Antiquity
SLA	*Studies in Luke-Acts*, ed. Keck and Martyn
SOEDER	Soeder, *Die apokryphen Apostelgeschichten und die romanhafte Literatur der Antike*
StANT	Studien zum Alten und Neuen Testament
StudTheol	*Studia Theologica*
SUNT	Studien zur Umwelt des Neuen Testaments
TAPA	*Transactions of the American Philological Association*
TDNT	*Theological Dictionary of the New Testament*, ed. G. Kittel and G. Friedrich
TheolLit	*Theologische Literaturzeitung*
TRu	*Theologische Rundschau*
TU	Texte und Untersuchungen
Wiss. Zeit. U. Rostock	*Wissenschaftliche Zeitschrift der Universtaat Rostock*
WMANT	Wissenschaftliche Monographien zum Alten und Neuen Testament
YCS	*Yale Classical Studies*
ZNW	*Zeitschrift für die neutestamentliche Wissenschaft*
ZPE	*Zeitschrift für Papyrologie und Epigraphik*
ZWT	*Zeitschrift für wissenschaftliche Theologie*

NOTES

1. LUKE-ACTS:
THE EYE OF THE STORM

1. Surveys of research: GASQUE; Mattill, "Luke as Historian"; HAENCHEN, 14–50, 106–32; McGiffert and Hunkin (*BEG CHR* 2:363–433); and more recently, Grässer, "Acta-Forschung"; Plümacher, "Acta Forschung"; idem, "Lukas als griechischer Historiker."

2. The Paul of Acts as the "real Paul": Bruce, "Is the Paul of Acts the Real Paul?" As not the "real Paul": Vielhauer, "On the 'Paulinism' of Acts," *SLA* 33–50.

3. The traditional name Luke is used as a convenience. The Book of Acts seems to claim some eyewitness participation, one of its historical problems. As Cadbury (*BEG CHR* 2:209–64) demonstrated, this conclusion would naturally lead to Luke. This attribution is all but untenable.

4. Among some of Ramsay's able modern exponents are Bruce, Gasque, and Marshall, the last with more reservations.

5. Dibelius's studies, originally written between 1923 and 1947, have been of great importance for subsequent research. The bulk of Cadbury's scholarly output, beginning with his 1919 dissertation, was devoted to Luke and Acts.

6. So, e.g., Cadbury's 1957 review of HAENCHEN; GASQUE, 244–47.

7. As in the commentaries of MARSHALL and SCHNEIDER. No discussion of Acts dare overlook HAENCHEN.

8. This is the implication of Haenchen's review of research: HAENCHEN, 14–50, 106–32.

9. This is the problem of the "western text."

10. HAENCHEN (81–90, 550–53) is probably too skeptical but presents the issues.

11. DIBELIUS, 1–25. See also S. Johnson, "A Proposed Form-Critical Treatment of Acts."

12. The Fourth Gospel presents similar problems and raises similar accusations, but there, at least, comparison with the Synoptic Gospels is fruitful.

13. See nn. 6, 7 above.

14. E.g., see HAENCHEN, 224, 640, 709–10, 740. Other examples will appear in the course of subsequent discussion.

15. Luke 4:16–30 is mostly a Lukan composition; 23:6–12 may be a similar case. Revision: Luke 7:36–50; 21:5–37. Rearrangement: Luke 9:51—19:27. Instances could be multiplied.

16. Hedging: DIBELIUS, 123–37; CADBURY, 133; CONZELMANN, 6. See also n. 35 below.

17. HAENCHEN, 120.

18. Synchronism: CREED, 48–50, 307–9; FITZMYER 1:453–58. See also Schürer, *HJP* 1:561–73; Bultmann, *John*, 643 n. 3.

19. In particular, note the notorious problems raised by the "universal census" under Quirinius. See the recent discussion by Schürer, *HJP* 1:399–427. One crux in Acts is the reference to historical figures in Gamaliel's speech (5:34–39), mentioning, out of order, one leader of the rebellion at the census and another who had not yet appeared. For a survey, see Krodel, *Acts*, 90–113.

20. Cadbury (*BEG CHR* 2:489–510) has not been superseded. See also FITZMYER and SCHNEIDER.

21. Parody: Lucian *A True Story* 2.32. See also Iambulus in Diodorus Siculus 2.55.1. Cadbury has good examples (*BEG CHR* 2:489–510).

22. Artemidorus's preface to *Oneirocriticon*, bk. 2, is verbally quite similar to Acts 1:1–14. The subject is dream interpretation. Novels: Note Chariton 5, 8; preface of Longus; preface of Antonius Diogenes; the beginning of the *Cyropaideia*. Lucian's *A True Story* demonstrates the use of the preface in utopian novels. In the biblical milieu the preface to the Greek translation of Sirach (not history) is interesting for comparison.

23. On verisimilitude, see p. 38 below.

24. Poor sources: BRUCE, 15. (What of Luke 3:1–2, where the source is known?) Most of the chronology of Acts derives from the mention of known persons (e.g., Gallio, Claudius) whose dates are elsewhere available.

25. Thus Acts 12:1–23, if it refers to Agrippa, implies that more than a decade has elapsed since the ascension. No one would guess this, nor imagine that chaps. 13—18 covered eight years.

26. "We cannot name any historian whom . . . Luke has taken as a model" (DIBELIUS, 183–85).

27. The literature is immense. In addition to the fine essay by Cadbury (*BEG CHR* 2:7–29), what I have made use of includes the writings of Attridge, Barwick, Bury, Dentan, M. Grant, Laistner, Lesky, North, Peter, Reitzenstein, Scheller, Shotwell, Syme, Ullman, and Walbank, as well as the commentaries of Homeyer and Avenarius on Lucian's *How to Write History*.

28. FITZMYER (1:114–25) concludes that Luke imitates the LXX. For use of biblical models, see Cadbury, *The Style*; Torrey, *The Composition and Date of Acts*; Tiede, *Prophecy and History*.

29. Thucydides was the model for the *Jewish War*, and Dionysius of Halicarnassus for the *Antiquities*.

30. For classics in education, see Marrou, *A History of Education in Antiquity*, 266–308. On mimesis, see Reardon, *Courants littéraires*, 3–12 and throughout.

31. Julian *Letter* 36.423d (LCL 3:120).

32. Lucian knew of such writings (*How to Write History* 16). He did not approve.

33. Ramsay thought of Tacitus's *Agricola* (*St. Paul*, 1, 23). CONZELMANN (p. 6) has been followed in detail by Steichele ("Vergleich") and Plümacher (*Lukas*). On the topic, see Reitzenstein, *Hellenistische Wunderzählungen*, 4–90; Ullman, "History and Tragedy." On the individual works, see Syme, *Roman Revolution*, 42–45, 67–81, 138–56; Ogilvie and Richmond's edition of the *Agricola*, 11–21.

34. *Letters to His Friends*, trans. Williams (LCL 371).

35. Reitzenstein (*Hellenistische Wunderzählungen*, 94–99) proposed this for Chariton. Perry extended the application to other novels (*Ancient Romances*, 146–47). By

including *3 Maccabees* in the list of Monographs, CONZELMANN (p. 6) opens the category to fiction.

36. Lucian *How to Write History* 15–16, 23–24; with the commentaries of Homeyer and Avenarius.

37. Lucian's view of such comparisons (Acts 4:19, 5:29) appears in *Peregrinus* 12. A hilarious example is found in *How to Write History* 25–26.

38. Josephus is a useful contrast. See Delling, "Josephus und das Wunderbare"; MacRae, "Miracle in the *Antiquities*"; as well as Kee, *Miracle*, 174–83.

39. HOMEYER, 218–19.

40. Observe the complaints registered in Lucian *How to Write History* 20.

41. Livy 39.8–18 (note the scope, a small portion of a single book).

42. See also Tacitus on Jews and Christians: *Histories* 5.1–13; *Annals* 15.44.

43. 2 Maccabees: See the works of Niese, Doran, and the references in Goldstein (*I Maccabees*, 108–46). Lucian presents a clear conventional picture of what conservative intellectuals regarded as bad history.

44. The structural outline of *Alexander* closely resembles that of Luke-Acts.

45. As SCHNEIDER (1:75) observes.

46. On *praxeis*, see p. 179 n. 40 below.

47. See Momigliano, "Pagan and Christian Historiography." On the relation of Luke to Eusebius, see Overbeck, *Über die Anfänge der patristischen Literatur*, 25; Nigg, *Die Kirchengeschicht-schreibung*, 1–3.

48. Esp. the letters. Presuming that Luke wrote some time after 90 C.E. (Conzelmann, "Luke's Place," *SLA* 298–316), it is not credible that he had not learned of Paul's letters and made use of those available. Acts knows about the use of letters to communicate policy. As Knox ("Acts and the Pauline Letter Corpus," *SLA* 279–87), following Goodspeed, maintained, Paul was the originator of the practice depicted in Acts 15.

49. For defenders, see n. 4 above.

50. See Koester, *Introduction to NT* 2:114–37; Ramsay, *St. Paul*, 273.

51. Thus, e.g., Goodspeed, *Introduction*, 208.

52. Issues include the meaning of baptism, the role of baptizer, and ecstasy. These disciples' views resemble those of Apollos, upon his first arrival, according to Acts.

53. Acts 18:19—19:1, probably a Lukan construction.

54. On the hypothetical Ephesian imprisonment of Paul, see Lohse, *Colossians*, 166, 188; Koester, *Introduction to NT* 2:130–31.

55. For this talent, see p. 35 below.

56. Paul was there accused of insufficient miracles, lack of power and prestige, poor speaking ability, and failure to have adequate credentials, including letters of recommendation. Acts attributes just these qualities to Paul and provides Apollos with a letter of recommendation (18:27).

57. HAENCHEN, 577.

58. Codex Bezae on Acts 2:45; 3:11; 4:18; 5:18–21; 8:37; etc. See also DIBELIUS (index, 288, s.v. "western text") and the commentaries.

59. CONZELMANN, 6 (a view already worked out in *The Theology of St. Luke* [German: 1953, 1957]).

60. Difficulties: See, in addition to n. 16 above, the comments of Steichele ("Vergleich," 104) and the nuanced judgment of Plümacher ("Lukas"). The parallels they point to are structural and stylistic. Each shies away from direct identification.

61. So one might conclude from the frequency of scholarly references to Schmidt, "Die Stellung der Evangelien."

62. Despite the conclusions of an earlier generation of philological giants—e.g., Norden, Reitzenstein, Weinreich, Wendland, and Wilamowitz.

63. See Lucian *How to Write History* 10.

64. See pp. 66, 103, 169 n. 1 below.

2. WHEN ALL SEEMS LOST:
ADVENTURE IN THE ACTS OF THE APOSTLES

1. See pp. 3–8 above.

2. See my dissertation "The Literary Genre of the Acts of the Apostles" (Harvard Univ., 1979); hereafter cited as PERVO.

3. See pp. 122–31 below.

4. Thucydides 1.22.4 is a classic. The so-called rhetorical (or tragic) historians of the Hellenistic age were inclined to promote history as light reading. Polybius (2.56ff.) criticizes this posture, followed by Lucian (*How to Write History* 9–10). See HOMEYER, 189; on history and tragedy, see Walbank and Ullmann, "History and Tragedy"; Scheller, "Hellenistica Historiae," 72–79. For the opposing position, see Dionysius of Halicarnassus *Roman Antiquities* 5.56.1; idem *To Pompeius* 3.11; Diodorus Siculus 1.3.5., 20.2.1. See also Cicero *De finibus* 5.19.51; idem *Letters to His Friends* 5.12; 2 Macc. 2:25; 15:39.

5. Lucian *How to Write History* 9 (LCL 6:15); idem *The Dance* 6 (LCL 5:219); Plutarch *Bravery of Women* 1.1.

6. Providence: See p. 74 below.

7. *Acts of Paul and Thecla* 20–27; *Acts of Thomas* 1–2, 21, 106, 141. See also *Acts of Andrew and Matthew* 2.14, 18.25; *Acts of Andrew* 2, 11. See *NTA* 2:403. Examples could be multiplied.

8. Apuleius, trans. Lindsay (*The Golden Ass*, 71–72).

9. Apuleius 9.9–10, 3.25, 4.23, 6.29–30, 10.6. Apuleius 9.9–10 and the parallel in Lucian (*The Ass* 41) are religious polemic. See Moehring, "The Persecution."

10. Chariton 1.5.10, 4.2. See also Xenophon of Ephesus (X. E. hereafter) 1.14, 2.6–7, 2.11.13, 8.3.12, 4.3, 4.6, 5.5; Longus 2.14.20. This list is far from complete.

11. Examples of the pattern, Dionysiac materials: Euripides *Bacchae*; *Homeric Hymn* 7. See also the Serapis inscription from Delos (ed. Engelmann) and Jonah. Ovid's sources for the *Metamorphoses* contained a number of parallel myths. Daniel 1—6 could represent a suitable immediate prototype for Acts. For Acts, note 3:1—4:31; 5:17–42; 12; 13:14–52; 14:1–5, 8–20; 17:1–10a, 10b–15; 18:1–8; 19:1–40. "Aretalogy" does not refer to a particular form or collection, such as the hypothetical Johannine "signs source," but to the various literary media and structures employed for proclaiming the virtues of a god or divine figure. The setting of aretalogy was in evangelism. Forms could include hymns, votive inscriptions, legends, even entire books. The plural "aretalogies" often designates spiritual biographies (as in Smith and Hadas, *Gods and Heroes*) but has long been employed for the hymns in which Isis publishes her accomplishments. By extension the term may apply to prose celebrations of the highest virtue. First Corinthians 13 is an "aretalogy" to love. Aretalogy is not a genre so much as a function.

12. The use of *dieprionto* in Acts 5:33 and 7:54 establishes the parallelism.

13. See also Cadbury, "Four Features of Lucan Style," *SLA* 87–102.

14. Like philosophers: Acts 3:11; 5:12, 42; 4:13–19; 5:29. The students of Jesus teach in a stoa, all but quote Plato, and stand up to tyrants with requisite courage.

15. Prison escapes: Most comprehensive is Weinreich, *Gebet und Wunder*, of which J. Jeremias gives a good summary in the article on *thyra* (esp. "Door Miracles in NT"), *TDNT* 3:175–76. See also SOEDER, 66–67, 151; Reitzenstein, *Hellenistische Wundererzählungen*, 121ff.; Kerenyi, *Griech.-orient. Romanliteratur*, 95–150. For a detailed discussion, see PERVO, 54–90. In addition to chaps. 4, 5, 12, and 16 of Acts, the following are important: Euripides *Bacchae;* Ovid *Metamorphoses* 3.511ff.; Nonnos 44–46; Longus 2.20–29; Pacuvius (LCL: *Remains of Old Latin* 2:272–74); Apollodorus *Bibliotheca* 3.5.1; *Ap. Ty.* 7–8, 4.44, 8.30; *T. Joseph* 8; *Acts of Thomas* 106–29, 142–63; *Acts of Andrew and Matthew* 2–3, 19–21; *Acts of Paul* (*P. Heid* 35–39, trans. in *NTA* 2:37–38); *Acts of Paul and Thecla* 17–24; *Acts of Philip* 120ff.; *Acts of Pilate* 12–16; *Recognitions* 2.9, 9.38; Lucian *Toxaris* 28ff.; Chariton 3.7, 4.2–3; X. E. 3.12, 4.4; Iamblichus (Photius *Bibliotheca* 74a–78a); Heliodorus 8.6ff., 9.2, 10.7ff.; Apuleius 6.9–24; Achilles Tatius 2.14–15, 3.9ff., 5.23ff., 6.2ff., 7.7ff., 8.14–15.

16. The Dionysiac material, as in Euripides, Pacuvius, Ovid, and Nonnos is "primitive" aretalogy.

17. Peter is thereafter "whisked offstage" to reappear only once in Acts 15, and then briefly.

18. Acts 12 is presumably from a source, one that had already introduced the Jewish or Christian agency of an angel.

19. Cf. *Ap. Ty.* 8.38; X. E. 4.4.1; *Acts of Thomas* 127.

20. On "secularized aretalogy," see pp. 93–95 below. Note, however, the strictures below on distinguishing historicity by reference to "supernatural" criteria (pp. 22, 53). The Delian worshipers of Serapis no doubt saw their legal victory as a miracle, secondarily elaborated with mythical features. Pausanias 9.16.6 is revelatory.

21. Xenophon clearly introduced the element of miracle into a crucifixion story borrowed from Chariton (X. E. 4, 2).

22. In Lucian's *Toxaris* 33, *ti prospeson* leads to the escape. See also the fortuitous events in X. E. and Achilles Tatius. Chaireas's rescue in Chariton was also due to chance events. *Toxaris* 33 may be a "rationalized" account of the usual miracle.

23. In Achilles Tatius 5.3ff. the hero slips off his chains to have sex with one other than his true love, then boldly escapes by donning female dress.

24. Again, *Toxaris* 33 is anything but "natural."

25. See p. 74 below.

26. HAENCHEN, 257, 502–3. Ramsay rationalizes the event in a brief meditation on the (presumably eternal) frailty of Turkish prisons (*St. Paul*, 220–21).

27. Zeller ("Griechische Parallele") already noted the similarity of the friendship novella in Lucian *Toxaris* 28–33 to Acts 16. A formal parallel to the jailer in Acts is the helmsman of *Homeric Hymn* 7. Later writers introduced him into the Pentheus legend, rather sentimentally. Ovid makes the helmsman a priest (*Metamorphoses* 3.581–691), as does Pacuvius, and Nonnos also integrates this figure into his Pentheus episode.

28. Codex Bezae already attempted to set Acts right by having the officials respond to the numinous. X. E. 4.2–4 is similar.

29. Cf. Schmeling, *Xenophon of Ephesus*, 50, 90.

30. On the jailer's status, see Vielhauer, *Geschichte*, 158 n. 3.

31. Roman citizens were not subject to arbitrary punishments. That Silas too held the franchise comes as a bit of a surprise. Luke probably assimilated his situation to that of Paul, whose Roman citizenship looms large in Acts.

32. Peter, in Acts 12:3, where his imprisonment creates suspense.

33. SOEDER, 151. See also Morard, "Souffrance et martyre dans les Actes apocryphes," *LAaa* 95–108.

34. On this scheme, see p. 19 above.

35. *Satire 6*, trans. Humphries (*The Satires of Juvenal*, 86).

36. Note SOEDER's summary, 151–52. On Luke's view of sex, see p. 181 n.79 below. On Encratism, see Tissot, "Encratisme et Actes apocryphes," *LAaa* 109–19.

37. On this persecution, see Acts 8:1b–3; 9:1–2; cf. 22:4.

38. Underlying the account is a split between two factions. HAENCHEN 297–98 says that the existence of two groups was inconceivable for Luke. In fact, Luke lived in an age when the existence of multiple and competing Christian factions could not be overlooked. See also M. Smith, "The Reason," 263. The flight of disciples is a *topos*, as in *Ap. Ty.* 3.37–38. The contrast between Luke and Acts visibly demonstrates the transforming power of the Spirit at Pentecost.

39. On this, see p. 72 below.

40. Only cynics will wonder why Barnabas was spared.

41. Dorothy Sayers's parody is illustrative. Lord Peter Wimsey confronts his brother-in-law, a policeman recently mugged by a criminal:

> It beats me, . . . the way these policemen give way over a trifling accident. In the Sexton Blake book . . . the great detective, after being stunned with a piece of lead-piping and trussed up for six hours in ropes which cut his flesh nearly to the bone, is taken by boat on a stormy night to a remote house on the coast and flung down a flight of stone steps into a stone cellar. Here he contrives to release himself from his bonds after three hours' work on the edge of a broken winebottle, when the villain gets wise to his activities and floods the cellar with gas. He is most fortunately rescued at the fifty-ninth minute of the eleventh hour and, pausing only to swallow a few ham sandwiches and a cup of strong coffee, instantly joins in a prolonged pursuit of the murderers by aeroplane, during which he has to walk out along the wing and grapple with a fellow who has just landed on it from a rope and is proposing to chuck a hand grenade into the cockpit. And here is my own brother in law . . . giving way to bad temper and bandages because some three by four crook has slugged him on his own comfortable staircase. (*Murder Must Advertise* [New York: Avon Books, 1967], 95)

Similarly the beaten apostles return to their task of proclamation (Acts 5:42). Paul, beaten so badly that he must be carried, rouses himself in Acts 21:38 to deliver a public oration.

42. Apparent death (*Scheintod*): See entries in indexes of both Kerenyi (*Griech.-orient. Romanliteratur;* also pp. 124–43) and Merkelbach (*Roman und Mysterium;* also p. 83). See also SOEDER, 87; Wehrli, "Einheit," 142–44; Perry, *Ancient Romances*, 320; Schmeling, *Chariton*, 100.

43. Achilles Tatius, trans. Gaselee (LCL 379).

44. Chariton 4.3; X. E. 2, 1, 13. Other examples include Heliodorus 7.6, 10.34. Ovid (*Metamorphoses* 3.697–700) reveals the adaptation of the aretalogical tradition to Greco-Roman concepts of adventure writing.

45. Luke 12:11–12 and 21:12–15 show that Luke knew of oppressive measures

taken against believers in his own day. Comparison with Mark and Q suggests that Luke omitted the eschatological element—indicating that such circumstances characterized the church of his own time.

46. See also pp. 72, 83 below.

47. Examples: Sinonis and Rhodanes (Iamblichus) fled the city because of a jealous king. Persecution is also a major element in Antonius Diogenes, as Bürger noted (*Studien*, 10–11).

48. In epic the wrath of a god often motivates wanderings. Novels tend to contrast blind fate (*tychē;* cf. Apuleius 11.5) to the providence of a particular god—Aphrodite in Chariton ("of Aprodisias"), Isis in Apuleius.

49. Jewish novels: Religion in Esther and *3 Maccabees*, jealousy in *Joseph and Asenath*. Apollonius experienced both political and religious persecution, like the apostles. Politics is also the theme in Chion of Heraclea's brief epistolary novel. Political and religious factors are often difficult to distinguish in works of a national character, including the Egyptian pieces linked to Nectabeno, Sesonchosis, and Alexander, no less than Jewish novels like Judith and Esther.

50. Persecution in Apoc. Acts: See the survey in SOEDER, 150–59.

51. See HAENCHEN, 389.

52. See pp. 19–21 above.

53. On the vision before death: Eusebius *H. E.* 2.23.1–2, 9.23.6–7; *4 Macc.* 6.5–6; *Ascension of Isaiah* 5.7; *Acta Carpi* et al. 39, 42; *S. Cononis* 5; *Ap. Ty.* 8.4. See also Betz, *Lukian*, 132 n.6; Cadbury and Lake (*BEG CHR* 4:84); CONZELMANN, 51.

54. SCHNEIDER 1:43.

55. On the editing of the Stephen narrative, see p. 66 below. Martyrological terms include *synarpazo, hypoballo, epithenai cheiras ep',* and *syrein.* The standard lexicons and the indexes of Lipsius-Bonnet (*AAA*) establish their technical quality.

56. Doubtless derived from Jewish hagiography, which had already begun to use the pagan tradition, as Hadas shows in *The Third and Fourth Books of Maccabees;* so too with M. Smith, *Gods and Heroes*, 87–97. See also Bieler, *Theios Aner* 1:44ff.; Musurillo, *Acts of the Pagan Martyrs*, 236–46.

57. E.g., van der Meer, *Augustine*, 513–27.

58. See Delehaye's discussion: *Les passions*, 171–230.

59. Thus von Dobschütz, "Der Roman," 102. Zimmerman (review of Soeder and Blumenthal, 1407) rejects this, wrongly in my estimate.

60. See the list in CADBURY, 312–13. It scarcely needs to be stated that Luke's treatment of the Jewish people is reprehensible to present-day Jews and Christians. He presumably exploited ancient anti-Semitism and has contributed to its modern descendants. Affirmation of the nonhistorical character of these accusations will, I hope, help diminish their repetition.

61. Political issues: Who controlled Damascus at that time (whenever it was)? See Lake (*BEG CHR* 5:193); HAENCHEN, 334–45; *HJP* 1:579–82.

62. Cf. Lake (*BEG CHR* 5:194).

63. The verbal resemblance to 2 Cor. 11:32–33 is fascinating. Perhaps the source was a rumor circulated to discredit Paul by describing his cowardice. For the stereotyped handling of the incident here, see Marxsen, *Introduction*, 18.

64. In favor of this are the frequentative imperfect-tense verbs in Acts 9:19b, and the repeated words in 9:24, 29–30. Nothing here is foreign to the style, method, or viewpoint of Luke.

65. On Acts 14:19, see p. 26.

66. See pp. 21, 23–24, 63.

67. Corinth: Acts 18:12–17. See pp. 45, 60 below.

68. See pp. 9–10 above, and further, pp. 37–63 below.

69. Lucian (*Alexander* 56) indicates how the readers might have construed the plot: Alexander allegedly bribed the captain to heave Lucian and friends overboard.

70. The actual reason for moving overland was to gather up the Collection, on which see p. 41 below.

71. On their oath, see pp. 32–33 below.

72. Luke 1:3 and Acts 18:25–26 and 24:22 suggest that *akribesteron ta peri* refers to questions of belief.

73. Cf. Livy 39.11.3.

74. HAENCHEN, 645–50 (quote, p. 650). Problems: Pharisees defend Paul with violence one day but keep silent the next when murder is planned. The march to Antipatris would have required more than one night. The force was too large a part of the garrison to risk. Ramsay solved the problem of the youth's discovery: Paul's family was, of course, influential and he overheard talk at home (*St. Paul*, 35).

75. Bribery, mentioned in Acts 24:26–27, is a logical suspicion, but not introduced here. Codex Bezae had it in mind already in 23:24.

76. On such inconsistency, see PERVO, 20–21. Edmund Crispin has one of his characters, a writer of thrillers, observe, "Characterisation seems to me a very overrated element in fiction. I can never see why one should be obliged to have any of it at all, if one doesn't want to. It *limits* the form so" (*Buried for Pleasure* [New York: Harper & Row, 1980], 35).

77. The readers would probably draw appropriate conclusions about Paul's death also: adversaries pursued him there and corrupted justice.

78. See Bickermann, *Four Strange Books of the Bible*, 171–87, on Esther. Note also the court intrigue in Daniel 3 and 6 and the Ahikar novel. The elders who plotted to have Susanna killed would have found kindred souls in the Sanhedrin described by Luke.

79. Artapanus 429c, 432d, 433–34a. See also pp. 118–22 below.

80. Intrigue in Chariton: See Heiserman, *The Novel*, 77–87.

81. Achilles Tatius 7. Diogenes and Iamblichus used plots in their mechanism. See also Longus 1.19–22, 4.11–31; Heliodorus 5.20; Apuleius 2.31–3.11. Numerous examples could be added.

82. Crowds drawn by miracles: Acts 2:1–6; 2:41; 3:1–11; 4:4; 14:8–11. Preaching: 13:44; Apoc. Acts (*Acts of Thomas* 37, 71; *Acts of John* 26, 31); see SOEDER, 158–62; E. Peterson, "Heis Theos." Critique in *The Ass* 37–41//Apuleius 8.25–31; Juvenal *Satire* 6.511–91; Josephus *Antiquities* 18.65–80; Lucian *Alexander;* idem *Peregrinus.* Missionary methods: Nock, *Conversion;* Georgi, *Die Gegner;* and the dissertations of J. Peterson ("Missionary Methods") and Liefeld ("Wandering Preacher"), as well as the works of Gerd Theissen.

83. Crowd reactions give the speeches an aretalogical tone. See Acts 2:41; 4:4; 5:14, 16; 13:48; 14:1; 17:4. For inspired speaking, note esp. Stephen (6:8, 10).

84. "Rending garments" is oratorical: Cadbury (*BEG CHR* 5:269–77); B. Gaertner, "Paulus." Texts: Appian *Civil War* 1.66; Dio Chrysostom 35.9; Chariton 1.3.4, 5.2.4; *Acts of Thomas* 16.

85. *Aeneid*, trans. Fitzgerald (*The Aeneid*, 8).

86. *Ap. Ty.* 1.15. See also 4.1.8; Apollonius *Letters* 75–76. On the practice: Lucian

Demonax 9; Philostratus *Lives of the Sophists* 531 (Polemon). Discussion: Bowersock, *Greek Sophists*, 26.

87. Chariton, trans. Blake (*Chariton's Chaereas and Callirhoe*, 40, 65). See the excursus, pp. 81–85 of this chapter.

88. Examples: Apuleius 4.28–29; X. E. 5.13–15; Chariton 1.1, 1.11–12, 3.3, 4.1, 5.3–6, 8.1, 8.6; Longus 4.33; *3 Macc.* 1.17, 5.24–46; Apuleius 2.12, 2.27, 3.2, 4.16, 7.13, 8.6; Achilles Tatius 6.3, 7.9; Herpyllis; *Ap. Ty.* 46, 50, 6.38, 8.15; *Alexander Romance* 2.2; Heliodorus 1.19, 2.27, 4.19, 7.5, 7.8–9, 10.17. Literature: SOEDER, 158–62; Musurillo, *Acts of the Pagan Martyrs*, 252–54.

89. Texts: Acts 2:12; 14:4; 17:32; 23:7; 28:24. On civic factions, see MacMullen, *Enemies*, 170–71; Baldson, *Romans and Aliens*, 39.

90. Achilles Tatius, trans. Gaselee (LCL 371).

91. Other examples: Heliodorus 1.14, 8.9; Achilles Tatius 7.10, 7.14; Apuleius 2.29; Chariton 5.8; *Pseudo-Clementine Recognitions* 1.8.10; *Acts of Philip* 4.37; *Acts of Paul* 3.32.

92. So Millar, *The Roman Empire*, 199. Seltman likens it to a "newspaper account" (*Riot in Ephesus*, 58–76).

93. E. Peterson ("Heis Theos," 199) speculates that the source of Acts 19 was a novel. For a disturbance in Ephesus, see Achilles Tatius 7.9. Note also the reference in nn. 88, 91 of the present chap. Martyr texts: Polycarp 8.3ff.; Pionius 7.1. Literature: MacMullen, *Enemies*, 169–79, 339–46; Browning, "The Riot"; Colin, *Les villes*, esp. 105 nn. 3, 4; C. P. Jones, *Roman World*, 19–25. *Acts of John* 31 brings to a close what Paul began.

94. See pp. 9–10 above.

95. Religious disputes: MacMullen (*Enemies*) knew of such only regarding Judaism and Christianity, and in Egypt. This is generally correct, especially if disputes over religious privileges, such as the title *Neokoros*, are not at heart religious.

96. Mobs are a literary motif in Martyr Acts also, but fear of the mob was genuine. See Musurillo, *Acts of the Christian Martyrs*, liii.

97. See Acts 17:6–7; 24:25; as well as the famous passage in Suetonius *Claudius* 25 referring to a riot instigated by a certain "Chrestus," probably involving Christians; and Tacitus *Annals* 15.44. Some would have accepted Nero's blame of the Christians. Revelation 18—19 does nothing to allay such suspicions.

98. Galba was steadfast, but not Commodus. Justinian wavered, not Theodora: Herodian 1.12–13; Cassius Dio 72.13; Plutarch *Galba* 17.

99. "Barbarous superstition" was a more or less technical Roman term for an unacceptable cult. Pliny *Letters* 10.96.8 applied this phrase to Christians. See Wilcken, *The Christians*, 48–50, 66–67.

100. For instance, *Ap. Ty.* 1.15, 4.8, 6.38.

101. Auerbach: Tacitus *Annals* 1.16–17 (*Mimesis*, 29–35); Ammianus Marcellinus 7.15 (*Mimesis*, 43–53). Auerbach does not give sufficient attention to ancient novels. In general he observes that novelists tend to stress the extraordinary rather than the everyday. One may say much the same of Acts.

102. MacMullen, *Enemies*, 168–171. Some texts with close resemblances to Acts 19: Chariton 1.5, 3.2; Heliodorus 7.8–9, 8.9, 10.8, 10.18.

103. Apuleius, trans. Lindsay (*The Golden Ass*, 66–67). See also Apuleius 10.6; Heliodorus 1.13–14, 4.19; Achilles Tatius 7.9, 10.1; *The Ass* 53; *Ap. Ty.* 45–46, 4.10; *Acts of John* 31; *Acts of Paul* (cf. *NTA* 2:370).

104. Stoning: Heliodorus 1.13–14; *Ap. Ty.* 50, 4.10; Apuleius 2.28, 4.6; *Acts of Paul* (cf. *NTA* 2:353); *Acts of John* 1; *Acts of Philip* 73 (10). There are many references in various texts to this form of popular justice. See Blinzer, "The Jewish Punishment"; W. Michaelis, "Lithazō, ktl.," *TDNT* 4 (1967): 267–68. See also MacMullen, *Roman Social Relations*, 66: "Stoning . . . was a common form of group vengeance."

105. For views on the date and provenience of Susanna, see Moore, *Daniel, Esther*, 77–92. (The Theodotionic text of Sus. 60 conforms more closely to the conventions of Greek popular literature than does the LXX.)

106. *3 Macc.* 1.17–23 (LXX describes punishment and adds a miracle); 5.24, 26 (cf. Acts 14:18).

107. So Judge, *The Social Pattern*, 47. For a similar view, see Ehrhardt, "Construction and Purpose of Acts," 20.

108. For further remarks on this passage, see pp. 39–40 below.

109. One hundred twenty was the requisite number for a small Sanhedrin, "scarcely an accident," as Cadbury and Lake shrewdly remark (*BEG CHR* 4:12). G. Bornkamm notes that the Christian assemblies resemble the Sanhedrin rather than the synagogue ("Presbys, ktl.," *TDNT* 6 [1968]: 651–83, esp. 663).

110. *Episkopē* is technical here: s.v. *BAGD*.

111. Lots: Lake (*BEG CHR* 5:15); Conzelmann, 25; Nock, *Essays* 1:255; and the practice of both political (Roman senate: Livy 23.2) and religious (Jerusalem temple) bodies. Reference to Qumran texts may illuminate Luke's ultimate source but not his intent.

112. See Haenchen, 159–62; Conzelmann, 24–25; Zehnle, *Peter's Pentecost Discourse*, 93; Renie, "L'election de Mathias"; Schneider 1:214.

113. Both diction and viewpoint are "early Catholic," as implied by Cadbury and Lake (*BEG CHR* 4:15).

114. *Plēthos* is technical for both religious and political groups: s.v. *BAGD;* Deissmann, *Bible Studies*, 323–24; Poland, *Griech. Vereinswesens*, 168, 333; Cadbury and Lake (*BEG CHR* 4:47–48); Haenchen, 230 n. 1. On the parallel usage of Qumran, see Fitzmyer, "Jewish Christianity in Acts in Light of the Qumran Scrolls," *SLA* 245–46.

115. On the historical situation, see Conzelmann, 43–44; Haenchen, 266–69.

116. "Those of circumcision" must include every Christian in Jerusalem to that point and not the party Luke proposes.

117. Haenchen, 174. On the parallel structure of Acts 11 and 15, see Hurd, *Origin*, 35–41.

118. Dibelius concludes "The Apostolic Council" with the observation that Galatians 2 is the only account of the meeting (Dibelius, 100). Some defenders of Acts harmonize the two accounts. Others, following Ramsay, find two different meetings described. A recent provocative effort to differentiate the two has been made by Achtemeier ("An Elusive Unity").

119. Including Titus, who ended on Luke's cutting-room floor, indirect testimony to the intensity of the dispute.

120. Haenchen, 445.

121. On the practice of collegia and other bodies imitating the solemn prose of municipal structures, see the remarks of MacMullen (*Roman Social Relations*, 76, 82). See also Lewis and Reinhard, *Roman Civilization* 2:276.

122. Cf. the function of decrees in Esther, *3 Maccabees*, and various fictional works.

123. Dibelius awards the name "apostolic council" only to Acts 15 (DIBELIUS, 100). Either Luke or the sources must have been familiar with Galatians 2 and various rumors, as Linton argues ("The Third Aspect"). Decrees and mandates issued under the names of the Twelve were subject to frequent updating, a practice that begins here with the "western text." Cf., e.g., the *Didache, Epistula apostolorum, Apostolic Constitutions*.

124. Problems: What happened to the Collection? Why was Paul arrested? Did he take Gentiles into the temple? What position do James and friends take on all this? See Jervell, *Luke*, 194.

125. This is precisely the thesis of *1 Clement*, which is more or less contemporaneous with Acts. See Jaeger, *Early Christianity*, 12–26, 113–18. Luke was unlikely to have been in the dark about all such unpleasantness of his own day. Like Clement he appeals to an idealized past, but he does this by telling stories.

126. On order alone: The Twelve, then the Seven (who seem to evaporate); Peter is in charge. In Acts 12–15 elders appear with the Twelve; James is prominent. By chap. 21 the Twelve have disappeared and James leads. There are no bishops or deacons. Not one of these transitions is explained. The reader must infer them from the church assemblies. See Klein, *Zwölf Apostel*, 202–16.

127. Already observed by Rohde, *Der greich. Roman*, 527.

128. Chariton, trans. Blake (*Chariton's Chaereas and Callirhoe*, 45).

129. See Chariton 1.11, 5.3, 8.6; Apuleius 3.2; Heliodorus 1.19, 2.27, 4.19, 7.5, 7.8–9, 10.17; *Ap. Ty.* 46, 50, 1.15, 4.8, 6.38; X. E. 5.13–15; Achilles Tatius 7.16; Dio Chrysostom 7.23ff.

130. MacMullen, *Enemies*, 172.

131. Origen makes a favorable comparison of Christian assemblies to pagan meetings (*Contra Celsum* 3.27–29). Philosophers often complained about urban assemblies, as does Musonius Rufus xlix (ed. Lutz, 142.19–28).

132. The locus classicus of all accounts is, of course, the *Apology* of Plato. Literature: Hadas and Smith, *Gods and Heroes*, 49–97; MacMullen, *Enemies*, 46–94.

133. See also p. 43 above.

134. The speech is creedal in form. On *parrēsia* as a quality of philosophers, see H. Schlier, "Parrēsia, parrēsiazdomai," *TDNT* 5 (1967): 871–86. The Socrates reference is *Apology* 29d. See also Sophocles *Antigone* 450–60; 2 Macc. 7:2; *4 Macc.* 5.16–38.

135. Difficulties: Peter and John are arrested for preaching resurrection but attacked for a healing (Acts 4:2–7). Fear of the crowd looms large in 4:29–30 but is not a factor in 4:2–3. And the court releases the two despite evidence that warning would fail. In fact, Luke wished to make a typical rebuff of practicing magic (cf. Acts 3:12–13 with *Pseudo-Clementine Recognitions* 5.70 and Mark 11:27–28). Luke can turn crowds on and off like a faucet (see esp. 14:8–20). Commentaries: CONZELMANN, 35; HAENCHEN, 220–23.

136. HAENCHEN, 224.

137. See also pp. 19–21, 23–24 above, and pp. 62–63 below.

138. HAENCHEN, 252.

139. Flaws: If Gamaliel's advice is accepted, warning and whipping are inappropriate. The Sanhedrin overlooks the mysterious disappearance of the whole group. A solution: Luke has composed the episode. Gamaliel acts like a great orator. His speech is Lukan in content. The incident closely resembles Acts 4. The escape ends with legal vindication, like chap. 16.

140. See also pp. 28–29 above.

141. Acts 6:15 and 7:55 appear to be the editorial seam made by inserting the speech, as noted by DIBELIUS, 158.

142. Detailed discussions: DIBELIUS, 168–69; CONZELMANN, 52–53; Burchard, *Dreizehnte Zeuge*, 23–31. Lynch mob: CONZELMANN, 52; HAENCHEN, 295–96; Burchard, *Dreizehnte Zeuge*, 29.

143. The content of this sermon is more Lukan than some have proposed. It is fundamentally congenial with the view of Luke and need not be derived from a source.

144. For more on this episode, see pp. 61, 65, 71, 72 below.

145. Ramsay, *St. Paul*, 246.

146. So HAENCHEN, 527. On the status of the Areopagus in the first century C.E., see Barnes, "An Apostle on Trial"; Colin, *Les villes*, 84; HAENCHEN, 519 n. 1.

147. Both Acts and ancient novels relate to Greece mainly in archaizing terms. See Conzelmann, "The Address of Paul on the Areopagus," *SLA* 218; Kerenyi, *Griech.-orient. Romanliteratur*, 55–56. See also Chariton 1.11; Apuleius 10.7.

148. *Epilambanō* in Acts refers to arrest. Barnes ("An Apostle") gives arguments for considering this to be a trial. On my position, see Cadbury and Lake (*BEG CHR* 4:213). Conzelmann's statement that Luke is "absolutely unambiguous" in reporting trials ("The Address of Paul," *SLA* 219) is in error.

149. HAENCHEN, 528.

150. Already imitated in the *Acts of Philip* 6 (1)ff.

151. Acts 17:34 appears to be some sort of tradition. 1 Thess. 3:2 implies no real success at Athens. Even Nock sees little tradition here (*Essays* 2:831).

152. Others: Gallio's brother's famous pupil Nero and later governors such as Pliny.

153. See p. 60 below.

154. Lysias did not give up easily, as Acts 21:34 and 22:24 imply. By 23:28 he was able to tell the procurator that Paul was probably innocent, but he never appeared to give testimony.

155. Cf. John 18:22–23. An amusing parallel is Achilles Tatius 8.1.3.

156. Haenchen strains to rationalize this action (HAENCHEN, 637–43). The high priest should have been identifiable.

157. Difficulties: The bizarre slapping incident; the threat of a death sentence, which is not within the Sanhedrin's prerogative, at an examination which is not supposed to be a trial; and the incredible behavior of the tribune who "does not personally interrogate Paul, but trots out the Roman Citizen before a Jewish court" (CONZELMANN, 127).

158. Note that three of this speech's seven verses consist in *captatio benevolentiae* (initial appeal to the hearers; 24:2–5). This is not a formal speech of prosecution but is merely enough to set issues and evoke a juridical atmosphere. See HAENCHEN; Plümacher, *Lukas als hellen. Schrift.*, 25; CONZELMANN, 133.

159. Problems: Festus goes from good to bad and back again. Paul appeals a proposed change of venue, rather than reject the offer. Those who violated the temple law on Gentiles could be killed without trial, as indicated by the extant portions of the warning inscription. Nowhere does Luke introduce these Gentiles allegedly brought into the sacred place.

160. BRUCE, 481.

161. Delehaye, *Les passions*, 171–226; idem, *Legends of the Saints;* Musurillo, *Acts of the Christian Martyrs*, 11. Musurillo notes that accuracy in reporting is a criterion for forged Martyr Acts. This is the problem of verisimilitude.

162. Evidence in the form-critical sense. If accuracy in details of local government and color or other information were the only criterion for establishing facticity, one would have to promote Apuleius's *Metamorphoses* to the rank of history and accept the Apoc. Acts as works of especial historical merit.

163. Some minor parallels: Apollonius enjoys a kind of relaxed custody after initial interrogation (7.40), enjoys conversations with highly placed individuals (7.17–33), and has the good fortune to find a biographer who can make the readers privy to the private words and thoughts of prominent people (7.16).

164. So Perry, *Ancient Romances*, 143.

165. Chariton, trans. Blake (p. 77); Apuleius, trans. Lindsay (p. 21). Achilles Tatius 7.9.1 is another good example.

166. Other examples: Achilles Tatius 7.7–8.14; Heliodorus 8.9ff., 10: 25ff.

167. *Acts of Thomas* 106, 126, 129, 142, 164. See also *Acts of Andrew* 3 (*AAA* 2/1:39); SOEDER, 200.

168. *3 Macc.* 4.14–21 uses registration to introduce a delay and has the king fall asleep in 5:10–21.

169. Nock, *Essays* 1:170–71. See also Delehaye, *Les passions*, 197–207. See further p. 134 below.

170. Thus the stories of Samson and Delilah, David and Bathsheba, and Susanna were easily made into popular films with more sex than Hollywood usually then allowed. Hagiography drips with examples. See also the *nekyia* literature in which the faithful are edified by glimpsing the fate of the damned (e.g., Lucian *Menippus* 14).

171. Whipping: Chariton 4.2; Longus 2.15; X. E. 2.6; *The Ass* 16, 18, 22, 28, 38–39, 42; Apuleius 6.9–10. Literature: Kerenyi, *Griech.-orient. Romanliteratur*, esp. 123–24; Merkelbach, *Roman und Mysterium;* s.v. *Geisselung* in both of their indexes. Legal: Waldstein, "Geisselung"; Schneider, "Mastigoō, ktl.," *TDNT* 4 (1967): 515–19.

172. Apuleius, trans. Lindsay (p.75).

173. Acts 22:24–25 is discussed on pp. 26–27 above. See also Achilles Tatius 7.12.7–8; SOEDER, 164–65. Passages like *4 Macc.* 8.12 and 12.19 offend modern taste, as does much hagiography. For references to the Apoc. Acts, see SOEDER, 150–58.

174. Crucifixion: Kerenyi, *Griech.-orient. Romanliteratur*, 109–50.

175. Hengel, *Crucifixion*, 88; see also 48–49, 81.

176. Luke 9:51—19:44 depicts Jesus' journey to Jerusalem with references to travel (e.g., 9:52; 14:1) but with no itinerary detail; this is unlike Acts, where journeys can be mapped.

177. Travel narrative is defined as two or more consecutive verses describing travel, including references to lodging and notes about hosts. Acts 28:3–6 appears to fit the travel genre; stories of native reaction to shipwrecked travelers are common.

178. By this we mean the period of Paul's work as an independent missionary. Luke agrees on its importance, but for different reasons.

179. Itinerary style: See the literature in n. 182 of the present chap., and the quote from Lucian *A True Story* 1.6, as well as the excursus on p. 57 below.

180. Spirit: Acts 16:6–7; 20:22. Prophecies: Acts 16:9–10; 21:10–12.

181. Acts 20—21 relates incidents involving the previously neglected east coast. Acts 20:7–12 reveals that this is schematic, for it presumes an earlier mission (cf. 2 Corinthians 12—13; Talbert, "An Introduction to Acts," 57).

182. Note BRUCE, 450. Selected examples: EPIC: *Odyssey* 5.291–92; *Aeneid* 1.81ff. DRAMA: Euripides *Helen* 408ff.; Plautus *The Rope*. OTHER: Juvenal *Satire* 12; Horace *Odes* 1.3, 5.13–16; Phaedrus 4.23; Dio Chrysostom 7; Lucian *Philosophies for Sale* 1; *T. Naphtali* 6. NOVELS: Ninus; Metiochus; Herpyllis; Chariton 3.3.5; X. E. 2.12; Heliodorus 1.22ff., 4; Achilles Tatius 3.1–5; Petronius 114; Longus 1.31; Chion of Heraclea 4; Jonah; *Pseudo-Clementine Homilies* 1.12. APOC. ACTS: *Acts of Philip* 3.33; *Acts of John* 8–9 (Prochorus). See other references in PERVO. Literature: SOEDER, 42–44, 48–49; Norden, *Agnostos Theos*, 34ff., 313–14, 323–24; Rohde, *Der griech. Roman*, 183–327; Plümacher, *Lukas als hellen. Schrift.*, also Casson, "The Isis"; Pokorny, "Die Romfahrt"; McCasland, "Ships"; idem, "Travel"; Praeder, "Narrative Voyage"; Robbins, "By Land and by Sea."

183. HAENCHEN's statement on p. 710 is thus otiose.

184. In particular, Lucian *A True Story* 1.6.28–29; Petronius 114; Achilles Tatius 4.14.8.

185. See both HAENCHEN and Haenchen, "Acta 27."

186. Wellhausen, *Kritische Analyse*, 54; DIBELIUS, 205–6.

187. *A True Story*, trans. Harmon (LCL 1:253–55); the original Greek should be consulted.

188. Stengel (*De Luciani Veris Historiis*) finds the specific target here to be Iambulus. See also Rohde, *Der griech. Roman*, 190–93; Betz, *Lukian*, 90 n. 5. From Lucian himself one could list *The Ship* 8–9 and *On Salaried Posts* 19. *Philosophies for Sale* 1–2 reads like a summary of Acts 27:

> I listened to them while they spun yarns about their shipwreck and unlooked-for deliverance, just like the men with shaven heads who gather in crowds at the temples and tell of third waves, tempests, headlands, standings, masts carried away, rudders broken, and to cap it all, how the Twin Brethren appeared (they are peculiar to this sort of rhodomontade), or how some other deus ex machina sat on the masthead or stood at the helm and steered the ship to a soft beach where she might break up gradually and slowly and they themselves get ashore safely by the grace and favour of the god.
>
> Those men, to be sure, invent the greatest part of their tragical histories to meet their temporary need, in order that they may receive alms . . . and how they first sailed in, with the sea apparently calm, and how many troubles they endured through the whole voyage by reason of thirst . . . and finally how they stove their unlucky lugger on a submerged ledge or a sheer pinnacle and swam ashore. (trans. Harmon, LCL 3:413–15)

189. Motifs: LATE DEPARTURE: Chariton 3.5.1; Heliodorus 5.17; and others. Düring calls this a *topos* (*Chion of Heraclea*, 88). PASSENGERS WITH SUPERIOR KNOWLEDGE: Herpyllis; *Ap. Ty.* 5.18; Chion 4; and others. JETTISONING CARGO: Jonah 1:5; ridiculed by Juvenal *Satire* 12.74 and Achilles Tatius 3.2.9. BOAT: Achilles Tatius 3.4; Petronius 102; Heliodorus 5.24. FRIENDLY (OR HOSTILE) BARBARIANS: X. E. 2.2.4; Petronius 114; Dio Chrysostom 7.5. (cf. Lucian *A True Story* 1.28–29; 2.46). See Cadbury, *Book of Acts*, 24–25; and further references in PERVO, 211.

190. The data, mainly assembled from commentaries and grammars, are given in PERVO.

191. Seven of about thirty "literary usages" are found in the sections considered by HAENCHEN and others to be Lukan additions to a source: Acts 27:9b–11, 21–26, 31, 33–38.

192. Ramsay, *The Bearing of Recent Discovery*, 207.

193. HAENCHEN, 709 (German, 624: *Mittelpunkt*).

194. SOEDER, 74 (*Mittelpunkt*). See also F. Pfister, "Apostelgeschichten," 163–71; H. Kraft in *AAA* 1/1:1–2 holds the same view.

195. Thus Stephen (Acts 6:8–10); Philip (Acts 8:5–13, 26–40); Peter (Acts 10; 11).

196. Ramsay, *St. Paul*, 22.

197. See the discussion on pp. 134–35 below.

198. The wording (*Statheis en mesō* + gen.) is precisely that of the opening of the Areopagus address (17:22)!

199. HAENCHEN, 704.

200. For such imperturbability in the midst of a storm at sea, see the famous anecdote about Pyrrho (Diogenes Laertius 9.68):

> When his fellow passengers on board a ship were all unnerved by a storm, he [Pyrrho] kept calm and confident, pointing to a little pig in the ship that went on eating, and telling them that such was the unperturbed state (*ataraxia*) to which the wise man should keep himself. (trans. Hicks, LCL 2:481)

201. That all will be saved because of Paul has its parallel in Lucan *Pharsalia* 5.578–93 (Caesar).

202. John: Acts 3—4; 8:14–25 (esp. awkward in 3:4–5 of one of the "pillars" of Gal. 2:9). Even in Acts the name of Barnabas tends to precede that of Paul: Acts 13:2, 7; 14:12, 14 (most probably from sources).

203. SOEDER, 46–58, gives many references to the Apoc. Acts. For various novels note the role of Damis (*Ap. Ty.*), Polycharmus (Chariton), and Clinias (Achilles Tatius).

204. They are present only in the editorial "we."

205. Protection of voyagers was one of the major functions of gods in antiquity, including not only the Dioscuri but also Poseidon, Isis, and Serapis. The aretalogical character of Acts 27 is apparent in comparison with Lucian *Philosophies for Sale* 1–2, quoted in n. 188 above. Pokorny ("Die Romfahrt") perceives that Acts 27 is a miracle story, however strained his interpretation may be. See also Zehnle, *Peter's Pentecost Discourse*, 38; Praeder, "Acts 27:1—28:16"; Miles and Trompf, "Luke and Antiphon"; LaDouceur, "Hellenistic Preconceptions of Shipwreck"; Theissen, *Miracle Stories*, 102. Also worthy of comparison to Acts 27 is Aelius Aristides *Hieroi Logoi* 2.11–14, with many parallels in detail and general agreement in theme.

206. Nock wondered, in a slightly more serious vein, how the diary would have survived (*Essays* 2:823).

207. Travel of the goddess explains the foundation of cι   sites in the *Homeric Hymn to Demeter*. Euripides' *Bacchae* 13–25 reflects the appeal of exotic and distant locales. The first books of Diodorus Siculus's *Universal History* show that by the beginning of the common era worldwide travel was normative for gods and heroes. The classic discussion of the literature is in Rohde, *Der griech. Roman*, 167–287. See also Reitzenstein, *Hellenistische Wundererzählungen*, 35–83; SOEDER, 21–51. On missionary travel, see Liefield, "The Wandering Preacher." For travel in the novella, see Trenker, *The Greek Novella*, 115–20.

208. See the comments of Reardon, *Courants littéraires*, 341–42.

209. On Luke's use of "the Way", see esp. W. C. Robinson, "On Preaching the Word of God (Luke 8:4–21)," *SLA* 131–38.

210. Travel in Apoc. Acts: SOEDER, 21–48. See her reflections on the Book of Acts (pp. 48–50).

211. Conzelmann, *Theology of St. Luke*, 213.

212. Haenchen describes the manner in which Luke has interwoven stories from separate sources about Philip and Peter so that wherever Philip goes, there Peter will follow shortly after ("Simon Magus," 278). Most interpreters who assign Luke a significant role in the editing and composition of Acts attribute this passage to him.

213. Acts 8:1–4 and 11:19–20 appear to derive from the same source, probably reflecting the Antiochene traditions.

214. The so-called famine relief (Acts 11:27–30) is probably inspired by the Collection. Had Paul previously brought such funds to Jerusalem, Gal. 2:10 would read differently, as Krodel notes (*Acts*, 100). Cf. Achtemeier, "An Elusive Unity."

215. Ramsay had experienced the geography firsthand. Knowing the difficulty of this overland climb, he found a deus ex machina: Paul got malaria and sought the highlands (*St. Paul*, 89–97).

216. Ramsay's maps (*St. Paul*) are not always current. The distance from Iconium to Antioch is about three hundred kilometers on major roads, and one passes several large cities. Whereas Luke is aware of sites and distances on the coast, he does not give an impression of knowledge in 13:1—14:23. Nor does he note that Antioch and Lystra are Roman colonies. Iconium was probably in Lycaonia. Lystra and Derbe were not twin cities in a different region from Iconium, as one would readily infer from Acts.

217. Von Harnack had remarked that this itinerary was strange (*Acts of the Apostles*, 94–96). Broughton puzzled over why they did not move on to Apameia rather than follow such a circuitous route ("Three Notes").

218. The Bar Jesus/Elymas episode is localized in Cyprus. Little tradition emerges in the Antioch material, but there appear to be sources for Lystra, or at least traditions (Acts 14:8, 20 appears to reveal a seam). On the whole, however, the "first journey" lacks the kind of color and detail that gains Luke such warm praise from historians in chaps. 16—20. Still, Luke seems unwilling to invent more than the statement that Paul preached in synagogues at Salamis and Perga, for instance (13:5; 14:25), and that he ordained presbyters (14:23).

219. On Acts 16:6–10, see p. 73 below. Paul's break with Antioch, an event not forgotten there and accessible to those who used Antiochene traditions, is omitted from this account.

220. La Piana, "The Roman Church," 211. Rome was the goal of the leader of every new movement, as well as of writers and artists: Juvenal *Satire* 3.62; Tacitus *Annals* 15.44.3; Sallust *Cataline* 37.5. Literature: La Piana, "The Roman Church"; Georgi, "Forms of Religious Propaganda," 124; Streeter, *Primitive Church*, 67. On Rome as the "end of the earth," see CONZELMANN, 22.

221. The famous note by Suetonius (*Claudius* 25; see n. 97 of the present chap.) requires rejection of the notion.

222. Thus, despite Acts 18:2 and 28:15, Paul begins his mission in Rome as he does all others.

223. On the geography of the *Acts of Paul*, see Schneemelcher, "Die Apostelgeschichte," 246–47.

224. Alexander collects tribute from Italy before proceeding to found Alexandria! This name was not drawn from a hat.

225. Liefeld takes it for granted that Acts uses travelogues to attract a readership ("The Wandering Preacher," 72–73).

226. Travel was exhausting. The *Hieroi Logoi* of Aelius Aristides do not give a rosy picture of 2d-century c.e. travel, even after due allowance has been made for neurosis and hypochondria. *The Ass* and Apuleius's *Metamorphoses* are exaggerated but generally realistic in their depiction of the rigors of travel. With the exception of the practitioners of certain occupations, travel was uncommon for the nonrich. On this subject, see Casson, *Travel in the Ancient World*.

227. 2 Cor. 11:23–27 probably summarizes obstacles an unprotected traveler might have to face: rivers, robbers, wilderness, sea dangers, toil and hardship, hunger and thirst, cold and exposure.

228. Ships are always at hand and the road poses no obstacles. For "swift travel" in novels and Apoc. Acts, see Chariton 3.2.14, 3.6.1, 8.6.1; *The Ass* 56; *Acts of Thomas* 3; *Acts of Peter* 5; *Acts of Andrew and Matthew* 7. Literature: SOEDER, 86; Kerenyi, *Griech.-orient. Romanliteratur*, 98–102; idem, review of SOEDER, 304.

229. See nn. 232, 234 on this p.

230. *Itinera Hierosolymitana*, ed. P. Geyer. For a discussion of this material, together with a translation of some texts, see Wilkinson's edition of *Egeria*.

231. From the *Itinerarium* of Antonius Placentius (6th cent. c.e.), see Geyer's edition (p. 159), as well as the account of the Bordeaux Pilgrim, Peter the Deacon's *De locis sanctis* ("On the Holy Sites"), and the famous *Peregrinatio Egeriae*.

232. Robbins discusses these matters ("By Land and by Sea"). The most famous example is the *periplous* of Hanno (GGM 1:1–14). Norden's comments and findings are still worthy of examination (*Agnostos Theos*, 4–5, 313–27). No reading of secondary literature can, however, replace examination of the texts, many of which are collected by Mueller.

233. *A True Story* 1 and 2 of Lucian is replete with examples, one of which is quoted above (p. 51). Achilles Tatius 3.1–5 is often compared with Acts 27. X. E. 1.11–12 and 4.1 are quite similar to Acts, as is *The Ass* 36–41.

234. Plümacher ("Wirklichkeitsfahrung") and Praeder ("Narrative Voyage," 186–222) have some good observations but seem to demand too much, in my judgment.

3. DIVERSIONS LESS ADVENTUROUS:
OTHER FORMS OF ENTERTAINMENT IN ACTS

1. *Duties*, trans. H. De Romestein (*ANF* 2d series 14:18). Bultmann, "Christianity as a Religion of East and West," 232.

2. Ancient humor: Duckworth (*Roman Comedy*, 305–9) discusses Aristotle *Nicomachean Ethics* 117b; idem *Poetics* 1449a; Plato *Laws* 7.816; idem *Philebus* 48ff.; Cicero *De oratore* 2.235ff.; Quintillian *Institutio oratoria* 6.3. On this topic, see also Cebe, de Saint Denis, Segal, and Suess. For humor in novels, the most extensive survey and discussion is that of Anderson, *Eros Sophistes*. For the NT, note W. F. Stinespring, *IDB* s.v. "humor." For Luke, see McLachlan (*St. Luke*) and Jonsson (*Humor and Irony in NT*). The latter two lack profundity.

3. Arrowsmith shows how the activity of translation exposes the problem of criteria for assessing humor ("Lively Conventions").

4. An amusing domestic crisis: The lost coin (Luke 15:8–10). Humor: The impor-

tunate friend and the unjust judge (Luke 11:5–8; 18:1–8). The problems raised by attempts to moralize the parable of the unjust steward (Luke 16:1–8) are notorious.

5. Punishment miracles: *Acts of Thomas* 8.51; *Acts of Peter* 3.14; *Acts of Paul* 11.6; Heliodorus 4.19; Apuleius 8.13. These are but a few examples. There are examples from the Epidauros collection: nos. 7, 11, 22. Note the treatise by Plutarch *On the Delays of the Divine Vengeance.* Literature: Lake (*BEG CHR* 5:29–30); Nock, *Conversion*, 80, 91; Nestle, "Legenden." See the examples in Acts 1:19–20; 5:1–11; 9:8; 13:6–12; 19:13–16.

6. Discussion: HAENCHEN, 236–41; Conzelmann, *1 Corinthians*, 78.

7. Acts 12:7: *Aggelos . . . pataxas.* 12:23: *eptaxen . . . aggleos.*

8. HAENCHEN, 323.

9. Thus Luke seeks to laugh off Paul's appearance before Gallio, which has become for NT historians one of the underpinnings of Pauline chronology. The burlesque humor is seen by CONZELMANN (p. 107) and Jonsson, *Humor and Irony in NT* (p. 216).

10. Mark 5:3–15; and commentaries, e.g., Klostermann, *Markusevangelium.*

11. MARSHALL (p. 285) finds Acts 17:22 probably ironic. BRUCE (p. 360) remarks on the piquancy of *ekklesia* in 19:32.

12. Mordecai and Haman: Esther 6:11–12 vs. 3:2; 1:17–19 vs. 5:1–2, 8. These are examples of ironic contrast in Esther.

13. A bit less subtle is the attempt of Anchialos to ravish Anthia with his "weapon" only to perish on the point of his sword. The author explains this link for the unobservant (X. E. 4.5). He was obviously proud of it. See also Schmeling, *Xenophon of Ephesus*, 49. Similar punishments were the fate of the wicked elders in Sus. 62, doing to them as they would have done to their neighbors.

14. Chaste lion: *Acts of Paul*, from Coptic papyrus, as translated in *NTA* 2:289. Talking dog: *Acts of Peter* 9–11. Perhaps the ancient readers were less naive and better humored about such episodes than some more recent critics. See also pp. 126–27 below. Animals and humans living peaceably together are a sign of Utopia: Isa. 11:2–5; Mark 1:11. Converse with animals characterizes the "divine man."

15. Anderson reluctantly notes the humor here but states that biblical precedent would make it edifying enough (*Eros Sophistes*, 60).

16. Poetic justice in novels: Heliodorus 8.7 (poisoner poisoned); Longus 2.25–30 (*Strafwunder*). Literature: Rohde, *Der griech. Roman*, 304–6. For more subtle types of irony, see Perry, "Chariton," 123–27; Anderson, *Eros Sophistes;* Wolff, *Greek Romances*, esp. 213–71. Walsh shows that Apuleius's novels not only are moralizing but also warn against the very sins that led Lucius (and others) into difficulty (*The Roman Novel*, 148–49).

17. Not least of all, ancient humor: Duckworth, *Roman Comedy*, 307; and perceptively, Richlin, *The Garden of Priapus.*

18. The terminology comes from Exod. 12:21 (Passover slaughter of lambs).

19. Cf. Jonsson, *Humor and Irony in NT*, 209–10.

20. The source was probably in popular preaching (DIBELIUS, 21). On this passage, see also p. 21 above; Weinrich, *Gebet und Wunder*, 150–54. On humor in aretalogy, note Epidauros tablets 8, 35, 37. See also Boll, "Zum griech. Roman," 10; Merkelbach, *Roman und Mysterium*, 86–87; A. Oepke, "Iaomai, ktl.," *TDNT* 3 (1965): 194–215, esp. 208; Werner, "Zum *Loukios E Onos*," 240–41. On the foot, see n. 7 above. HAENCHEN (p. 386) regards the death of the guards as almost comic.

The images of this passage are initiatory: paschal season, sleep, light, rising, putting on garments, passing barriers (the portal is a symbol of Passover). Symbolically they depict the redemption of believers through baptism. See also Moule, *Birth*, 34.

21. On Acts 16:16–18, see also p. 63 below. Iamblichus's novel has a similar person, on which see Rohde, *Der griech. Roman*, 399 n. 2.

22. DIBELIUS, 19. See also CONZELMANN, 111; Jonsson, *Humor and Irony in NT*, 217; and p. 9 above.

23. HAENCHEN, 578; cf. *Acts of John* 33. On the riot, see also pp. 9–10, 37, 63 above.

24. See further Plümacher, *Lukas als hellen. Schrift.*, 98–100; Oster, "The Ephesian Artemis." The use of *diopetēs* (19:35), evoking an aniconic image of Artemis like that worshiped by the barbarous Taurians (who performed human sacrifices) is perhaps a slander. The temple of Artemis looms large in novels: X. E. 1.11, 5.15, of course; Achilles Tatius 6.3, 7.2–3; *Antheia* (*Griechische Roman-Papyri*, ed. F. Zimmerman, 79–80); *Ap. Tyre* 37, 40–49; *Acts of John* 37–47.

25. Despite Ehrhardt, *Framework of NT Stories*, 79.

26. On the *Satyricon*, see Walsh, *The Roman Novel*, 79. *The Ass* 29–30 illustrates the penchant for violence. *The Ass* 35–41//Apuleius 8.24–9.10 show burlesque humor in the service of polemic. Anderson (*Eros Sophistes*) finds burlesque parody not only in Achilles Tatius but also in Heliodorus. His work contains a wide survey of humor in the ancient novel. Apuleius 3.2ff. and Achilles Tatius 7–8 are examples of the use of humor in legal procedures.

27. Hagiography: Delehaye, *Legends of the Saints*, 153. There is more than a little humor in the *Lausaic History* and the various monastic traditions and collections. *Acts of Peter* 14 is a fine illustration of such rowdy material: Simon is beaten by his slaves, with fists, sticks, and stones, anointed with the contents of chamber pots, and then cast into the street.

28. Problems include the reception of the missionaries of a new god for old gods; the local reaction, which was excessive even for barbarians, since other healings do not create this much excitement; and the pairing of Zeus and Hermes at a cultic site, together with their veneration as healing gods. See HAENCHEN, 431. HAENCHEN (432–33) and CONZELMANN (179–80) agree that a form of the legend of Baucis and Philemon underlies the account. BRUCE (p. 281) invites comparison of the two accounts and MARSHALL (p. 237) all but accepts it.

29. Nock, *Essays* 2:660 n. 43.

30. Many examples are given in SOEDER (95–98).

31. Alexander usually rejects honors, but not so in 1.22.7 and 2.14.

32. DIBELIUS, 8 n. 61. See also Cadbury, *The Book of Acts in History*, 24–26; Plümacher, *Lukas als hellen. Schrift.*, 21; Cadbury and Lake (*BEG CHR* 4:342); HAENCHEN, 715–16. Such natives were to be feared, as in Dio Chrysostom 7.1ff.; Iamblichus; Apuleius 2.14; Lucian *A True Story* 1.21; X. E. 3.12.2; Vergil *Aeneid* 6.351–61.

33. X. E. 2.2.4, an important parallel to Acts 28:1–7; Heliodorus 1.5–7; 5.7.

34. Nock, *Essays* 2:831. For a description of Athens based upon literature, see Strabo 9.16.396. Conzelmann makes comparison with travel books, in "Luke's Place," *SLA* 298–316. See also pp. 44–45 above and pp. 71–72 below on this passage.

35. Piety: Sophocles *Oedipus Colonnus* 260; Josephus *Against Apion* 2.130. Curios-

ity: Lucian *Icaromenippus* 24; Thucydides 3.38.5; Demosthenes *Philippic* 1.10; Pausanias 1.17.1; Strabo 9.1.16; Livy 14.27.

36. Imitation: *Acts of Paul* 11.1.

37. DIBELIUS, 17–19. See also CONZELMANN, 115.

38. E.g., Ignatius's descriptions of his pending martyrdom in *Romans* 4; Melito *On the Passover* 16–29; and, to a degree, the Pastoral Epistles, esp. 2 Timothy with its appeal for sympathy: "Only Luke is with me" (2 Tim. 4:11).

39. One can observe this in Luke's treatment of the Passion of Jesus. See Tiede, *Prophecy and History in Luke-Acts*, 78–79, for a discussion of the parallel sections of Luke to Acts 20–21, and the details of Luke 15:15–16 (prodigal son).

40. By Acts 8:3 Paul has become a raging persecutor in his own right. Luke's addition has a sentimental quality.

41. DIBELIUS, 12. For other pathetic miracles in Luke and Acts, see CADBURY, 237–38. The Asclepius tradition has many similar accounts, as in Epidauros 11. Cadbury and Lake (*BEG CHR* 4:111) recognized the appeal of the pathetic scene to the author.

42. The Latin tradition in Acts 9:39 which speaks of "coats and dresses which she made for them" was admired by Dibelius and Zahn (DIBELIUS 13 n. 1).

43. Acts 20:7–12, discussed on pp. 65–66 above.

44. See the Passion predictions of Mark 8:31 pars. On the meaning of *dei*, see W. Grundmann, "Dei, ktl.," *TDNT* 2 (1964): 21–25, esp. 23. Cf. the Zoilus letter 6 in Deissmann's *Light from the Ancient East*, 152–61, and the Serapis inscription from Delos 1.

45. On the itinerary style, see p. 57 above. On the entourage, see Haenchen's quote from Overbeck (HAENCHEN, 581).

46. Cadbury finds this scene one of the most touching of its kind in literature (CADBURY, 238). See also the detailed study by Michel, *Die Abschiedsrede des Paulus;* Budesheim, "Paul's *Abschiedsrede*."

47. The correspondence between Paul's farewell address and the Pastorals has been observed since at least Harnack's *Acts of the Apostles* (p. 129). See also the more recent studies by Wilson (*Luke and the Pastorals*) and Quinn ("The Last Volume of Luke").

48. Longus, trans. Hadas (*Three Greek Romances*, 16–17). See also Achilles Tatius 1.11; X. E. 1.10, 3.3, 3.7, 5.1; Chariton 3.10; Apuleius 3.7–8; 4.26–27.

49. A few examples: Chariton 1.14, 3.8, 5.10; X. E. 4.6. Christian: *Xanthippe and Polyxena* 26. The "you may do as you wish to my body, but . . ." speech is a *topos* in novels, Apoc. Acts, and hagiography.

50. X. E., trans. Hadas (*Three Greek Romances*, 82).

51. Chariton, trans. Blake (*Chariton's Chaereas and Callirhoe*, 45). Cf. also *Acts of Thomas* 68; *Acts of Peter* 5–6.

52. Kroll (*NTA* 2:169–70). See also Plümacher, "Apokryphe Apostelakten," 67.

53. See *The Third and Fourth Books of Maccabees*, ed. Hadas, 33. *3 Macc.* 4.2–10 and 5.46–49 are florid examples. Judith 7—9 contains a siege description the character of which is clear. On pathos in novels and martyrdoms, see also Wehrli, "Einheit," 147; Musurillo, *Acts of the Pagan Martyrs*, 252–53.

54. Nock's *Conversion* is the classic statement of the propaganda value of the marvelous and exotic (see p. 106). The adventurous element was rarely of interest to epitomators, but note the fragments of Iambulus; Diodorus Siculus 1.55–60; and the ad-

ventures in Lucian's *A True Story*. Rohde's discussion is still valuable (*Der griech. Roman*, 167–309, esp. 167–287).

55. Oscar Wilde, according to Finley, "Utopianism," 20.

56. CONZELMANN, 5; Easton, *The Purpose of Acts*, 35.

57. Vergil (LCL 1:29) typifies the pagan hope. See also Georgi, "Who Is the True Prophet?"

58. Visits to "primitive societies": See Lovejoy and Boaz, *Primitivism*, vol. 1. Philosophical societies: See the still useful work of Zeller, *Die Philosophie der Griechen* 3/2:284. Iamblichus's *Life of Pythagoras* 168 is one of the most frequently cited parallels to Acts 4:32–33.

59. Utopian description in *Aristeas*: See Hadas, *Aristeas to Philocrates*, 47; Tcherikover, "Jewish Apologetic Literature."

60. So Plümacher, *Lukas als hellen. Schrift.*, 17–18; Hengel, *Property and Riches*, 81; Countryman, *The Rich Christian*, 76–78; Grant, *Early Christianity*, 100—to give a sample of modern authorities.

61. Luke's sources would appear to regard such action as extraordinary, preserved in the tales of Barnabas and Ananias. Similar actions by Marcion and Cyprian were long remembered. See also *Xanthippe and Polyxena* 31; Athanasius *Life of Antony* 2–3.

62. On this matter, see the references in L. T. Johnson, *Literary Function*, 1–2.

63. Cadbury, *The Book of Acts in History*.

64. The basis is probably astrological, as argued by Cumont, J. Thomas, Weinstock, and others. Luke had no interest in promoting astrology, but such catalogues symbolized all the nations under heaven, i.e., the zodiac.

65. On linguistic diversity as a primitive gift to be restored with the return of the Golden Age, or lost for good, see Philo *On the Confusion of Tongues;* Josephus *Antiquities* 1.1.4; *T. Judah* 25; Plutarch *Isis and Osiris* 47.

66. The repetition in Acts 2:7–8, 11–12 suggests that the catalogue was added, probably therefore by Luke.

67. Cadbury (*The Book of Acts in History*, 16–17), Dinkler ("Philippus"), and Plümacher (*Lukas als hellen. Schrift.*, 13) stress Luke's contribution to the exotic appeal of the text. *1 Clement* 20.8 also demonstrates the interest in Ethiopia in Christian circles more or less contemporaneous with Luke-Acts. Note the interesting and cogent remarks of Plümacher (p. 13).

68. On the style and diction of the episode, see HAENCHEN, 111; SCHNEIDER 1:198–99 and the references there.

69. See pp. 64, 74, 76 above; Cadbury, *The Book of Acts in History*, 21–27.

70. See the examples in SOEDER, 103–12.

71. Lake gives a very judicious account of the difficulties in the Jerusalem description (*BEG CHR* 5:474–86). Despite the customary praise of Luke's knowledge of details, one should not overlook Acts 16:12 (a serious error), and the use of *stratēgos* for *duumvir* and other offices, including chief of the temple police. On politarchs, one should consult Ferguson, *Legal Terms*, 65–66, 74; *New Doc* 2 (1977):34–35.

72. Chariton, trans. Blake (*Chariton's Chaereas and Callirhoe*, 13).

73. So Hallstrom, "De Curiositate Atheniensium," 57–58. See also Apuleius 10.7; Heliodorus 3.1. Apollonius's visit to Athens inspired Norden's classic work. See *Agnostos Theos* 35–55; *Ap. Ty.* 4.17–22, which Norden studies. See also Lake (*BEG CHR* 5:240–51); and pp. 44–45 above.

74. Persian court: Esther. The alleged accuracy of detail here has occasioned a debate. Note also the court scenes in Daniel and the "Tobiad Romance" cited by Josephus, as well as *3 Maccabees*. On Esther, where the debate most closely parallels Acts, see Moore (*Esther*, lix); Bickerman (*Four Strange Books*, 171–240).

75. *Archaios:* Acts 15:7, 21; 21:16. The use of the LXX "biblical" style would also contribute to "archaizing" the work.

76. Acts 1:8: On its function, see Kümmel, *Introduction*, 158.

77. To which one should compare the *argumenta* and opening speeches of ancient drama.

78. Addition A to Greek Esther relates the dream; addition F interprets it—a neat inclusio. Moore notes that the Greek text makes providence the leading theme (*Daniel, Esther, Jeremiah*, 8).

79. X. E. 1.6.2 is the subject of much ridicule and some discussion:

Why yearn ye to learn the end of disease or its beginning? Both a single malady holds fast, and hence the solution issues. Yet perceive I for these twain fearful suffering and toil protracted. Both shall flee o'er the brine pursued by pirates. They shall be laden with fetters by men who live by the sea. For both a bridal chamber will serve as a tomb, and fire the destroyer. And by the floods of the river Nile upon holy Isis, the savior goddess you will thereafter bestow rich gifts. But after their woes their lot grants a fortune that is better. (trans. Hadas, *Three Greek Romances*, 76)

80. Introductory oracles: Apuleius 2.12 (parody), 4.32; Achilles Tatius 1.3; *Ap. Ty.* 1.4–5; Longus 1.7–8; Heliodorus 2.35; Antonius Diogenes; Petronius frag. 44; Jonah 1:1; Apoc. Acts (examples in Soeder, 44–46, 171, 180); *Pseudo-Clementines.* H12, 8.4.

81. Commands: Acts (1:15–26); 8:26, 29; 9:6, 11, 15; 10:5; 12:7; 13:2, 20; 16:6, 9; 18:9; (20:22); 22:17, 21; 23:11; 27:23.

82. Travel: X. E.; Antonius Diogenes. Other commands are *Ap. Tyre* 46; Heliodorus 3.11; *Ap. Ty.* 1.23; Apuleius 11.26. See Rohde, *Der griech. Roman*, 305.

83. So Soeder, 175; cf. 44–45, 171, 180. Soeder does not try to distinguish between canonical and apocryphal Acts in this matter.

84. Wikenhauser ("Religionsgeschichtlich Parallelen") assembles most of the evidence. Alexander: Josephus *Antiquities* 11.329ff. Caesar: Suetonius *Julius* 32 (Alea jacta est; "the die is cast"). Text: Acts 16:6–9.

85. Double dreams: Wikenhauser ("Doppelträume") again gives numerous instances. He stresses their folkloristic character. Kerenyi calls them aretalogical (*Griech.-orient. Romanliteratur*, 166). Both are correct. For examples from novellas, see Wendland, *De Fabellis Antiquis*, 27–28. A large number occur in novels, e.g., *Joseph and Asenath* 14–15; Chariton 1.12; Petronius 104; Apuleius 11.1–3; 11.6, 11.21–22, 11.26–27; Longus 1.7–8; Heliodorus 3.11–12, 3.18.

86. Burchard (*Dreizehnte Zeuge*, 59–86) compares Acts 9 to Apuleius and *Joseph and Asenath*. The source problem of Acts 10:1—11:18 is perhaps more complicated than Haenchen allows (345–63). See Schneider 2:61–64. Luke does appear responsible, however, for linking Peter's vision with Cornelius's visitation by an angel and thus obtaining the effect of a double dream.

87. Achilles Tatius 4.1–8. Leucippe turns down Clitophon on the basis of a dream: Artemis promised aid if she would remain a virgin until marriage. He remembers a dream of his own. Attempting to worship Aphrodite, he found the temple door shut.

A woman in the form of the cult statue appeared and promised that he would soon be admitted and be made her priest (i.e., would have sex shortly).

88. Acts 9:15–16; 11:27–30; 18:9–11; 21:4–6, 8–14; 23:11; 27:23–24.

89. Suffering: E.g., X. E. 1.6; Antonius Diogenes; Apuleius 4.32. Note the parody in Lucian *A True Story* 2.27. Literature: SOEDER, 178–80. Promises: Apuleius 11.6 is famous. See also X. E. 1.6; Heliodorus 2.35; Chariton 5.5; Longus 2.23, 27.

90. Quote: Wendland, *Urchristlichen Literaturformen*, 329. Dreams and oracles in ancient novels: Rohde, *Der griech. Roman*, 304–5; 476–77, 492 n.3, 514 n.1; Grimal, *Romans*, xv–xviii; Kerenyi, *Griech.-orient. Romanliteratur*, 165–68; Haight, *Ancient Romances*, 30, 55, 83, 103, 133; idem, *More on Ancient Romances*, 39.

91. Providence in Luke: Cadbury, *The Making of Luke-Acts*, 303–6; Conzelmann, *Theology of St. Luke*, 151–54; Schulz, "Gottes Vorsehung bei Lukas"; G. Schrenk, "Boulomai, ktl.," *TDNT* 1 (1964): 629–37; M. A. Schmidt, "Horizō, ktl.," *TDNT* 5 (1967): 452–56.

92. Cawelti makes a number of useful comparisons to modern melodrama and popular fiction (*Adventure*, 44–47).

93. Discussion of providence in ancient novels: Rohde, *Der. griech. Roman*, 296–306; Kerenyi, *Griech.-orient. Romanliteratur*, 98, 101, 179–80, 190, 199; Merkelbach, *Roman*, 97; Auerbach, *Mimesis*, 443; Wehrli, "Einheit," 135; Reardon, "The Greek Novel," 298; idem, *Courants littéraires*, 357, 386.

94. Jewish novels: E.g., Greek Esther (see n.74 above); *3 Maccabees*. Apuleius transformed the story which exists only in the form known in *The Ass* into a testimony to Isis's providence. See Festugiere, *Personal Religion*, 75; Merkelbach, *Roman*, 6; Riefstahl, *Roman des Apuleius*, 29–33.

95. Romantic novels: Chariton, as described by Zimmerman ("Chariton," 333–35) and Schmeling (*Chariton*, 84). Note also X. E., which is more of a religious novel according to most but not all commentators. Longus, also often considered religious, expounds the theme of providence (4.24). There would seem to be universal agreement regarding the agency of providence in Heliodorus, beginning with Rohde (*Der griech. Roman*, 476).

96. Rohde, *Der griech. Roman*, 428.

97. Heliodorus in particular is so charged. See Rohde, *Der griech. Roman*, 476; Chalk, review of *Heliodorus*, 132; Wolff, *Greek Romances*, 183. The metaphor of humans as puppets was popular in antiquity. See some references in Dodds, *The Greeks*, 8–9. Winkler ("The Mendacity of Kalasiris") disagrees with this interpretation of Heliodorus.

98. See HAENCHEN (p. 362), summarizing Acts 10:1—11:18.

99. By "immature" I refer to those who prefer to blame their problems upon fate, or others, and see themselves as perpetual victims. See pp. 27–28 above, and the excursus on ancient novels and their readers, pp. 81–85 below.

100. Dio Chrysostom's *Oration* 11 is an entertainment, as are many of Lucian's shorter addresses. Among many works on rhetoric in the Roman world, see in particular the recent works of George Kennedy.

101. On the appeal of preaching in the patristic age, see MacMullen, *Christianizing the Roman Empire*, 64–65 and his references.

102. Mimesis in Luke: Plümacher, *Lukas als hellen. Schrift.*, 32–80, esp. 51–57. For literature of the period in general, note Reardon, *Courants littéraires*, 3–11.

103. This is also the conclusion of Veltman, "The Defense Speeches of Paul," 256.

104. DIBELIUS, 138–61. Another classic survey is that of Cadbury, *The Making of Luke-Acts*, 184–91; idem (*BEG CHR* 5:402–27). Cf. Plümacher, *Lukas als hellen. Schrift*. Comparison of Luke's speeches with contemporary rhetoric is a fruitful line of current scholarship.

105. Stylistic unity: DIBELIUS, 179.

106. Parallel speeches: See p. 76 below.

107. Both Cadbury (*BEG CHR* 5:404) and DIBELIUS (179–80) refer to Luke's love for direct speech. This is a popular feature of his style, popular because it is more vivid. Omniscience is a narrative license of novelists.

108. Interruption: DIBELIUS, 160–61. Examples: Acts 2:36; 7:53; 10:44; 17:32; 18:14; 19:28; 22:22; etc. It is, according to Veltman ("The Defense Speeches of Paul," 256 n. 44), common in defense speeches, and the technique was employed by historians. For novels, see, e.g., Chariton 1.7.2.10–11, 2.11.6, 3.4.3, 5.8.1, 8.7.2; Petronius 2–3, 38, 98; Heliodorus 4.19.

109. Acts 5:35–36; 19:35–36; 25:14–15; 26:30–32. Paul can claim that he still is a Pharisee, and James can serve as his defender. Jervell has a number of examples (*Luke and the People of God*, 153–207).

110. Plato had been dead for over a decade, Lysias for almost two generations. The views of Demades and Demosthenes have been inverted. See the comments of Kroll (*Historia Alexandria magni*) on the *Alexander Romance* 2.4.4 (the section runs from 2.2.5–2.5.1).

111. Examples: Achilles Tatius 5.15ff.; *Metiochus* (on which see *Griechische Roman-Papyri*, ed. F. Zimmermann, 297). For rhetorical exercises see Apuleius 2.8–9. See the discussion of rhetorical duels and related matter in SOEDER, 206–7.

112. On these two styles, see Kennedy, *Art of Rhetoric*, index (p. 644) s.vv. "Asianism," "Atticism," and the references provided.

113. *Ninus*, end of frag. AII, beginning of AIII.

114. The two letters in Acts are the best NT examples of the "Hellenistic letter" form. Lysias's letter (23:26–30) shows an unusual degree of hypotaxis. Acts 15:24–26 is the only true period in Acts. For formal comparison, see the texts in Welles (*Royal Correspondence*). For style and function, note 1 Macc. 14:25–45, which may have been a model. MacMullen gives examples of the aping of municipal decrees by guilds and the like (*Roman Social Relations* 76, 82). Luke probably did not invent the prohibitions contained in the decree, but he is almost certainly responsible for their form.

115. Sallust is an apt comparison. *Jugurtha* 9, 24, and *Cataline* 35, 44, contain letters. He identifies them as his own work with "Quarum sententia." When Bruce finds the Lysias letter "true to life" he is not establishing more than verisimilitude.

116. Some examples: Chariton 4.5.6, 8.4.1.5–6; X. E. 2.5.1.4, 2.12.2; Iamblichus (Photius 77–78); Heliodorus 5.9, 8.3, 10.2; Achilles Tatius 1.3, 5.18, 5.20. See love letters in Petronius 129–30. Chion wrote a short novel in letters. Some of the Cynic collections have a similar function. See Malherbe, *The Cynic Epistles*. The *Alexander Romance* may have been in letter form in the first edition. An English analogy is Richardson's *Pamela* (a novel in letters).

117. For speeches in the Apoc. Acts, see SOEDER, 204–11. (The *Pseudo-Clementines* contain enough speeches to satisfy the most pronounced craving.)

118. On Lydia's status, see Horsley in *New Doc 2* (1977): 25–32.

119. Ramsay, *St. Paul*, 21–22.

120. For the biographical approach, see, e.g., the beginning of Philo's *Life of Moses*.

121. Acts 16:35; 21:39; 22:3–4, 25–29; 26:4–10.

122. Acts 17:16–24 is usually presumed to be the best display of Paul's Greek education, but the defense speeches in chaps. 24 and 26 are also worthy of note.

123. Bowersock noted that only three of Philostratus's subjects were of low- or middle-class origin. Sophists were nearly always wealthy and notable (*Greek Sophists*, 21–22, 31).

124. Acts 28:16–17, 30–31. Cf. Acts 24:23. In Rome Paul could hold meetings in a facility large enough for the Jewish leadership and address a sizable group.

125. Ramsay notes that Julius "looks up" to Paul (*St. Paul*, 55).

126. The studies of Countryman, Gager, R. Grant, Judge, Malherbe, Meeks, and Theissen, among other recent contributions, destroy the romantic myth about Christianity as a purely proletarian phenomenon. On the other hand, the majority of Christians were of relatively low status until the 4th cent. Even in the days of Augustine the conversion of a prominent person was a momentous occasion. Note Origen *Against Celsus* 3.15; Minucius Felix *Octavius*, 9ff. See Gager, *Kingdom and Community*, 94; A. H. M. Jones, "Social Background," 17–18. A classic picture is that of Friedlander, *Roman Life* 3:206–11. Rohrbach provides a good survey of the modern debate ("Methodological Considerations").

127. Not many Jews could hold Greek citizenship, scarcely one who had left Tarsus in infancy. Nock can cite only a few examples (*Essays* 2:960–63). Sherwin-White also notes problems (*Roman Law*, 56–57). The citizenship is based on Acts. As Conzelmann observes (*1 Corinthians*, 277 n. 129), 2 Cor. 11:23–25 does not read in support of Roman citizenship. The account of Paul's appeal in Acts proves nothing. Garnsey concludes that Paul usurped the position of a much more prominent type of person than himself ("The *Lex Julia*," 185). Noncitizens, such as Ignatius, could also be dispatched to Rome. See *Les epîtres d'Ignace*, ed. Camelot, 9 n. 1, for a list and discussion.

128. For contempt of the rabble, see Acts 17:5; for workers, 19:24–41. Paul's status in Acts is difficult to reconcile with his practice of a trade. Hock (*Social Context*) has wrestled with this issue from a different perspective. MacMullen (*Roman Social Relations*, 114) describes the low status of craftsmen.

129. On the "Upward mobility" of new religions, see the remarks of Georgi ("Socioeconomic Reasons") and Theissen (*Social Setting*). The tales in Josephus *Antiquities* 18.65ff. and Juvenal *Satire* 6 give good examples.

130. "Petite bourgeoisie" refers to cultural factors rather than economic position. It refers not only to those members of a cosmopolitan society with some education and wealth (and many ambitions) but also to those with considerable money deterred by status from finding an appropriate place in social life. The latter are parodied by Petronius in his famous description of Trimalchio and friends. On them see my "Wisdom and Power" and the literature cited there. Finley (*The Ancient Economy*) and Rohrbach ("Methodological Considerations") show that "middle class" is not an appropriate designation for members of Greco-Roman society.

131. See Dibelius and Conzelmann, *The Pastoral Epistles*, 39–41, for discussion of this ideal, one feature of so-called early Catholicism.

132. "Virtue Rewarded" is the subtitle of Richardson's *Pamela*.

133. Perry, *Ancient Romances*, 115; Trenker, *Greek Novella*, 170.

134. For a discussion of Acts 25:23, see p. 75 above.

135. Civic pride: E.g., Chariton 7.3; X. E. 3.2; Achilles Tatius 6.16; Heliodorus 1.22; *Acts of Paul and Thecla* 27; *Alexander Romance* 1:31–32; all are similar to Acts 21:39. See also Apuleius 3.11, 8.23, 10.25; Chariton 1.1, 2.5; X. E. 3.2. For evidence that civic pride did not recede in Roman times, see C. P. Jones, *Roman World of Dio,* 75.

136. Hellenic pride: Chariton 2.5; Heliodorus 1.8.20.25; *Calligone* 25ff. (*Griechische Roman-Papyri*, ed. F. Zimmerman); *Ap. Ty.* 1.34–35, 2.27, 3.12.

137. Education: Chariton 2.5, 6.7, 7.6.25; *Ap. Tyre* 4; *Ap. Ty.* 1.7. On learning, see MacMullen, *Roman Social Relations*, 107.

138. As in Chariton 1.2.14, 2.6, 6.4.

139. A list of references to "leading citizens" from ancient novels would be lengthy. Some examples are in Philonenko's edition of *Joseph and Asenath* (p. 129) and in Rohde (*Der griech. Roman,* 443 n. 1). Jewish novels were not immune: e.g., Esther 1:1; Sus. 1–4.

140. Even monarchs act like the bourgeois: the Persian king is quite attracted to Esther (5:1a–2b) as well as to Callirhoe (Chariton 5.3). On the latter, see Perry, *Ancient Romances,* 132. The pirate leader is a bourgeois sort in X. E. Although the kings and satraps are of high status, their values resemble those of the reader.

141. Burchard notes this (*Dreizehnte Zeuge,* 37–38). The context of these claims is often ignored in research.

142. *Ap. Ty.* 1.4.7, 4.35, 4.44, 5.10.27ff., 7.4, 7.16.

143. Chariton 2.5, 4.2. X. E. reveals the nadir to which this device may descend, Heliodorus its artistic potential (Winkler, "The Mendacity of Kalasiris," 94–95).

144. So Levin, "To Whom Did the Ancient Novelists Address Themselves?"

145. Ludvikovsky, *Recky Roman* (French summary); Lavagnini, *Studi,* 53–54. See also Perry, *Ancient Romances,* 5, 63, 98–100.

146. This is the view of Anderson (*Eros Sophistes*), Reardon ("The Greek Novel," 165–71), and Levin ("To Whom Did the Ancient Novelists Address Themselves?"). Each of these authors has sophistic novels in view.

147. On the social standing of early Christians, see n. 126 above.

148. The most frequently cited references are Julian *Letter to a Priest* 301C (LCL 2:326); Philostratus *Letter* 66 (LCL 534) addressed to Chariton. Lucian's *A True Story* parodies travel novels. Dio of Prusa could borrow many features of contemporary novels for his *Euboicus* (*Oration* 7), but without giving the genre formal recognition, as Jouan observes ("Les thèmes romantiques," *EA* 38–39).

149. For the style of Chariton, see *Kallirhoe,* ed. Plepelits, 5. X. E. is even less sophisticated. The *Chione* and related fragments are very similar to Chariton. See Gronewald, "Metiochus Parthenope"; idem, "Roman"; Mähler, "Metiochus-Parthenope Roman." Cadbury stressed the resemblance of Chariton to the latter half of Acts (*Book of Acts in History,* 8).

150. See references in n. 146 above.

151. See also the discussion of providence, p. 74 above.

152. Highet, *The Classical Tradition,* 165. See also the remarks of Schmeling in *Xenophon of Ephesus,* 135.

153. Schmeling, *Xenophon of Ephesus,* 131–41: "Ancient novels appealed to the same audience in which the early Church found its members and in which it sought converts" (p. 141). Hägg agrees (*The Novel in Antiquity,* 81–108).

154. See Bultmann's characterization of the Golden Rule as "naive egoism" (*History*

of the Synoptic Tradition, 103). Also see Douglas, *Purity and Danger,* 81: "Explanations of events . . . couched in notions of good and bad fortune . . . are implicitly subjective notions ego centered in reference."

155. Notable examples are Callirhoe (Chariton), Chariclea (Heliodorus), and Thecla (Apoc. Acts).

156. The 2d-cent. c.e. *P. Michaelidae* of Chariton confirms what is also apparent from the final sentence: that the woman's name alone was used in the title. Parthenope was certainly the major character of the novel traditionally called *Metiochus and Parthenope.* See Gronewald and Mähler (n. 149 above). The practice of naming all novels after a couple is Byzantine. Many originally bore geographical names, others of a person.

157. Miralles, *"Eros as Nosos," EA* 20–21, with reference to Plutarch and Galen. 1 Corinthians 7 offers a view more or less opposed to marriage. The Pastoral Epistles reflect the viewpoint of those who regard marriage as a necessary institution. Rhetorical studies included among their stock essays the topic of whether males should marry. Juvenal *Satire* 6 is probably the best-known example of the negative answer. Cf. also *Acts of Thomas* 12.

158. Hägg, *The Novel in Antiquity,* 95–96. See also MacDonald, *The Legend and the Apostle;* Davies, *The Revolt of the Widows.*

159. See the data summarized by Molinié (*Chariton,* 12).

160. Plepelits points to many of these in his commentary *Kallirhoe.*

161. So all the critics, based largely upon the work of Bartsch ("Charitonroman") and Fr. Zimmermann ("Chariton und die Geschichte").

162. Just as one can appreciate Acts without picking up the references to Socrates in 5:29 and 17:16–21, not to mention the numerous allusions to the LXX.

163. It is possible to compare use of similar material by Alexandrian and Latin poets. Callimachus's *Aitia,* e.g., treats love stories and local legends with a wealth of erudition and affectation far surpassing anything in the earlier novels. See Reardon, *Courants littéraires,* 317.

164. See the works listed in n. 126 above. On the lack of firsthand data about women in literary sources, see Finley's suggestive "The Silent Women of Rome."

165. Often in translation, as in the Clementine literature, and possibly, *Ap. Tyre.*

166. Heiserman begins his study of the ancient novel with Apollonius of Rhodes (*The Novel before the Novel*). For a discussion of romantic elements in Vergil, see Soady, "Romance Elements," *EA* 40–41. Many examples could be adduced from 1st-cent. c.e. epic. On history as the ancient equivalent of serious fiction, see Bury, *Ancient Greek Historians,* 175. Sallust's monographs read like novels. Cicero was well aware of this potential and looked forward to just such an exciting depiction of his own consulship (*Letters to His Friends* 5.12).

167. See the references in n. 148 above. Although Byzantine, Photius is an example of a cultured gentleman (and prelate) who devoted some of his reading to the productions of popular and other novelists.

4. THE ANCIENT NOVEL:
ITS ORIGINS AND NATURE

1. Praeder does not accurately represent my position when she states that I regard Acts as entertaining rather than theological ("Luke-Acts and the Ancient Novel," 269).

2. See Schneemelcher and Schäferdiek (*NTA* 2:175); Kaestli, "Les Principales orientations," *LAaa* 49–67.

3. See SOEDER, 188–215; Blumenthal, *Formen und Motive;* the separate introductions to the several Acts in *NTA* 2; Vielhauer, *Geschichte*, 693–718; Plümacher, "Apokryphe Apostelakten"; *LAaa*.

4. An example is *NTA* 2, where 411 pages are devoted to a survey of Christian novels, concluding with the *Travels of Barnabas*, the book SOEDER (p. 183) found most like the canonical Acts in form.

5. On the Apoc. Acts, see Dobschütz, "Roman," followed by Soeder, who was in turn followed by the contributors to *NTA*. Note also Vielhauer, *Geschichte*, 715–17; Plümacher, "Apokryphe Apostelakten," 63. See also various contributions to *LAaa*.

6. Rohde's *Der griech. Roman* was reprinted as recently as 1974, although the text is that of 1876.

7. For recent views on the Second Sophistic, see Reardon, "The Second Sophistic and the Novel"; Anderson, *Ancient Fiction*.

8. Lesky states that prior to Rohde others had made similar proposals (*History*, 857 n. 2).

9. Rohde, *Der griech. Roman*, on love, 11–166 (12–177); on travel, 167–287 (388–544). [Page numbers of later editions are given in parentheses.]

10. See the summary of Rohde's process, in ibid., 242–47 (262–64).

11. Ibid., 250–51 (269). Since Rohde's day possible fragments of the novel have been located but without bearing on his theory. Rohde had to rely upon the summary of Photius alone.

12. Schmid's appendix to the 1914 edition of Rohde's *Der griech. Roman* already set out the need for revision. See also Lesky, *History*.

13. Heinze, "Petron," 509; Bürger, *Studien*, 5–6. Rohde observed this, without drawing a similar conclusion (*Der griech. Roman*, 274–75 [295]). Love is really the major theme only in Longus. There is a vast difference between the idea of love presented in Hellenistic poetry and the goals of perfect fidelity and perpetual commitment communicated by the novels. Heliodorus is, in some ways, the most "sophistic" of the novels, and the least interested in love. See Perry, *Ancient Romances*, 75–76, 123. On adventure as predominant, see Ludvikovsky, *Recky Roman;* Warren, *History of the Novel*, 42; Murray, *Literature*, xxiii–xxiv. See also Reardon, *Courants littéraires*, 322, and pp. 105–10 below.

14. Schwartz, *Fünf Vorträge*, 138. There is further discussion of Schwartz below. Rohde, *Der griech. Roman*, xix–xx (1974), reports on early reviews and opinions.

15. Most discussions of Rohde focus upon the revision caused by papyrus discoveries. He had placed Chariton at the end of the chronological sequence.

16. *Ap. Tyre* was not a love story, nor was the Greek novel that is alleged to have stood behind the *Pseudo-Clementines*. On these, see Perry, *Ancient Romances*, 285–93.

17. Reardon, *Courants littéraires*, 314.

18. Notably by such NT scholars as Conzelmann and Haenchen, who speak of "required adventures" and the like (CONZELMANN, 6; HAENCHEN, 170). Perry is but one of many who have denounced this approach. See also Schissel, *Entwicklungsgeschichte*, 12; Lavagnini, *Studi*, 9, 200; Zimmermann, review of Soeder and Blumenthal, 1406; idem, "Zum Stand," 60–61; Grimal, *Romans*, vii; Wehrli, "Einheit," 135–36. No leading student of the ancient novel propounds this view today.

19. Analogies from modern cinema and television come readily to mind.

20. Reardon includes a substantial discussion of *mimesis* in literature of the imperial age (*Courants littéraires*, 3–11, 99–232).

21. The issue is no longer regarded as certain, Hägg having entered substantial objections ("Ephesiaka").

22. This is the inference of Mähler, "Metiochus-Parthenope," 19.

23. Not to mention the embarrassment of having to exclude the *Iliad* because it lacks love and travel!

24. The most extensive study of motifs is probably Calderini's *Le avventure*. Soeder regarded it as axiomatic, and Lesky supports the approach. Motifs aside, Rohde grasped the importance of the changing attitude toward love and the individualism emergent in Hellenism, even if the critical tools for assessing this were not yet available. His analysis of the extant novels, value judgments aside, is excellent, and his eye for detail has not been surpassed.

25. Schwartz, *Fünf Vorträge*, 147.

26. Livy will provide some examples, as will Josephus, as demonstrated by Braun (*Griech. Roman*).

27. Perry denounces all evolutionary schemes applied to literature (*Ancient Romances*, 3–43, esp. 37).

28. Note Schwartz's treatment of the couple, suicide, and sentimental love (*Fünf Vorträge*, 62–65).

29. Thiele, "Zum griechischen Roman." See also Barwick, "Gliederung"; Kerenyi, *Griech.-orient. Romanliteratur*, 18–20. Historiography has been judged primary by Chassang, Calderini, Rattenbury, Ludvikovsky, and others. See lists in Ludvikovsky, *Recky Roman*, 149; Trenkner, *The Greek Novella*, 180 n. 2; Reardon, "The Greek Novel," 295 n. 11. It is now generally accepted, albeit without emphasis upon "degeneration."

30. See also p. 134 n. 35 above.

31. For Rohde's views on the novella and novel, see *Der griech. Roman*, 5–8, 583 (1974). See also Schissel, *Entwicklungsgeschichte*, 1–12; Braun, *History and Romance*, 44–104; Trenkner, *The Greek Novella;* Helm, *Antike Roman*, 10; Wehrli, "Einheit."

32. Lavagnini, *Studi*. The 1950 reprint reaffirms his views (xi, 199–205). Lavagnini worked with local legends preserved, he presumed, in Parthenius and fragments like Callimachus's tale of Acontius and Cydippe (*Aetia* 3, frags. 67–75).

33. Lavagnini, *Studi*, 25.

34. Lavagnini discussed the "oriental" material (ibid., 57–80). He noted (p. 201) that in 1938, Braun (*History and Romance*) did not credit him with propounding this theory.

35. Perry was enthusiastic in his 1923 review of Lavagnini. *Ancient Romances* (42–43) presents Perry's mature reflections, with recognition of indebtedness (p. 33). See Reardon, *Courants littéraires*, 316–17, for a recent assessment of Lavagnini's contribution.

36. Ludvikovsky, *Recky Roman*. I rely upon the French summary. Perry finds Ludvikovsky essentially correct but inclined toward superficiality (*Ancient Romances*, 34–43).

37. Weil, "La Ninopédie." *La Ninopédie* was his designation for the novel about Ninus.

38. Despite disapproval, demand was sufficient to enable a reissue of Kerenyi's *Griech.-orient. Romanliteratur* in 1962.

39. A striking example is the "empty tomb" scene in Chariton 3.3.1–3.

40. Nock, *Essays* 1:169–76. For cautious approval, see Hadas, *Hellenistic Culture*, 181; idem, *Three Greek Romances*, ix. For incautious disapproval, see Perry, *Ancient Romances*, 336 n. 17. For Reardon's reaction, see below. Kerenyi's own comments may be found in *Griech.-orient. Romanliteratur*, 289–96.

41. Kerenyi, "Die Papyri."

42. E.g., Reardon, *Courants littéraires*, 343; Hägg, *The Novel in Antiquity*, 90; Altheim, *Literatur und Gesellschaft*.

43. Perry (*Ancient Romances*, 32, 336 n. 17) had no interest in Altheim.

44. Reardon has a criticism of details, with admiration of his basic idea (*Courants littéraires*, 321).

45. Kerenyi (*Antike Roman*, 9–10) regarded Merkelbach's method (*Roman und Mysterium*) as "oversimplified." Burchard tries to compare the two by way of form and redaction criticism (*Dreizehnte Zeuge*, 63 n. 46).

46. For a serious view of Merkelbach, see Turcan, "Le Roman 'Initiatique.'" Perry would do no more than refer to M. Smith's vitriolic review, 336 n. 17. Chalk ("Mystery Cults") received the work favorably. See Merkelbach's studies of Apuleius and Longus (*Roman und Mysterium*, 1–90, 192–224).

47. Merkelbach on Chariton (*Roman und Mysterium*, 339–40).

48. In Perry, "Chariton and His Romance."

49. Perry, *Ancient Romances*, 11.

50. Ibid., 18–30.

51. Ibid., 175.

52. Ibid., 3–43.

53. Ibid., 87. See also p. 137 below.

54. Ibid., 40.

55. Ibid., 85. In his italicized definition (pp. 44–45) Perry includes "spiritual edification," which in his view must somehow differ from instruction.

56. Ibid., 85. Heliodorus receives kindred judgment (pp. 107–8).

57. Ibid. "All Greek romances, except . . . comic . . . are what would be called today historical novels" (p. 78). "The principal virtue of Chariton's novel, apart from adventure . . . lay in its sentimental idealism, its *inner* force, which was meant for the edification of naive readers. . ." (p. 99). See also p. 5. This is not quite true. Achilles Tatius and Longus claim to interpret paintings, thus eluding the charge of false history.

58. Petronius appears to be Epicurean in sentiment, but the *Satyricon* is no ideal novel for the edification of teenagers, students, and housewives.

59. There is more on these clichés below, p. 103.

60. Reardon's manuscript for *Courants littéraires* (1971) was apparently complete before Perry's *Ancient Romances* appeared in 1967. He thus responds primarily to Perry's "Chariton and His Romance," of 1930. Direct dialogue with *Ancient Romances* is essentially confined to his footnotes.

61. Reardon, *Courants littéraires*, 322.

62. Therefore the impassioned declarations that life without x is impossible. One cannot exist without the other because without the other the identity of each is incomplete. Apuleius's Latin novel explores a similar theme, by way of marriage symbolism in the tale of Cupid and Psyche, religiously in the case of Lucius.

63. Reardon, *Courants littéraires*, 343–45. See pp. 390–99 for Reardon's thorough critique of Merkelbach.

64. For a possible Amenophis novel, see *P. Oxy.* 3011.

65. The concluding inferences are mine, not Reardon's.

66. See my 1985 review of Anderson's *Eros Sophistes*.

67. See also Anderson's *Studies in Lucian's Comic Fiction*. Forthcoming works on Petronius, Apollonius of Tyana, and Iamblichus are promised in the preface to *Ancient Fiction*, v–vi.

68. Anderson's hesitation at accepting a religious interpretation of Apuleius may reflect his bias against religion. See *Ancient Fiction*, 76, 198–207; *Eros Sophistes*, 87–90.

69. Hägg's *Novel in Antiquity* is a revision in English of a work first issued in Swedish, *Den antika Romanen* (1980).

70. I.e., in the Acta of the International Conference on the Novel, in *EA*.

71. So Anderson, "The Greek Novel," *EA* 169.

72. Among writings not mentioned above, Haight's three volumes of *Essays on Ancient Romances* and her English translation of the A-text of the *Alexander Romance* have also helped shape my views. Haight approached the subject with enthusiasm and charm, if not consistent depth. Scobie's two volumes of essays (*Aspects; More Essays*) on the ancient romance contain much that is provocative. Giagrande has restated a case for viewing love poetry as fundamental, in his article "On the Origins of Greek Romance." Wehrli's "Einheit" is very suggestive. The various contributions of F. Zimmermann are valuable, and the articles of Reardon summarize the Greek novel or supplement his major work. Helpful surveys: Lesky, *History*, 857–71; Wilamowitz-Moellendorf, *Griech.-lat. Literatur*, 184–191, 257–263; Wendland, "Der Roman," in *Einleitung* 1:240–42.

The introductions to various editions and translations, and the monographs and commentaries upon individual novels, are too numerous to list but have been of great utility. Whatever deficiencies Twayne's World Authors' Series may have in other regards, its works on ancient novels (Corbett, McCulloh, Sanday, Schmeling) are of good quality. K. Plepelits's contributions to the series Bibliothek der Griechischen Literatur, produced by Hiersemann, are excellent.

The bibliography on Latin novels is relatively immense. Walsh offers a solid introduction in *The Roman Novel*. For a survey of recent work on Petronius, see Sullivan, "Petron." On Apuleius, see Tatum, *Apuleius*, as well as *Aspects of the Golden Ass*, ed. Hijmans and van der Paardt.

General studies of the novel can broaden critical horizons, reveal parallel developments, and suggest direct influence. The growth of specialization leaves few willing or able to venture beyond a limited focus. The older works of Wolff (*Greek Romances*) and Dunlop (*History of Prose Fiction*) remain useful for analysis of content and technique. Some standard histories, like Stevenson's *The English Novel* (1–54) and Warren's *History of the Novel* (1–81), briefly survey earlier works as background to their subject. Watt sees no direct connection between ancient and later novels, but he presents this as an assertion rather than an argument (*The Rise of the Novel*). Heiserman, although not a classicist, dares to read ancient novels through eyes formed by modern critical methods. Classically oriented students of the ancient novel have begun to experiment with modern methods. Hägg's *Narrative Technique* reveals interesting possibilities. Auerbach's *Mimesis* is a study of remarkable breadth long admired by those who have little time for reading much literary criticism. More recently the writings of Bakhtin have begun to appear in English (*The Dialogic Imagination*). The breadth of Bakhtin's erudition eclipses even that of Auerbach. Bakhtin's phenomenological perspective upon the novel includes many remarkable insights expressed in opaque prose. Few reflect the combination of so wide a mastery of material and so profound a concept of method.

Other general studies of fiction that have contributed to my point of view include Forster, *Aspects of the Novel;* Frye, *Anatomy of Criticism;* Booth, *The Rhetoric of Fiction* (on which see also Comstock, "Wayne C. Booth, Pluralist"). Application of contemporary literary criticism to biblical texts is an academic growth industry. One relevant example treating material somewhat similar to Acts is Culpepper's *Anatomy of the Fourth Gospel.*

73. Perhaps the first to propose an oriental background to the Greek novel was Huet in 1671 (*Traité de l'origine des romans*). Rohde discussed the notion in *Der griech. Roman,* 4–5, 38–55, 183–84, 578–601. Braun (*History and Romance*) is a full-fledged proponent, supported by Hengel (*Judaism and Hellenism* 1:112). See also Kerenyi, *Griech.-orient. Romanliteratur;* Weinreich, *Griech. Liebesroman,* 27; Grimal, *Romans,* 97; Lesky, *History,* 858. Barns ("Egypt and the Greek Romance") is receiving increasing approval. And the acceptance of oriental sources by Reardon, Anderson, and Hägg indicates the trend toward a consensus.

74. Thus, e.g., Kerenyi, *Griech.-orient. Romanliteratur,* 13; Weinreich, *Griech. Liebesroman,* 30; Scobie, *More Essays,* 3; and many others, esp. Perry, *Ancient Romances,* 46–47.

75. So Gual ("Le roman grec," *EA* 99–105), who takes note of *mythos, drama, historia, diēgema, plasma, pathos, syntagma.* Philostratus's *Letter* 66 uses *logoi* (of Chariton, probably the novelist). Julian's *Letter* 89, 301b, writes of *historias eidos* and *erotikai hypotheses.* Macrobius's *Commentary on the Dream of Scipio* 1.2.8 speaks of *argumenta fictis causibus.* Suidas uses the term *historikos* for novelists. Literature: Rohde, *Der griech. Roman,* 350 (376) n. 3; Perry, *Ancient Romances,* 74–75.

76. So Hägg, *The Novel in Antiquity,* 101–3.

77. Initiation scenes are prominent in the fragments of *Iolaus, Lollianus,* and *Monica* (if the last is not some sort of amusing hoax), not to mention Petronius.

78. Seaford, *Pompeii,* 42–43.

79. The Antiochene wall illustrations of *Parthenope* and *Ninus* come to mind, on which see the comments of Mähler in "Metiochus-Parthenope," 1–2, 19. See also Levin, "To Whom Did the Ancient Novelists Address Themselves?" 29. Perhaps some of the Pompeian frescoes illustrate novels rather than classical myth. This practice still would be a slight cultural cut above Trimalchio, Petronius 29.9.

80. For an alternative approach, see Praeder, "Luke-Acts and the Ancient Novel"; idem, "Narrative Voyage."

81. Therefore a biological model is more valid than Perry allows (*Ancient Romances,* 12).

82. See Hägg, *The Novel in Antiquity,* 4. Schmeling (*Xenophon of Ephesus,* 111) describes the novel as representative of the real world, the romance as illustrative of the real world. Frye discusses "romance" both as "mode" and as "form" (*Anatomy,* 33, 304–7). Romance modality depicts a world "in which the ordinary laws of nature are slightly suspended" and the heroes are superior in degree (not kind) to ordinary people (p. 33). The essential formal difference "lies in the concept of characterization. The Romancer does not attempt to create 'real people' so much as stylized figures" (p. 304). These observations are quite apt. Because in everyday modern parlance "romance" is derogatory, I prefer to use "novel" as a general term, recognizing that most ancient novels are "romances" in Frye's sense.

83. "Near-novel" was a category at the International Conference on the Ancient

Novel in 1976 (see *EA*), and Cizek speaks of "prenovels," a type he sees as ongoing, in "Les structures du roman antique," *EA* 106–28.

84. The elder Pliny *Natural History* pref. 6.

85. Praeder, "Luke-Acts and the Ancient Novel," 279.

86. Since the earliest known novels were didactic or historical, the efforts to exclude them from consideration only further complicate the task of tracing the history of the genre.

87. These three complementary approaches resemble the major theories advanced to account for the novel's origins.

88. For example, Tobit, *Joseph and Asenath*, and Esther, brief enough to be short stories, but too complex in structure.

89. The two most recent versions of *The Life of Apollonius of Tyana*, those of Hadas and Smith (1965) and Bowersock and Jones (1970), are summary abridgments.

90. So Auerbach, *Mimesis*, 20–66.

91. See pp. 12–13 above.

92. On the use of biographical titles see p. 84 above.

93. Older traditions were not abolished, witness the Homeric quality of Alexander's deeds in the *Alexander Romance*, and Chaireas's imitation of Alexander in Chariton. Ludvikovsky stresses the shift toward new heroic models in *Recky Roman*. I use "transcendent" as an alternative to the derogatory "escapist." Schmeling refers to the adjustments for survival required by Hellenism and points out that classical heroes refused to bend and were tragically shattered, whereas the heroes of the novels are willing to bend but do not break (*Xenophon of Ephesus*, 122).

94. This definition is a revision of Perry (*Ancient Romances*, 44–45), who added "private capacities and . . . interests and emotions," thereby excluding historical and religious novels.

95. Discussed above, pp. 77–81.

96. See the remarks of Cawelti, *Adventure*, 9, quoting an essay by R. Warshow.

97. On sea travel as a symbol, see Reardon, *Courants littéraires*, 342–43. The sea, and travel thereupon, are also potent symbols in Scripture, including such NT passages as Mark 4:35–41; 6:45–52.

98. See also the discussion of "secularized aretalogy," pp. 93–95 above.

99. Such miscellanies are typical of the Second Sophistic. A.T. *Ap. Ty.* and Heliodorus delight in diversions on various topics.

100. Reardon, "Second Sophistic and the Novel"; Anderson, *Eros Sophistes;* and a number of the contributors to *EA*.

101. Reardon ("The Greek Novel," 296) criticized Perry for generalizing the sentimental quality that is most marked in Chariton. Henry Fielding observed, "There are a set of religious, or rather moral writers, who teach that virtue is the certain road to happiness, and vice to misery, in this world. A very wholesome and comfortable doctrine, and to which we have but one objection, namely, that it is not true" (*Tom Jones*, preface to book 15).

102. See Anderson, *Eros Sophistes.*

103. On this matter Rohde and Perry were in error. *Iolaus* was probably comic, as was *Lollianus*. Iamblichus and Antonius Diogenes may well have exceeded the fully surviving romantic novels in realism. The moral bias of Byzantine and medieval Christians was a major factor in the transmission of novels. (As recently as 1956 an expurgated version of Longus was issued [replaced by an unexpurgated edition in 1968] in the Penguin Classics series.)

104. See Anderson, *Ancient Fiction*, 43–61.

105. See Kerenyi, *Griech.-orient. Romanliteratur*. Books could, of course, be published in readings, but as books rather than "living" oral genres. The same eras witnessed the rise of "book" religions, including Judaism, Christianity, Manicheism, and Islam.

106. Exceptions support the principle. The stage endured, but without enduring new works and with the tendency to transform, abridge, excerpt, and replace the old. The largest edifices were devoted to games and races rather than to drama.

107. Perry makes an analogy to the history of English literature (*Ancient Romances*, 44–79).

108. Heisermann says that the romance is a "luxury of . . . a state of society, when boundaries of exploitation and therefore of interesting danger, are almost infinite" (*The Novel*, 115). On boundary and miracle, see Theissen, *Miracle Stories*.

109. Consult a NT concordance under *dynamis* and *exousia*. For non-Christian material, see Nock, *Essays* 1:34–45; Nilsson, *Greek Piety*, 103–10.

110. See Revelation 21—22 and the commentaries on relevant verses. Parallels from Lucian are *A True Story* 2.11–16 (parodies of utopian works common enough to arouse his ire).

111. Even in Chariton, Callirhoe deals with each of her husbands, deceiving Chaireas about her communication with Dionysios. Longus plays with the readers' feelings, leading them to spend the first part of the book eager that the children will discover sex and the second part fearful that they will not postpone its consummation.

112. Bilbo reflects on the merits of signing off with "They all lived happily ever after." "It is," he says, "a good ending, and none the worse for having been used before" (J. R. R. Tolkien, *The Fellowship of the Ring* [Ballantine ed.], 353).

113. Cf. the syncretistic method of assimilation and acculturation used in texts such as the Isis aretalogies. On the process of character change see Perry's review of Braun's *History and Romance*.

114. Suetonius diplomatically describes Augustus's family as *Velitris praecipuam* (prominent at Velitrae; *Augustus* 1). Syme is more blunt: "The grandson of a small-town banker" (*Roman Revolution*, 229). The former slaves to whom I refer are the freedmen of Ptolemaic Egypt and the early empire who held major positions in the state. See my remarks in "Wisdom and Power" on the social status of former slaves.

115. Compare current feminist critique of the paperback romances produced in immense quantities for mainly female readers.

116. The diffusion of the *Alexander Romance* is the most spectacular example. Note also the profusion of romantic-novel literature in various languages.

117. Perry blames the novel's failure to flourish on the Christianization of the empire (*Ancient Romances*, 124). Gibbon might be pleased, but the large-scale production of Christian entertainment literature must be taken into account. The International Conference on the Ancient Novel (1966) included a number of contributions on the continuation of the novel in various manifestations. When hagiography became stagnant and unappealing, humanist Byzantines revived the composition of romantic fiction.

118. Cizek's "Les structures du roman antique" (*EA* 106–28) is a full paper, not an abstract.

119. Praeder, "Luke-Acts and the Ancient Novel." It is difficult for me to understand how Praeder can infer that I seek to define the genre on the basis of typical features alone.

120. "Sequential" is subject to qualification, as Praeder admits (ibid., 291 n. 14), with a reference to Heliodorus. Novels may treat of a group or people, *3 Maccabees* being an example.

121. See p. 134 below.

122. This definition is that of Heisermann (*The Novel*, 59), to whose reflections I am indebted.

5. HISTORICAL NOVELS:
PAGAN, JEWISH, AND CHRISTIAN

1. Cicero speaks of "that Cyrus whom Xenophon portrayed not with historical fidelity but for establishing an image of just government" (Cyrus ille a Xenophonte non ad historiae fidem scriptus sed ad effigiem iusti imperi, *Letter to Quintus* 1.1.23). See also Diogenes Laertius 3.34 (with reference to Plato *Laws* 694–95, apparently); Dionysius of Halicarnassus *Letter to Pompeius* 4.

2. Antisthenes also wrote about Cyrus, according to Diogenes Laertius 6.16. Heracles was a favorite subject for such expositions.

3. The most noted is the love story about Araspas and Pantheia. On its moralism, see Breitenbach, "Xenophonon von Athen," 1717–18.

4. So Onesicrates, according to Diogenes Laertius 6.84.

5. Braun (*History and Romance*, 5) also posited a *Manes Romance*, based upon Plutarch *Isis and Osiris* 24. Ecology dictates the prominence of Egyptian evidence.

6. Only the *Alexander Romance* is not fragmentary, and the existing editions are perhaps centuries removed from the first. The Ninus texts are fragmentary, and the existence of an underlying "national romance" is hypothetical.

7. Patriotic literature of one culture may be preserved by others. The Arthurian saga derives from Romano-British resistance to English invaders but lived on to acquire an erotic element as a romance written in French. Arthur ultimately became a folk hero of the very English whose ancestors he had fought!

8. Perry presumes that "Hellenistic individualism" ousted oriental patriotism and left room for love (*Ancient Romances*), but the *Alexander Romance* includes his love for Roxanne, and Tobit contains a love story without abandoning its didactic quality. Perry dates Ninus at ca. 100 B.C.E., following Rattenbury.

9. The resurgence of Parthia might have given impetus to revision of the material. On oriental resistance to Hellenistic and Roman rule see Eddy, *The King Is Dead*; MacMullen, *Enemies of the Roman Order*, 192–242.

10. Dedications: Antonius Diogenes; *Aristeas* (and Acts). Concocted sources: *Ap. Ty.* (presumably); Antonius Diogenes; and the various forged letters and decrees, such as those in Esther. X. E. and *Ap. Tyre* make use of inscriptions to create an illusion of reality. *3 Maccabees* opens with an apparently credible historical narrative (which it is; see *The Third and Fourth Books of Maccabees*, ed. Hadas, 16–17). The incipits of Esther, Judith, and *Joseph and Asenath* precisely follow the model of later biblical historians. *Artapanus* offers an amphiboly, two different accounts of the Red Sea crossing (436b), one rational, the other miraculous, thus aping historiographical distance. This is all hocus-pocus, as is *Aristeas's* polemic against romancers (322; see *The Third and Fourth Books of Maccabees*, ed. Hadas, 51–62).

11. Petronius 29.9. The Campanian villas give numerous examples of Homeric scenes, none of games.

12. Apocalyptic writings are likely to oppose assimilation very strenuously. A kind

of dual loyalty is apparent in many American citizens whose fondness for the homeland of their ancestors in no way mitigates their superpatriotism.

13. On these works, all of which, save the allegedly epitomized 2 Maccabees, are
fragmentary, see now the edition of Holladay, *Fragments* 1:189–243, with bibliography there and in idem, *Theios Aner*, 199–200. The following relies upon *Theios Aner*,
199–232; Freudenthal, *Hell. Studien*, 143–74; Braun, *History and Romance*, 26–31,
99–102; Hadas, *Hellenistic Culture*, 96–98; Georgi, *Die Gegner*, 148–62; Collins
and Poehlmann, "Artapanus"; Tiede, *Charismatic Figure*, 146–77; and the works of
Schürer, Schwartz, Wendland, Heinemann, Weinreich, Altheim, Dalbert, Hengel.
Most regard Artapanus as a novel. Holladay discusses the genre and is reluctant to label it history (*Theios Aner*, 215–18). For a very recent survey, see Attridge, "Historiography," in Stone, CRINT 2/2:166–68.

14. So Hadas, *Hellenistic Culture*, 96.

15. As in *T. Joseph* 3–9 and Josephus *Antiquities* 2.39–59, on which see Braun,
History and Romance; Pervo, "Testament of Joseph and Greek Romance." Since Polyhistor had already summarized Joseph's rise to power from Demetrius (424d), he
avoided repetition.

16. On parallels with Sesostris (= Sesonchosis), see Tiede, *Charismatic Figure*,
146–77. Artapanus could have used a similar source, of course, and not a novel alone.

17. Jealousy: Artapanus 432d. Oath and ambush: 434a, 433c. Cf. Acts 22:12–24;
25:1–12; *Joseph and Asenath* 26–29.

18. By means of "elephantiasis," the first known case, thus making him a *protos
heuretes* (discoverer) of sorts.

19. Miracles exhibit the power of the divine name (Artapanus 434c–35a). For a
comparison of Artapanus with the biblical account, see Tiede, *Charismatic Figure*,
170–76.

20. As Holladay observes in *Theios Aner*, 227–28.

21. Such as reluctance to accept his call; Artapanus 434c vs. Exod. 3:1—4:17.

22. Tiede emphasizes this aspect in *Charismatic Figure*.

23. Artapanus 434c gives a general reference to the people's suffering, and 433a requires Jews to wear special garments—of linen! The building program becomes the
task of Moses' militia, composed mainly of Jewish peasants (433a).

24. It is not appropriate to object that Alexander Polyhistor accepted Artapanus as a
source. Universal historians made happy use of legendary, even mythic, material if
they chose. See the rationale of Diodorus, bk. 4, pref. Eusebius made use of the
Apoc. Acts as sources (Streeter, *Primitive Church*, 7), and Augustine believed that
Apuleius related his own actual transformation into an ass (*City of God* 18.18).

25. The most famous reservations are Origen's criticism of Susanna and Jerome's
questions about a number of deuterocanonical/apocryphal writings. Antiquity also
witnessed criticism of the Apoc. Acts.

26. The differences between the MSS. and versions of many of these works reflect a plurality of editions rather than simple MS. "variations."

27. Mark 4:35–41 shows considerable influence from the text of Jonah. See Cope,
Matthew, 96–98.

28. Works like the *Genesis Apocryphon, Jubilees*, various lives of the prophets, and
the *Martyrdom of Isaiah* should not be overlooked. Not all of these are "novels." For
the present purpose I include novellas, like Bel et Draco, and collections of novellas,
as in Daniel 1—6.

29. Hengel conjectures the existence of a "Tobiad romance" (*Judaism and Hellenism*, 88, n. 237). The Tobiad material in Josephus *Antiquities* 12.158–236 is filled with plots, sex, status issues, and various motifs found in such fiction. The material from Josephus surveyed by Braun (*Griech. Roman*) suggests that other novels existed.

30. For understanding of the sapiential novel I am indebted to John Strugnell's lectures on intertestamental literature, Harvard Univ., 1972. In 1976 I attempted to link *Joseph and Asenath* with that tradition, in "Joseph of Asenath and the Greek Novel." Secondary literature on these relatively neglected writings has been recently enhanced by the appearance of the Anchor Bible and the Jüdische Schriften aus hellenistischer Zeit series, as well as *The Old Testament Pseudepigrapha*, ed. Charlesworth.

31. For a survey see Nicklesburg, *Jewish Literature*, 19–42, 105–9, 169–75, 258–64. Eissfeldt (whose introductions are generally useful) has little use for the chauvinism of Esther and Judith (*Old Testament*, 512, 587). He would uphold Luther's condemnation of Esther as normative for Christians.

Jewish, like romantic, novels tended to prefer the Persian period. In both cases this is not only nostalgic but provides opportunity for "coded" criticism of the ruling power. *3 Maccabees* and *Aristeas* are more or less contemporary in setting. There is no "rule" that ancient fiction had to restrict itself to the distant past.

32. Even Tobit, Esther, and Judith have their basis in legend or myth. The Esther/Mordecai Ishtar/Marduk correspondence is well known. Did the Tobiads lend their name to Tobit?

33. See n. 10 of the present chap.

34. Canonical questions intervene. Protestant rejection of Judith and Tobit has resulted in little opposition to viewing them as novels. Esther, however, has been staunchly defended, on the (unstated) grounds that God will not inspire fiction.

35. Collections of proverbs: *Ahikar* 8.1–41 (taught to the tune of a hickory stick); Tobit 4:5–21; 12:6–10. Through its influence upon both Tobit and the *Life of Aesop*, *Ahikar* is an ancestor of both Jewish and Greek popular novels.

36. Esther and *3 Maccabees* deal with calendar reform (the addition of a festival), as does *Jubilees* (lunar versus solar controversy). The problem of the relationship between Esther and *3 Maccabees* is notorious. *Aristeas* defends the LXX.

37. On the significance of the love theme in Jewish writings, see Stiehl in Altheim and Stiehl, *Aramäische Sprache*, 200. Correspondences between *Joseph and Asenath* and romantic novels are given by Philonenko (*Joseph et Asenath*, 43–48) and throughout his commentary.

38. This appears to be the implicit view of SOEDER and those who follow her, albeit with critical reservations: Vielhauer, *Geschichte*, 715–16; Plümacher, "Apokryphe Apostelakten"; and the contributors to *LAaa*.

39. See p. 8 above.

40. "Aretalogy," a hotly debated subject, does, to be sure, describe in general the religio-historical character of the Apoc. Acts but is probably not suitable to designate a genre. As a catchall for religious propaganda of missionary religions, the word is applied to many genres, including hymns, miracle stories, and accounts of conversions. It is also used to designate religious or philosophical biographies. The latter is controverted. See Tiede, *Charismatic Figure*; Georgi, *Die Gegner*; Holladay, *Theios Aner*; Hadas and Smith, *Heroes and Gods*—the last with texts and discussions of earlier literature.

Praxeis likewise comprehends a number of genres describing the deeds of gods, heroes, and humans. The term is in general an accurate description of the structure of the Apoc. Acts but is not easily restricted to a single genre. See SCHNEIDER 1:74; and the basic discussions in Wikenhauser, *Apostelgeschichte*, 94–112; Pfister, *NTA* 2:163–65; Vielhauer, *Geschichte*, 713–18; Plümacher, "Apokryphe Apostelakten," 54–65; Kaestli, "Les principales orientations," *LAaa* 57–67.

41. Both Kerenyi and Zimmermann, in their critical reviews of Soeder, demonstrate that the Apoc. Acts are not romantic novels. This position, shared by SOEDER (p. 216), does not prove that they are not historical novels. See also Rattenbury's review of Helm's *Antike Roman*.

42. Recent research, exemplified by the Suisse Romande group responsible for major studies and new editions of the Apoc. Acts, lays great stress upon the differences between and among the writings.

43. *NTA* 2:174.

44. MacMullen, *Paganism*, 95–97; idem, *Christianizing the Roman Empire*.

45. *NTA* 2:172.

46. However disappointing to some theologians, popular theology was far more determinative for the history of Christian doctrine than learned formulations. See Carpenter, *Popular Christianity;* von Harnack, *A History of Dogma* 1:150–222; 4:268–350.

47. On the *Acts of Thomas*, see Bornkamm, *NTA* 2:425–41, and the literature discussed there, as well as brief discussions in Vielhauer, *Geschichte*, 710–13; Plümacher, "Apokryphe Apostelakten"; *LAaa*.

48. On the *Acts of Andrew*, see Hornschuh, *NTA* 2:392–94; J.-M. Prieur, "La figure de l'apôtre," *LAaa* 121–39. See also references in n. 47 above.

49. The speeches in *Acts of Andrew* are far more intellectual in tone than even the Areopagus address of Acts 17. I refer to Hornschuh's reconstruction of the martyrdom, *NTA* 2:416–23.

50. For a reconstruction of the early history of Johannine theology, see R. E. Brown's *Epistles of John* and his references. For the debate on the theology of the *Acts of John*, see *NTA* 2:212–14 (Schäferdiek); and Junod and Kaestli, *Acta Iohannis* 2:679–702.

51. Notably Schneemelcher, *NTA* 2:259–75.

52. *Acts of Peter* 4 (*NTA* 2:283).

53. Cf. Acts 20:18–35; 8:4ff. Cf. also the Pastorals, e.g., 1 Tim. 4:1–10. See Koester's comments, in *Trajectories*, 156–57.

54. *NTA* 2:272–75.

55. Schneemelcher, *NTA* 2:322–51, esp. 350.

56. Bousset's classic history of the development of Christology placed the main burden upon popular piety and worship (*Kyrios Christos*, 282–384).

57. Tertullian's famous remarks are in *On Baptism* 17. Schneemelcher accepts this criticism as theological (*NTA* 2:373). To speak of *a* theology of the *Acts of Paul* is an oversimplification, since there appear to have been different editions of it with different orientations (Kasser, "Acta-Pauli, 1959"). The best-preserved and longest extant portions contained in *P. Ham* and *P. Heid* are in view here, for these provide the best support to Schneemelcher's assertions.

58. On the polemical character of the *Acts of Paul*, see also Bauer, *Orthodoxy and Heresy*, 39–42, 100–102; and the literature in n. 47 above.

59. *NTA* 2:273.

60. For Schneemelcher this is a deficit (*NTA* 2:349), but why he needs to observe that they are not treatises is not clear, since they make no such claims.

61. Thus the lengthy survey of Fitzmyer finds a certain lack of consistency (*Luke* 1:143–258). See my 1984 review of Fitzmyer on this point. Bousset's remarks about *1 Clement* have much in common with the theology of Luke (*Kyrios Christos*, 367–82).

62. Schneemelcher, *NTA* 2:350–51.

63. On use of Paul's letters, see the notes in C. Schmidt's edition of the *Acta Pauli*, and the speech discussed by Kasser ("Acta Pauli, 1959," 55–56).

64. Schneemelcher and Schäferdiek, *NTA* 2:173.

65. To which group it is not likely that Schneemelcher and Schäferdiek would assign themselves. It is a sign of desperation when such scholars imply the normative character of Lukan theology. See *NTA* 2:167–88.

66. *NTA* 2:173–74. See also SOEDER, 74.

67. Achtemeier, "Jesus and the Disciples," 170. The entire paragraph is a good corrective to the generalizations of Schneemelcher and Schäferdiek, e.g., *NTA* 2:174.

68. As admitted by Schneemelcher and Schäferdiek, *NTA* 2:176.

69. For the *Acts of Paul*, see *Acta Pauli*, ed. C. Schmidt, 198–216. Detailed lists may be found in PERVO, 368–75.

70. *NTA* 2:174. Protection of her virginity is a constant need of Thecla, for which she receives continual divine assistance. See also the *Act of Peter* (*Nag Hammadi Library*, 475–77; BG 8502.4) for a combination of punishment miracle with protection of virginity (by paralysis, in this case a divine gift). See also the punishments in *Acts of Thomas* 8, 15–61; *Acts of John* 63–86, 113; *Acts of Peter* 2.15, 25.

71. *Acts of John* 68. See *NTA* 2:338–39 on the lion Paul baptized. Asses obey Thomas (39–40, 70, 74), and a serpent is featured in 30–33. See also Bieler, *Theios Aner*, 104–11; SOEDER, 110–11. See also the discussion below, p. 128.

72. Reconstructed from papyri in *NTA* 2:373–80.

73. Achtemeier ("Jesus and the Disciples," 168–70) and Poupon ("L'accusation de magie," *LAaa* 71–85) discuss magic in Apoc. Acts.

74. See the sampling of liturgical material in Quasten, *Patrology* 1:129–43; and the index entries of "baptism" and "eucharist" in *NTA*. Luke scarcely mentions officials of local communities, in contrast to Apoc. Acts. See the indexes to *AAA* under the Greek and Latin terms for "bishop," "deacon," and "presbyter."

75. At points Schneemelcher and Schäferdiek allow that the Apoc. Acts are edifying in intent. See *NTA* 2:176, 330. Schneemelcher ("Die Apostelgeschichte," 42–43) sees the *Acts of Paul* as edifying. Most would agree. Perry would have been astonished to learn they were *not* edifying, since this is why he despised them (*Ancient Romances*, 86).

76. Schneemelcher and Schäferdiek, *NTA* 2:174, expressing the then *communis opinio*.

77. Ibid. The authors do not specify whether it is the issue of the delay of the Parousia or Jewish-gentile relations to which these passages (Acts 5:15; 19:12) are subordinated.

78. Orthodox objections to the Apoc. Acts were on other grounds. Most patristic authorities had nothing but admiration for their enthusiastic commendation of continence.

79. Luke prefers celibacy, as indicated by his editing of Mark and Q, and his special emphases. Most telling is Luke 20:34 vs. Mark 12:25. Luke 18:29 adds "wife" to

the list of what was given up for the gospel's sake according to Mark 10:22. Luke 11:27–28 does not support the notion that woman's role is the production of babies. Luke alone lists marriage as a reason for not accepting the invitation to the banquet (14:20). Codex Bezae does not admire Luke's use of women and prefers to make them "wives" if possible, rather than missionaries. Celibacy accompanies women who prophesy: blessed Virgin Mary, Anna, Philip's four daughters. See also Cadbury, *The Making of Luke-Acts*, 272; Pervo, "Social and Religious Aspects of the Western Text," 235–40.

80. See the detailed treatment in SOEDER, 154–55, 90–148. On sex in the Apoc. Acts, see also Tissot, "Encratisme et Actes apocryphes," *LAaa* 109–19.

81. See Acts 17:1–15 on the problem of the view that only in Apoc. Acts do women converts lead to trouble.

82. Photius, who was properly attentive to such matters, gave Heliodorus high marks on sex, but did not approve of Iamblichus and found Achilles Tatius simply unacceptable. Rohde took Longus to task in *Griech. Roman*, 549–51. The fragments of *Lollianus* and *Iolaus* suggest that many of the more scabrous works disappeared. Some of the lacunas in Petronius may be due to censorship. A lacuna in Chariton might refer to a contemplated rape. Another confused place in the text coincides with Callirhoe in the bathtub. She, in a fit of pique, can refer to her husband's former boyfriends. On these textual questions, see the Budé edition of Chariton by Molinié (22–41). On changing views toward sex in late antiquity, see Dodds, *Pagan and Christian*, 32–33. One means for preserving novels was to claim that their authors had later repented and risen to episcopal dignity. This made their earlier works a valuable *Vorgeschichte*, like that in the *Confessions* of Augustine. M. Grant reports a more modern-sounding solution: monks prepared a pocket edition of Longus with the added protection of ecclesiastical writings on opening and closing leaves (*The Climax of Rome*, 126).

83. 1 Corinthians 5—7 and passages such as 1 Tim. 2:8–15 suggest that some interesting stories could have been told in both Luke's day and Paul's.

84. Callirhoe (Chariton) actually married another man. By the time of Heliodorus (4th cent. C.E.) one could write a pagan novel about a woman ashamed to have her arm bared, even when her life was at stake (Heliodorus 10.15).

85. Hagiography is replete with exhibition of women nude in the theater, threats of rape, and condemnation to brothels. Not all of this was fiction.

86. Talking animals: Num. 22:21–35; 2 Kings 2:24; Mark 1:13. An altar speaks in the vision of Rev. 16:7. The *Lausaic History* includes an animal story (23.4). For animals in hagiography, see Duckett, *Wandering Saints*, 15–16.

87. Aelian's *Historical Miscellanies* and *On Providence* contain a number of animal stories. The Pythagoras tradition includes a number of encounters with the animal world. Apollonius of Tyana is a friend and admirer of elephants and other species.

88. Fig tree: Mark 11:12–14, 20–26. Bugs: *Acts of John* 6.

89. The animal in *Acts of Thomas* symbolizes the human body; so Bornkamm, *NTA* 2:430; *Acts of Thomas* 68–81.

90. *Acts of Peter* 9–13.

91. The association between Paul's story and the tale of Androcles would readily occur.

92. Perhaps literary competition encouraged writers of Apoc. Acts. to publish something more remarkable and exciting than ever before. However distant from immediate participation in the Second Sophistic, the authors of the Apoc. Acts were

quite possibly influenced by some of its extravagances. Kaestli ("Les principales orientations," *LAaa* 62) criticizes Soeder's "teratological" category on the basis that it is mainly in later Apoc. Acts.

93. The Apoc. Acts are not altogether devoid of literary pretensions, on which Plümacher ("Apokryphe Apostelakten," 65–68) and Vielhauer (*Geschichte*, 700–703) make some useful observations.

94. *NTA* 2:172. Travel plays but a small role in the *Acts of Peter*. Are they therefore to be stricken from the list of *Apoc. Acts*?

95. Schneemelcher and Schäferdiek, *NTA* 2:169–72, with reference to the work of Dibelius, Conzelmann, and Haenchen on Acts.

96. *NTA* 2:170. Prieur's work on the *Acts of Andrew* indicates what may be discovered in this and other *Apoc. Acts*. See *LAaa* 121–39. When Vielhauer (*Geschichte*, 714), e.g., asserts that Acts and the Apoc. Acts differ in genre because the speeches in the latter do not mark historical turning points, he appears to mix categories. Such differences refer to theological rather than literary distinctions. Similarly, the contributors to *LAaa* 71–158, esp. Bovon ("La vie des apôtres," 141–58), speak of the apostles' playing essentially different roles. In the Apoc. Acts they function more as revealers than communicators of the message of Jesus. This is important, but it is not a sound basis for generic distinction. Moreover, in the only place in Acts where a sermon is preached to a purely pagan audience, Paul functions as the revealer of an unknown God: "That which you seek to worship despite your ignorance, that is what I am proclaiming to you" (Acts 17:23).

97. Ramsay, *St. Paul*, 21.

98. See p. 66 above.

99. See pp. 50–51 above.

100. Even Ramsay regarded Acts 1—5 as largely legendary (*St. Paul*, 367–72) and did not introduce them as evidence of Luke's historical acumen.

101. This is the position of Schneemelcher and Schäferdiek (*NTA* 2:172–74).

102. SOEDER, 188–215.

103. Note the Thecla material, in which Paul plays an often secondary and sometimes cowardly role, the stories of Mygdonia and others (*Acts of Thomas* 82–130), the episode of Drusiana and Callimachus (*Acts of John* 63–86), and the opening chaps. of the *Acts of Peter*.

104. On episodic technique in historians and Acts, see Plümacher, *Lukas als hellen. Schrift.*; on the Apoc. Acts, see idem, "Apocryphe Apostelakten," 66.

105. *The Travels of Barnabas* 1–2 (*AAA* 2/2:292) echoes Luke's preface. Note also the introduction to "Linus's" edition of Peter's martyrdom (*AAA* 1/1:1–2) and the synchronism in the *Acts of John* (*AAA* 1/1:151). Best of all is perhaps the incipit of the *Passion of St. Bartholomew*, imitating the opening of Caesar's *Gallic Wars*! The *Lausiac History* begins with the strongest claims for authenticity, claims few would now wish to endorse. On the use of the first person, see SOEDER, 211–14. *Acts of Thomas* begins with the first person, and it emerges in the *Acts of Peter* 4. See SOEDER for many examples; also Plümacher, "Apokryphe Apostelakten," 54.

106. Worship: A terse note in Acts 2:42; the unison, miracle-working prayer in 4:24–31; reference also to prayer in 13:1–3 and 15:30–31. Baptism is noted but not described, the references to imposition of hands created confusion for later Christians (e.g., 8:14–17; 19:1–7), and the Eucharist is alluded to only in passing at 2:32 (presumably); 20:7; and 27:35 (presumably). This is scanty compared with the detailed reports in various Apoc. Acts.

107. So Dibelius, 181. The major exception occurs in the early section, in the incident about Ananias and Sapphira.

108. Acts 11:19–21; 13:1; 15:1; 18:24–28. All but the last refer to Paul or Pauline issues.

109. Visitation: Acts 14:22, 41; 15:41; 20:2. On pastoral activity, see esp. 20:7–12 (miracle story); 20:17–35 (farewell address).

110. Acts 20:28 implies a pastoral role for *presbyteroi* (*post mortes apostolorum*), and aligns them with bishops, which is perhaps polemical. Acts 14:23 has Paul ordaining presbyters, a notion refuted by his letters. On the Seven, see p. 40 above. Luke may have cared for the office of deacon no more than for bishops and tried to bury both. Acts 13:1–3 mentions "prophets and teachers," almost certainly from a source. Here they emerge only to commission Paul and Barnabas. Agabus and Philip's daughters are also prophets but without indications of formal status.

111. Achtemeier ("Jesus and the Disciples," 172) notes the crowd's honoring of Peter as a god in *Acts of Peter* 29 and contrasts this with Acts 10:25–26, suggesting that in at least one case the Apoc. Acts blur the distinction between missionaries and the god they serve. He overlooks Acts 28:6, a similar incident. In neither case does the writer express approval. Presumably, the object of this motif is not to deify the missionaries but to show how (benighted) pagans would understand them within their own categories. The real exception is *Acts of Thomas*, wherein the apostle functions as a master recruiting disciples to follow him. They worship not him, however, but the god he serves. From the *theios aner* perspective humans can exhibit the divine. Luke 3:38 and Acts 17:28 portray humans as divine offspring (thus capable of manifesting the *theion*). In Gnosticism humans have within them divine substance that brings basic identity with god: thus the *Acts of Thomas*.

112. Lukan theology has been hotly debated since Conzelmann's *Theology of St. Luke*. See also Grässer, "Acta-Forschung," 51–66; Plümacher, "Lukas als griech. Historiker"; Fitzmyer, *Luke*, 143–258.

113. Cf. Koester, *Trajectories*, 153.

114. On magic in Luke and the other Synoptics, see Hull, *Hellenistic Magic*.

115. References to magic in Acts: 3:12 (probably); 8:6–24; 13:4–12; 19:18–20.

116. For surveys of the issue in the Apoc. Acts, see n. 73 above.

117. I refer to Thomas Costain's *The Silver Chalice*.

118. *NTA* 2:272–74; esp. 273.

119. The texts are Acts 8:6–24. See the comments of Georgi (*Die Gegner*, 211) on the context. For recent discussion on the theology of Simon, see Meeks, "Simon Magus," 137–42. See also Koester, *Introduction* 2:326.

120. Personal conflict and the like: Acts 6:1–6; 7:8–12; 15:36–39. Most charges are regarded as slander, of course. That Luke treats the question of Torah in detail reveals that this is one issue about which he has something to say. Jervell's essays in *Luke and the People of God* and *The Unknown Paul* are provocative discussions of this matter.

121. *Acts of Paul* 8 (*NTA* 2:373–77).

122. Schneemelcher and Schäferdiek, *NTA* 2:170.

123. Petersen, *Literary Criticism*, 83.

124. Lukan parallelism and repetition have been discussed since the days of the Tübingen school. Cadbury, Morgenthaler, Mattill, Petersen, and Talbert have been among the contributors. Talbert (*Literary Patterns*) and Radl (*Paulus und Jesus*) are the most ambitious in scope. Praeder ("Parallelism") is an important critical study.

125. Jewish examples include Tobit and Esther (on the latter, see Moore, *Esther,* 1–2). Blumenthal (*Formen and Motive*) probably exaggerated the situation in the Apoc. Acts. SOEDER (189–92, 196–200) is balanced. For the novels, see esp. Schissel von Fleschenberg, Hägg, Wolff, and Heiserman. The technique can be rather mechanical, as in the following examples from X. E., or highly sophisticated, as in the interrelationships established by Apuleius.

126. X. E. has been selected as a popular work that is typical and imitative.

127. X. E.'s efforts to achieve this parallelism can be strained to the point of absurdity (e.g., X. E. 2.13, 4.6). This suggests how important it was to him.

128. Not all novelists employed these techniques so woodenly. Chariton, e.g., devotes lengthy sections to each character in turn. Esther and the story of Paul and Thecla are examples of interlacement. See SOEDER, 196–97, and in general, 188–202.

129. In the debate over the Divine-Man (*Theios Aner*) phenomenon there are frequent objections to the creation of a *Gesampttypos*. These objections are valid. What the "epiphanies" in romantic novels help clarify is the expression in many forms of what is at basis a common longing for transfigured existence. See Ogle, "The Trance," for some detailed comparisons of erotic to religious ecstasy.

130. Examples of the devices referred to in these paragraphs may be found in chaps. 2 and 3 of this book. Kaestli describes the Apoc. Acts as an "original creation of Christianity" but hastens to say that they were constructed through combinations of various genres ("Les principales orientations," *LAaa* 67).

CONCLUSION

1. This emerges most clearly in the essays of Bakhtin's *The Dialogic Imagination*.

2. Perry, following a quote from Croce, labeled all creative work as sui generis (*Ancient Romances,* 18). Booth calls this point of view no more than a half-truth (*Rhetoric of Fiction,* 377).

3. Haenchen's lack of attention to the problem of genre and his skepticism about sources are not unrelated. For some suggestions about sources, see PERVO, 551–53.

4. Tertullian (*On Baptism* 17) alleged that the presbyter who had composed the *Acts of Paul* out of love for the apostle was deposed.

5. Schweizer observes that by telling stories Luke did what Jesus did by telling parables (*Luke,* 61). Crossan concludes *Four Other Gospels* with some thought-provoking remarks on the relation of parable to Gospel, fact to fiction. Because my study has concentrated upon the various Acts, I have not taken the genre of Luke into question, apart from noting some differences between Luke and Acts. "Biographical novel" may be an appropriate characterization of the Gospel type.

6. Apocalyptic and gnosis are the most obvious examples of the theological impetus toward resistance or withdrawal.

7. This should not be read as suggesting that Luke's program was essentially political or secular or that his eschatology was entirely this-worldly. His vision does often approximate that of the pre-apocalyptic prophets. See Tiede, *Prophecy and History*.

8. This should not be taken to imply that Luke invented the vision he shares. He is the earliest surviving Christian writer to give it detailed expression. This vision has many points of contact with that of the Jewish apologists described by Georgi in *The Opponents,* 83–151.

BIBLIOGRAPHY

1. EDITIONS AND TRANSLATIONS OF
ANCIENT PROSE FICTION AND
RELATED LITERATURE

Under the designation by which the work is most commonly described in the text there are typically listed at least one edition in the original and an English translation.

Achilles Tatius.
   Leucippe and Clitophon. Ed. E. Vilborg. Stockholm, 1955.
   Achilles Tatius. Trans. and ed. S. Gaselee. LCL. Cambridge: Harvard Univ. Press, 1969.
   Leukippe und Kleitophon. Trans., intro., and comm. K. Plepelits. BGL 11. Stuttgart, 1980.
Aesop, Life of.
   Aesopica I. Ed. B. E. Perry. Champaign: Univ. of Illinois Press, 1952.
   Aesop without Morals. Trans. L. W. Daly. New York: Thomas Yoseloff, 1961.
Alexander Romance.
   Historia Alexandri Magni. Vol. 1. Ed. G. (= W.) Kroll. Berlin, 1958. Edition of the A-text.
   The Life of Alexander of Macedon. Trans. E. Haight. New York: Longmans, Green & Co., 1955.
Apocryphal Acts.
   Acta Apostolorum Apocrypha. Ed. R. Lipsius and M. Bonnet. 2 vols. in 3. New York, 1972. This is the standard, although inadequate, edition of the major Acts.
   New Testament Apocrypha. Vol. 2. Trans. and ed. R. M. Wilson; ed. E. Hennecke and W. Schneemelcher. Philadelphia: Westminster Press, 1965. Trans., with intros., of the major Acts of the 2d cent.
   Acta Pauli. Ed. C. Schmidt. Hildesheim, 1965. Coptic.
   The Nag Hammadi Library. Ed. J. M. Robinson. San Francisco: Harper & Row, 1978.
   Praxeis Paulou. Ed. C. Schmidt. Hamburg, 1936. Greek.
   Acts of Xanthippe and Polyxena. In *Apocrypha Anecdota*, ed. M. R. James. Cambridge, 1893.
Apocryphal Old Testament.
   The Apocryphal Old Testament. Ed. H. F. D. Sparks. Oxford: At the Clarendon Press, 1984.
Apollonius of Tyana (Ap. Ty.).
   Heroes and Gods: Spiritual Biographies in Antiquity. Ed. M. Hadas and M. Smith.

New York: Harper & Row, 1965. Contains a summary of *The Life*.

Philostratus: The Life of Apollonius of Tyana. 2 vols. Trans. and ed. F. C. Conybeare. LCL. Cambridge: Harvard Univ. Press, 1912.

The Life of Apollonius. Trans. C. P. Jones; ed., abridg., and intro. G. W. Bowersock. Baltimore: Penguin Books, 1970.

Apollonius of Tyre (*Ap. Tyre*).

Historia Apollonii Regis Tyri. Ed. A. Riese. Leipzig, 1893.

Apollonius Prince of Tyre. Trans. P. Turner. London: Penguin Books, 1956.

Apuleius.

Metamorphoseon. Ed. R. Helm. Leipzig, 1968.

Les metamorphoses. Trans., ed., and intro. P. Valette. Paris, 1940.

The Golden Ass. Trans. J. Lindsay. Bloomington: Indiana Univ. Press, 1962.

Aristeas.

Aristeas to Philocrates. Trans., ed., intro., and comm. M. Hadas. New York: Harper & Bros., 1951.

Artapanus.

Fragments from Hellenistic Jewish Authors. Vol. 1. Trans. and ed. C. Holladay. Chico, Calif.: Scholars Press, 1983.

Chariton.

Charitonis Aphrodisiensis: De Chaerea et Callirhoe. Ed. W. Blake. Oxford, 1938.

Chariton's Chaereas and Callirhoe. Trans. W. Blake. Ann Arbor, 1939.

Chariton. Trans., ed., and intro. G. Molinié. Edition Budé. Paris, 1979.

Chariton von Aphrodisias Kallirhoe. Trans., ed., intro., and comm. K. Plepelits. BGL 6. Stuttgart, 1979.

Chion of Heraclea.

Chion of Heraclea. Trans., ed., intro., and comm. I. Düring. Göteborg, 1951.

Dares and Dictys.

Dictys Cretensis. Ed. W. Eisenhut. Leipzig, 1893.

Dares Phrygius. Ed. F. Meister. Leipzig, 1873.

The Trojan War. Trans. and intro. R. Frazer. Bloomington: Indiana Univ. Press, 1966.

Dio of Prusa *Oration 7, The Euboicus*.

Dio Chrysostom. Vol. 1. Trans. and ed. J. W. Cohoon. LCL. Cambridge: Harvard Univ. Press, 1932.

Diogenes Laertius.

Diogenes Laertius. 2 vols. Trans. R. D. Hicks. LCL. Cambridge: Harvard Univ. Press, 1925.

Esther.

Esther. Trans., intro., and comm. C. A. Moore. Anchor Bible. Garden City, N.Y.: Doubleday & Co., 1971.

Daniel, Esther, and Jeremiah: The Additions. Trans., intro., and comm. C. A. Moore. Anchor Bible. Garden City, N.Y.: Doubleday & Co., 1977.

Euripides.

Bacchae. Ed., intro., and comm. E. R. Dodds. New York and London: Oxford Univ. Press, 1960.

Fragments and Summaries.

Collections of Fragments:

Eroticorum Graecorum Fragmenta Papyracea. Ed. B. Lavagnini. Leipzig, 1922.

"Romance: The Greek Novel," by R. M. Rattenbury. In *New Chapters in the History of Greek Literature*, ed. J. Powell, 211–57. Oxford, 1933.

Griechische Roman-Papyri. Ed. F. Zimmermann. QSGKAM 2. Heidelberg, 1936.

Each of these is quite incomplete. Rattenbury does include some trans. For a (still incomplete) listing of publication of subsequently discovered fragments, see Hägg, *The Novel*, 238.

Summaries (Antonius Diogenes and Iamblichus): Photius. *Bibliothèque.* 2 vols. Trans. and ed. R. Henry. Paris, 1959–60.

Heliodorus.

Heliodori Aethiopica. Ed. A. Colonna. Rome, 1938.

Les éthiopiques. 3 vols. Trans. J. Maillon; ed. R. M. Rattenbury and T. Lumb. Paris, 1935–43.

An Ethiopian Story. Trans. W. Lamb. London, 1961.

Iamblichus.

Babyloniaca. Ed. E. Habrich. Leipzig, 1960.

Ignatius.

Les epîtres d'Ignace. Ed. P. Camelot. SC 10. Paris, 1951.

Joseph and Asenath.

Joseph et Asenath. Trans., ed., intro., and comm. M. Philonenko. Leiden: E. J. Brill, 1960.

Studia Patristica, I–II. Ed. P. Batiffol. Paris, 1889–90.

"Ein vorläufiger griechischer Text von Joseph und Asenath," by C. Burchard. *Dielheimer Blätter zum Alten Testament* 14 (1979): 2–53.

Joseph and Asenath. Trans. and intro. C. Burchard. In *The Old Testament Pseudepigrapha*, ed. J. Charlesworth, vol. 1. New York: Doubleday & Co., 1983.

Judith.

The Book of Judith. Trans., ed., intro., and comm. M. Enslin and S. Zeitlin. Leiden, 1972.

Juvenal.

The Satires of Juvenal. Trans. and ed. R. Humphries. Bloomington: Indiana Univ. Press, 1958.

Lollianus.

Die Phoinikaka des Lollianos. Trans., ed., intro., and comm. A. Henrichs. Bonn, 1972.

Longus.

Longos. Trans., ed., intro., and comm. O. Schoenberger. Berlin, 1973.

Daphnis et Chloe. Trans., ed., intro., and comm. G. Dalmeyda. Paris, 1934.

Daphnis and Chloe. Trans. P. Turner. Baltimore: Penguin Books, 1968.

Lucian.

Histoire vraie (A true story). Ed. and comm. F. Ollier. Paris, 1962.

Wie man Geschichte schreiben soll (How to write history; Quomodo historia conscribenda sit). Trans., ed., and comm. H. Homeyer. Munich, 1969.

Lucian. 8 vols. Vols. 1–5, trans. A. M. Harmon; vol. 6, trans. K. Kilburn; vols. 7 and 8, trans. M. D. Macleod. LCL. Cambridge: Harvard Univ. Press, 1913–67.

Maccabees.

The New Oxford Annotated Bible. New York: Oxford Univ. Press, 1977.

The Third and Fourth Books of Maccabees. Ed. Moses Hadas. New York: Harper & Row, 1953. Intro., Greek text with facing annotated trans.

Martyr Acts.
   Acts of the Christian Martyrs. Trans., ed., and intro. with notes H. A. Musurillo.
      Oxford: At the Clarendon Press, 1972.
   Acts of the Pagan Martyrs. Trans., ed., and intro. with notes H. A. Musurillo. Ox-
      ford: At the Clarendon Press, 1954.
Petronius.
   The Satiricon. Ed., intro., and comm. E. T. Sage and B. Gilleland. New York,
      1969.
   The Satyricon and the Fragments. Trans. and intro. with notes J. P. Sullivan. Balti-
      more: Penguin Books, 1974.
Pseudo-Clementines.
   Die Pseudo-Clementinen. Ed. B. Rehm and F. Paschke. Berlin, 1965.
      There is an antiquated version in the *Ante-Nicene Fathers*, vol. 8, and a partial
      trans., with intro., in *NTA*, vol. 2.
Secundus.
   Secundus the Silent Philosopher. Trans. and ed. with notes B. E. Perry. APA Mon
      22. Ithaca, N.Y.: Cornell Univ. Press, 1964.
Tobit.
   The Book of Tobit. Trans., ed., intro., and comm. F. Zimmermann. New York,
      1958.
Vergil.
   The Aeneid. Trans. Robert Fitzgerald. New York: Random House, 1983.
Xenophon of Ephesus (X. E.).
   Les ephésiaques. Trans., ed., and intro. with notes G. Dalmeyda. Paris, 1962.
   Xenophontis Ephesii Ephesiacorum Libri V. Ed. A. D. Papanikolaou. Leipzig, 1973.
   Three Greek Romances. Trans. M. Hadas. Garden City, N.Y.: Doubleday & Co.,
      1953.

                              2. OTHER WORKS

Abbott, F. F. "The Origin of the Realistic Romance among the Romans." *ClassPhil* 6
   (1911): 257–70.
Achtemeier, P. J. "Jesus and the Disciples as Miracle Workers in the Apocryphal
   New Testament." In *Aspects of Religious Propaganda*, ed. E. Schüssler Fiorenza,
   149–86. South Bend, Ind.: Univ. of Notre Dame Press, 1976.
Albright, W. F. Review of Braun, *History and Romance. AJP* 66 (1942): 100–104.
Altheim, F. *Literatur und Gesellschaft im ausgehenden Altertum.* Vol. 1. Halle, 1948.
Altheim, F., and R. Stiehl. *Die aramäische Sprache unter den Achimeniden.* Frankfurt
   am Main, 1963.
Aly, W. "Aretalogoi." *RESup* 6:13–15.
Anderson, G. *Ancient Fiction: The Novel in the Greco-Roman World.* Totowa, N.J.:
   Barnes & Noble, 1984.
———. *Eros Sophistes.* ACS 9. Chico, Calif.: Scholars Press, 1982.
———. "The Greek Novel." In *EA* 165–71.
———. *Studies in Lucian's Comic Fiction.* Mnemosyne Supplement 2. Leiden: E. J.
   Brill, 1976.
Aristotle. *Poetique.* Trans. and ed. J. Hardy. Paris, 1965.
Arrowsmith, W. "The Lively Conventions of Translation." In *The Craft and Context*

of Translation, ed. W. Arrowsmith and R. Shattuck, 187–213. Austin: Univ. of Texas Press, 1964.

Athanasius. *The Life of St. Anthony.* Trans. and intro. with notes R. T. Meyer. ACW 10. Westminster, Md.: Newman Press, 1950.

Attridge, H. *The Interpretation of Biblical History in the Antiquitates Judaicae of Flavius Josephus.* HDR 7. Missoula, Mont.: Scholars Press, 1976.

———. "Prolegomena to a Study of Josephus." Cambridge, Mass., 1972. Unpub. paper.

Auerbach, E. *Mimesis: The Representation of Reality in Western Literature.* Trans. W. R. Trask. Princeton: Princeton Univ. Press, 1953.

Avenarius, G. *Lukians Schrift zur Geschichtsschreibung.* Meisenheim am Glan, 1956.

Bakhtin, M. *The Dialogic Imagination.* Trans. C. Emerson and M. Holquist; ed. M. Holquist. Austin: Univ. of Texas Press, 1981.

Balsdon, J. P. V. D. *Romans and Aliens.* Chapel Hill: Univ. of North Carolina Press, 1979.

Bardtke, H. *Das Buch Esther.* KzAT 17/5. Gütersloh, 1963.

Barnes, T. D. "An Apostle on Trial." *JTS* 20 (1969): 407–19.

———. "Legislation against the Christians." *JRS* 58 (1968): 32–50.

Barns, J. W. B. "Egypt and the Greek Romance." *MPER* n.s. 5 (1956): 29–36.

Barr, D. L., and J. L. Wentling. "The Conventions of Classical Biography and the Genre of Luke-Acts." In *Luke-Acts,* ed. Talbert, 63–88.

Barrett, C. K. *Luke the Historian in Recent Study.* Philadelphia: Fortress Press, 1970.

———. Review of Burchard, *Dreizehnte Zeuge. JTS* 24 (1973): 549–50.

Bartsch, W. "Der Charitonroman und die Historiographie." Diss., Univ. of Leipzig, 1934.

Barwick, K. "Die Gliederung der Narratio." *Hermes* 63 (1928): 261–87.

Bauer, W. *Orthodoxy and Heresy in Earliest Christianity.* Trans. and ed. R. Kraft and G. Krodel. Philadelphia: Fortress Press, 1971.

Bauernfeind, D. "Arete." *TDNT* 1:457–61.

Behr, C. H. *Aelius Aristides and the Sacred Tales.* Amsterdam, 1968.

Betz, H. D. *Lukian von Samosata und das Neue Testament.* TU 76. Berlin, 1961.

Beyschlag, K. *Clemens Romanus und der Frühkatholizismus.* BHT 35. Tübingen, 1966.

Bickerman, E. *Four Strange Books of the Bible.* New York: Schocken Books, 1968.

Bieler, L. *Theios Aner.* 2 vols. Darmstadt, 1967.

Blaiklock, E. M. "The Acts of the Apostles as a Document of First Century History." In *Apostolic History and the Gospel* (F. F. Bruce Festschrift), 41–54. Grand Rapids: Wm. B. Eerdmans, 1967.

Blinzer, J. "The Jewish Punishment of Stoning in the New Testament Period." In *The Trial of Jesus* (C. F. D. Moule Festschrift), 147–61. SBT 13. London: SCM Press, 1970.

Blumenthal, M. *Formen und Motive in den apokryphen Apostelgeschichten.* TU 48/1. Leipzig, 1933.

Boer, W. den. "Some Remarks on the Beginning of Christian Historiography." In *Studia Patristica.* TU 79:348–62. Berlin, n.d.

Boll, F. "Zum griechischen Roman." *Philologus* 66 (1907): 1–13.

Booth, W. *The Rhetoric of Fiction.* 2d ed. Chicago: Univ. of Chicago Press, 1983.

Bornkamm, G. "The Missionary Stance of Paul in I Corinthians and in Acts 9." In *SLA* 194–207.

————. *Paul*. Trans. D. M. G. Stalker. New York: Harper & Row, 1971.

Bousset, W. *Kyrios Christos*. Trans. J. Steely. Nashville: Abingdon Press, 1970.

Bovon, F. "La vie des apôtres: Traditions bibliques et narrations apocryphes." In *LAaa* 141–58.

Bovon, F., et al. *Les Actes apocryphes des apôtres*. Geneva, 1981.

Bowen, C. "Paul's Collection and the Book of Acts." *JBL* 42 (1923): 49–58.

Bowers, P. "Paul and Religious Propaganda in the First Century." *NovT* 22 (1980): 316–23.

Bowersock, G. *Greek Sophists in the Roman Empire*. New York and London: Oxford Univ. Press, 1969.

————. *Augustus and the Greek World*. New York and London: Oxford Univ. Press, 1965.

Bowie, E. L. "The Greek Novel." In *The Cambridge History of Classical Literature*. Vol. 1. Ed. P. E. Easterling and B. M. W. Knox. New York: Cambridge Univ. Press, 1985.

————. "The Greeks and Their Past in the Second Sophistic." In *Studies in Ancient Society*, ed. Finley, 166–209.

Braun, M. *Griechischer Roman und hellenistische Geschichtsschreibung*. FSRKAG. Frankfurt, 1934.

————. *History and Romance in Greco-Oriental Literature*. Oxford: Basil Blackwell, 1938.

Broughton, T. R. S. "Three Notes on St. Paul's Journeys in Asia Minor." In *Quantulacumque* (R. Harris Festschrift), ed. R. Casey et al., 131–38. London: Christophers, 1937.

Brown, P. "The Rise and Function of the Holy Man in Late Antiquity." *JRS* 6 (1971): 80–101.

Brown, R. E. *The Epistles of John*. Anchor Bible. Garden City, N.Y.: Doubleday & Co., 1982.

Browning, R. "The Riot of A.D. 387 in Antioch." *JRS* 42 (1952): 13–20.

Bruce, F. F. *The Acts of the Apostles*. Grand Rapids: Wm. B. Eerdmans, 1952.

————. "Is the Paul of Acts the Real Paul?" *BJRL* 58 (1976): 282–305.

————. "St. Paul in Rome." *BJRL* 46 (1964): 226–45.

Brunt, P. "The Roman Mob." In *Studies in Ancient Society*, ed. Finley, 74–102.

Budesheim, T. L. "Paul's *Abschiedsrede* in the Acts of the Apostles." *HTR* 69 (1976): 9–30.

Bultmann, R. "Christianity as a Religion of East and West." 1949. In *Essays*, trans. C. G. Greig, 209–33. London: SCM Press, 1955.

————. *The Gospel of John*. Trans. G. Beasley-Murray et al. Philadelphia: Westminster Press, 1971.

————. *The History of the Synoptic Tradition*. Trans. J. Marsh. 2d ed. New York: Harper & Row, 1968.

————."Zur Frage nach den Quellen der Apostelgeschichte." In *New Testament Essays: Studies in Memory of T. W. Manson*, ed. A. J. B. Higgins, 68–81. Manchester: Manchester Univ. Press, 1959.

Burchard, C. *Der dreizehnte Zeuge*. FRLANT 103. Göttingen: Vandenhoeck & Ruprecht, 1970.

————. *Untersuchungen zur Joseph und Asenath*. Tübingen: J. C. B. Mohr [Paul Siebeck], 1965.

Burckhardt, J. *The Age of Constantine the Great.* Trans. M. Hadas. New York: Pantheon Books, 1949.

Bürger, K. *Studien zur Geschichte des griechischen Romans*, part 2. Blankenburg a.H., 1903.

Bury, J. B. *The Ancient Greek Historians.* New York: Dover Pubs., 1958.

————. *Romances of Chivalry on Greek Soil: Romance Lecture.* Oxford, 1911.

Cadbury, H. J. "Acts of the Apostles." *IDB* 1:28–42.

————. *The Book of Acts in History.* New York: Harper & Bros., 1955.

————. "Erastus of Corinth." *JBL* 50 (1931): 42–58.

————. "Four Features of Lucan Style." In *SLA* 87–102.

————. *The Making of Luke-Acts.* London: SPCK, 1961.

————. Review of Haenchen, *Die Apostelgeschichte. JBL* 76 (1957): 65–66.

————. Review of O'Neill, *The Theology of Acts. JBL* 81 (1962): 197–98.

————. "Some Semitic Personal Names in Acts." In *Amicitiae Corolla* (R. Harris Festschrift), ed. H. Wood, 45–56. London, 1933.

————. "The Speeches in Acts." *BEG CHR* 5:402–27.

————. *The Style and Literary Method of Luke.* HTS 6. Cambridge, Mass., 1920.

————. "The Summaries in Acts." *BEG CHR* 5:392–402.

————. "We and I Passages in Luke-Acts." *NTS* 3 (1956): 128–32.

Calderini, A. *Le avventure di Cherea e Calliroe.* Milan, 1913.

Carpenter, H. J. *Popular Christianity and the Early Theologians.* Philadelphia: Fortress Press, 1966.

Cassidy, R. J., and P. J. Scharper, eds. *Political Issues in Luke-Acts.* Maryknoll, N.Y.: Orbis Books, 1983.

Casson, L. *The Ancient Mariners.* New York: Macmillan Co., 1959.

————. "The Isis and Her Voyage." *TAPA* 81 (1950): 43–56.

————. *Travel in the Ancient World.* Sarasota, Fla.: Samuel Stevens & Co., 1974.

Cawelti, J. *Adventure, Mystery, and Romance.* Chicago: Univ. of Chicago Press, 1976.

Cebe, J.-Ph. *La caricature et la parodie dans le monde romain antique des origines à Juvenal.* Paris, 1966.

Chalk, H. H. "Eros and the Lesbian Pastorals of Longos." *JHS* 80 (1960): 32–51.

————. "Mystery Cults and the Romance." *CR* n.s. 13 (1963): 161–63. Review of Merkelbach, *Roman.*

————. Review of Feuillatre, *Heliodore. CR* n.s. 21 (1971): 131–33.

————. Review of Schoenberger, *Longos. CR* n.s. 12 (1962): 210–12.

Charlesworth, J., ed. *The Old Testament Pseudepigrapha.* Vol. 1. Garden City, N.Y.: Doubleday & Co., 1983.

Chassang, A. *Histoire du roman.* Paris, 1862.

Cizek, E. "Les structures du roman antique." In *EA* 106–28.

Colin, J. *Les villes libres de l'Orient greco-romain.* Coll. Lat. 72. Brussels, 1965.

Collins, J., and R. Poehlmann. "Artapanus." Harvard Univ., 1970. Unpub. seminar paper.

Comstock, G. "Wayne C. Booth, Pluralist." *RSR* 10 (1984): 252–57.

Conzelmann, H. "The Address of Paul on the Aereopagus." In *SLA* 217–30.

————. *Die Apostelgeschichte.* HNT 7. Tübingen, 1963. ET: *Acts.* Hermeneia. Philadelphia: Fortress Press, 1987.

————. *First Corinthians.* Trans. J. W. Leitch. Hermeneia. Philadelphia: Fortress Press, 1975.

————. "Luke's Place in the Development of Early Christianity." In *SLA* 298–316.

————. *The Theology of St. Luke.* Trans. G. Buswell. Philadelphia: Fortress Press, 1982 [1960].

Cope, O. L. *Matthew: A Scribe Trained for the Kingdom of Heaven.* CBQMS 5. Washington, D.C.: Catholic Biblical Assn. of America, 1976.

Corbett, P. *Petronius.* New York: Twayne Pubs., 1970.

Countryman, L. W. *The Rich Christian in the Church of the Early Empire.* New York: Edwin Mellen Press, 1980.

Creed, J. *The Gospel according to St. Luke.* New York, 1930.

Crossan, J. D. *Four Other Gospels.* New York: Seabury Press, 1984.

Crowe, J. *The Acts.* NTM 8. Wilmington, Del.: Michael Glazier, 1979.

Culpepper, R. A. *Anatomy of the Fourth Gospel.* Philadelphia: Fortress Press, 1983.

Davies, S. L. *The Revolt of the Widows.* Carbondale: Southern Illinois Univ. Press, 1980.

Deissmann, A. *Bible Studies.* Trans. A. Grieve. Edinburgh, 1901.

————. *Light from the Ancient East.* Trans. L. Strachan. New York: Harper & Bros., 1927.

————. *Paul: A Study in Social and Religious History.* Trans. W. Wilson. 2d ed. New York: Harper & Bros., 1957 [1927].

Delehaye, H. *Les légendes hagiographiques.* Brussels, 1905.

————. *The Legends of the Saints.* Trans. V. Crawford. New York: Fordham Univ. Press, 1961.

————. *Les passions des martyrs et les genres littéraires.* Brussels, 1966.

Delling, G. "Josephus und das Wunderbare." *NovT* 2 (1958): 291–309.

————. "Magos-Mageia." *TDNT* 4:356–59.

Dibelius, M. *A Fresh Approach to the New Testament.* Westport, Conn.: Greenwood Press, 1936.

————. *From Tradition to Gospel.* Trans. B. Woolf. New York: Charles Scribner's Sons, 1935. Reprint. Greenwood, S.C.: Attic Press, 1971.

————. *Studies in the Acts of the Apostles.* Trans. M. Ling and P. Schubert; ed. H. Greeven. New York: Charles Scribner's Sons, 1956.

Dibelius, M., and H. Conzelmann. *The Pastoral Epistles.* Trans. and ed. H. Koester. Hermeneia. Philadelphia: Fortress Press, 1972.

Dinkler, E. "Philippus und der *Aner Aithiops.*" In *Jesus und Paulus* (W. G. Kümmel Festschrift), ed. E. Ellis and E. Grässer, 85–95. Göttingen, 1975.

Dobschütz, E. "Der Roman im Altchristlichen Literatur." *Deutsche Rundschau* 111 (1902): 87–106.

Dodds, E. R. *The Greeks and the Irrational.* Berkeley and Los Angeles: Univ. of California Press, 1968.

————. *Pagan and Christian in an Age of Anxiety.* New York: W. W. Norton & Co., 1970.

Doran, R. *Temple Propaganda.* CBQMS 12. Washington, D.C.: Catholic Biblical Assn. of America, 1970.

Dorey, T. A., ed. *Latin Biography.* London, 1957.

Dörrie, H. "Die griechischen Romane und das Christentum." *Philologus* 93 (1938): 273.

Douglas, M. *Purity and Danger.* London: Routledge & Kegan Paul, 1984.

Duckett, E. S. *The Wandering Saints.* New York: W. W. Norton & Co., 1959.

Duckworth, G. *The Nature of the Roman Comedy*. Princeton: Princeton Univ. Press, 1952.

Dunlop, J. *A History of Prose Fiction*. Vol. 1. Rev. H. Wilson. New York: AMS Press, 1969.

Dupont, J. "L'apôtre comme intermediaire du salut dans les Actes." *RevTheolPhil* 112 (1980): 342–58.

———. *Etudes sur les Actes des apôtres*. Paris, 1967.

———. *Nouvelles études sur les Actes*. Paris, 1984.

———. *The Salvation of the Gentiles*. Trans. J. Keating. Ramsey, N.J.: Paulist Press, 1979.

———. *The Sources of Acts*. Trans. K. Pond. New York: Herder & Herder, 1964.

Durham, D. B. "Parody in Achilles Tatius." *CP* 33 (1938): 1–19.

Easton, B. S. *The Purpose of Acts*. London, 1936.

Eddy, S. *The King Is Dead*. Lincoln: Univ. of Nebraska Press, 1961.

Ehrhardt, A. "The Construction and Purpose of the Acts of the Apostles." In *The Framework of the New Testament*, 64–102. Cambridge: Harvard Univ. Press, 1964.

Eissfeldt, O. *The Old Testament*. Trans. P. Ackroyd. New York: Harper & Row, 1965.

Engelmann, H. *The Delian Aretalogy of Sarapis*. Etudes préliminaires aux religions orientales dans l'empire romain 44. Leiden: E. J. Brill, 1975.

Enk, P. "The Romance of Apollonius of Tyre." *Mnemosyne* 4th series 1 (1948): 222–37.

Fascher, E. "Theologische Beobachtungen zu *Dei*." In *Neutestamentlichen Studien für R. Bultmann*, 228–54. Göttingen, 1954.

Feldman, D. M. "Chastity." *EncJud* 5:363–64.

Ferguson, W. D. *The Legal Terms Common to the Macedonian Inscriptions and the New Testament*. Chicago, 1913.

Festugière, A. J. *Personal Religion among the Greeks*. Berkeley and Los Angeles: Univ. of California Press, 1954.

Feuillatre, E. *Etudes sur Les éthiopiques de Heliodore*. Paris, 1966.

Finley, M. I. *The Ancient Economy*. Berkeley and Los Angeles: Univ. of California Press, 1973.

———. "The Silent Women of Rome." In *Aspects of Antiquity: Discoveries and Controversies*, 129–42. New York: Viking Press, 1969.

———. "Utopianism Ancient and Modern." In *The Critical Spirit* (H. Marcuse Festschrift), ed. K. Wolff and B. Moore, Jr., 3–20. Boston: Beacon Press, 1967.

———, ed. *Studies in Ancient Society*. London: Routledge & Kegan Paul, 1978.

Fitzmyer, J. *The Gospel according to Luke*. 2 vols. Anchor Bible. Garden City, N.Y.: Doubleday & Co., 1981–85.

———. "Jewish Christianity in Acts in Light of the Qumran Scrolls." In *SLA* 233–57.

Foakes-Jackson, F., and K. Lake, eds. *The Beginnings of Christianity*. 5 vols. New York: Macmillan Co., 1920–33.

Forster, E. M. *Aspects of the Novel*. New York: Harcourt & Brace, 1927.

Freudenthal, J. *Hellenistische Studien*. Vol. 1, *Alexander Polyhistor*. Breslau, 1874.

Friedlander, L. *Roman Life and Manners*. Trans. L. A. Magnus et al. 4 vols. New York: Barnes & Noble, 1965.

Frye, N. *Anatomy of Criticism*. Princeton: Princeton Univ. Press, 1965.

Gaertner, H. "Xenophon von Ephesos." *RE* 18:2056–89.

Gager, J. *Kingdom and Community: The Social World of Early Christianity.* Englewood Cliffs, N.J.: Prentice-Hall, 1975.

Garnsey, P. "The Criminal Jurisdiction of Governors." *JRS* 58 (1968): 51–59.

———. "The *Lex Julia* and Appeal under the Empire." *JRS* 56 (1966): 167–89.

Gärtner, B. "Paulus und Barnabas in Lystra: Zu Apg. 14, 8–15." *Svensk Exegetisk Årsbok* 27 (1962): 83–88.

Gasque, W. W. *A History of the Criticism of the Acts of the Apostles.* Grand Rapids: Wm. B. Eerdmans, 1975.

Georgi, D. "Forms of Religious Propaganda." In *Jesus in His Time*, ed. H. J. Schultz, 124–31. Philadelphia: Fortress Press, 1971.

———. *Die Gegner des Paulus im 2. Korintherbrief.* WMANT 11. Neukirchen: Neukirchener Verlag, 1964. ET: *The Opponents of Paul in Second Corinthians.* Philadelphia: Fortress Press, 1985.

———. "The Records of Jesus in the Light of Ancient Accounts of Revered Men." In *SBLSP 1972* 2:527–42.

———. "Socioeconomic Reasons for the 'Divine Man' as a Propagandistic Pattern." In *Aspects of Religious Propaganda*, ed. E. Schüssler Fiorenza, 27–42. South Bend, Ind.: Univ. of Notre Dame Press, 1976.

———. "Who Is the True Prophet?" In *Christians among Jews and Gentiles*, ed. G. W. E. Nickelsburg and G. W. MacRae, 100–126. Philadelphia: Fortress Press, 1986.

Geyer, P., ed. *Itinera Hierosolymitana Saeculi IIII–VIII.* CSEL 38. Vienna, 1898.

Giangrande, G. "Novel, Greek." *Oxford Classical Dictionary*, 2d ed., 739–40.

———. "On the Origins of Greek Romance." *Eranos* 60 (1962): 132–59.

Glava, Z. *A Study of Heliodorus and His Romance.* New York, 1937.

Goepp, P. "The Narrative Material of *Apollonius of Tyre*." *ELH* 5 (1938): 150–72.

Goldstein, J. *I Maccabees.* Anchor Bible. Garden City, N.Y.: Doubleday & Co., 1976.

Grant, M. *The Climax of Rome.* Boston: Little, Brown & Co., 1968.

Grant, R. *Early Christianity and Society.* New York: Harper & Row, 1977.

———. *Miracle and Natural Law.* Amsterdam: North-Holland Pub. Co., 1952.

Grässer, E. "Acta-Forschung seit 1960." *TRU* 41 (1976): 141–94, 42 (1977): 1–68.

Grimal, P. "A la recherche d'Apulée." *REL* 47 (1969): 94–99.

———. *Romans grecs et latins.* Tours, 1958.

Gronewald, M. "Ein neues Fragment aus dem Metiochus-Parthenope Roman." *ZPE* 24 (1977): 21–22.

———. "Ein neues Fragment zu einem Roman." *ZPE* 25 (1978): 15–20.

Grube, G. *The Greek and Roman Critics.* Toronto and Buffalo: Univ. of Toronto Press, 1965.

Gual, C. "Le roman grec dans la perspective des genres littéraires." In *EA* 99–105.

Hadas, M. *Hellenistic Culture.* New York: W. W. Norton & Co., 1972.

———. "Third Maccabees and Greek Romance." *Review of Religion* 13 (1949): 155–62.

———. "Third Maccabees and the Tradition of Patriotic Romance." *Chronique d'Egypte* 47 (1949): 97–104.

———, trans. *Three Greek Romances.* New York: Doubleday & Co., 1953.

Hadas, M., and M. Smith. *Heroes and Gods: Spiritual Biographies in Antiquity.* New York: Harper & Row, 1965.

Haenchen, E. "Acta 27." In *Zeit und Geschichte* (R. Bultmann Festschrift), ed. E. Dinkler, 235–54. Tübingen, 1964.

———. *The Acts of the Apostles*. Trans. and ed. B. Noble et al. Philadelphia: Westminster Press, 1971. [= *Die Apostlegeschichte*. 7th ed. Meyer. Göttingen, 1977.]

———. "The Book of Acts as Source Material for the History of Early Christianity." In *SLA* 258–78.

———. "Simon Magus in der Apostelgeschichte." In *Gnosis und das Neues Testament*, ed. K. W. Tröger, 267–79. Gütersloh: Mohn, 1973.

———. "'We' in Acts and the Itinerary." *Journal for Theology and Church* 1 (1965): 65–69.

Hägg, T. "Die Ephesiaka des Xenophon Ephesios—Original oder Epitome?" *Class. et Med.* 37 (1966): 118–61.

———. *Narrative Technique in Ancient Greek Romances*. Göteborg: Paul Astrom, 1971.

———. *The Novel in Antiquity*. Berkeley and Los Angeles: Univ. of California Press, 1983.

Haight, E. H. *Essays on Ancient Fiction*. New York: Longmans, Green & Co., 1936.

———. *Essays on Ancient Romances*. New York: Longmans, Green & Co., 1943.

———. *More Essays on Ancient Romances*. New York: Longmans, Green & Co., 1945.

Hallstrom, A. "De Curiositate Atheniensium." *Eranos* 14 (1914): 57–59.

Harnack, A. von. *Acts of the Apostles*. Trans. J. Wilkinson. New York, 1909.

———. *The Expansion of Christianity in the First Three Centuries*. Trans. J. Moffat. Freeport, N.Y.: Books for Libraries, 1972.

———. *A History of Dogma*. Trans. N. Buchanan. 7 vols. New York: Peter Smith, 1961.

Harris, B. F. "Appolonius of Tyana: Fact and Fiction." *JRelHist* 5 (1969): 189–99.

Heintze, W. *Der Klemsroman*. TU 40/2. Leipzig, 1914.

Heinze, R. "Petron und der griechische Roman." *Hermes* 34 (1899): 494–519.

Heiserman, A. *The Novel before the Novel*. Chicago: Univ. of Chicago Press, 1977.

Helm, R. *Der antike Roman*. Göttingen, 1956.

Hemer, C. J. "Luke the Historian." *BJRL* 60 (1977): 28–51.

———. "Paul at Athens." *NTS* 20 (1974): 241–50.

Hengel, M. *Acts and the History of Earliest Christianity*. Trans. J. Bowden. Philadelphia: Fortress Press; London: SCM Press, 1980.

———. *Crucifixion*. Trans. J. Bowden. Philadelphia: Fortress Press; London: SCM Press, 1977.

———. *Judaism and Hellenism*. Trans. J. Bowden. 2 vols. Philadelphia: Fortress Press; London: SCM Press, 1974.

———. "Maria Magdalena und die Frauen als Zeugen." In *Abraham unser Vater* (O. Michel Festschrift), ed. O. Betz et al., 243–56. Leiden, 1963.

———. *Property and Riches in the Early Church*. Trans. J. Bowden. Philadelphia: Fortress Press; London: SCM Press, 1974.

Highet, G. *The Classical Tradition*. New York: Oxford Univ. Press, 1957.

Hijmans, B. L., and R. van der Paardt, eds. *Aspects of the Golden Ass*. Amsterdam: John Benjamins, 1978.

Hock, R. *The Social Context of Paul's Ministry*. Philadelphia: Fortress Press, 1980.

Holladay, C. *Fragments from Hellenistic Jewish Authors*. Vol. 1. Chico, Calif.: Scholars

Press, 1983.

———. *Theios Aner in Hellenistic Judaism*. SBLDS 40. Missoula, Mont.: Scholars Press, 1977.

Huet, P. *Traité de l'origine des romans*. Paris, 1671.

Hull, J. M. *Hellenistic Magic and the Synoptic Tradition*. London: SCM Press, 1974.

Hunter, R. L. *A Study of Daphnis and Chloe*. New York and Cambridge: Cambridge Univ. Press, 1983.

Hurd, J. C. *The Origin of 1 Corinthians*. New York: Seabury Press; London: SPCK, 1965.

Huxley, H. H. "Storm and Shipwreck in Roman Literature." *Greece and Rome* 21 (1952): 117–25.

Jaeger, W. *Early Christianity and Greek Paideia*. Cambridge: Harvard Univ. Press, 1961.

Jervell, J. *Luke and the People of God*. Minneapolis: Augsburg Pub. House, 1972.

———. *The Unknown Paul*. Minneapolis: Augsburg Pub. House, 1984.

Johnson, L. T. *The Literary Function of Possession in Luke-Acts*. Chico, Calif.: Scholars Press, 1977.

Johnson, S. "Asia Minor and Early Christianity." In *Christianity, Judaism* (M. Smith Festschrift), ed. J. Neusner, 2:77–145. 4 vols. Leiden: E. J. Brill, 1975.

———. "A Proposed Form-Critical Treatment of Acts." *ATR* 21 (1939): 22–31.

Jones, A. H. M. *The Greek City*. London: Oxford Univ. Press, 1940.

———. "The Social Background of the Struggle between Paganism and Christianity." In *The Conflict between Paganism and Christianity in the Fourth Century*, ed. A. Momigliano, 17–37. Oxford: At the Clarendon Press, 1963.

Jones, C. P. *The Roman World of Dio Chrysostom*. Cambridge: Harvard Univ. Press, 1978.

Jonsson, J. *Humor and Irony in the New Testament: Illuminated by Parallels in Talmud and Midrash*. Reykjavík, 1965. Reprint. Leiden: E. J. Brill, 1985.

Jovan, F. "Les thèmes romanesques dans l'Euboikos de Dio Chrysostom." In *EA* 38–39.

Judge, E. A. "St. Paul and Classical Society." *JAC* 15 (1972): 19–36.

———. *The Social Pattern of Christian Groups*. London, 1960.

Juel, D. *Luke-Acts: The Promise of History*. Atlanta: John Knox Press, 1983.

Junod, E., and J.-D. Kaestli. *Acta Iohannis*. 2 vols. Turnhout: Brepols, 1983.

Juster, J. *Les juifs dans l'empire romain*. 2 vols. Paris, 1914.

Kaestli, J.-D. "Les principales orientations de la recherche sur les Actes apocryphes." In *LAaa* 49–67.

Karris, R. J. *Invitation to Acts*. Garden City, N.Y.: Doubleday & Co., 1978.

———. *What Are They Saying about Luke and Acts?* Ramsey, N.J.: Paulist Press, 1979.

Kasser, R. "Acta Pauli, 1959." *RHPR* 40 (1959): 45–57.

Keck, L., and J. Martyn, eds. *Studies in Luke-Acts* (P. Schubert Festschrift). Philadelphia: Fortress Press, 1980 [1966].

Kee, H. C. *Miracle in the Early Christian World: A Study in Sociohistorical Method*. New Haven: Yale Univ. Press, 1983.

Kennedy, G. *The Art of Rhetoric in the Roman World*. Princeton: Princeton Univ. Press, 1972.

Kerenyi, K. *Der antike Roman*. Darmstadt, 1971.

———. *Die griechisch-orientalische Romanliteratur.* Tübingen, 1927. Reprint, 1962.

———. "Die Papyri und das Problem des griechischen Romans." *Actes du 5e congrès international de papyrologie,* 192–209. Brussels, 1938.

———. Review of Soeder, *Die apokryphen Apostelgeschichten. Gnomon* 10 (1934): 301–9.

Klein, G. *Die Zwölf Apostel.* FRLANT 59. Göttingen: Vandenhoeck & Ruprecht, 1961.

Klijn, A. F. J. *The Acts of Thomas. NovTSup* 5. Leiden: E. J. Brill, 1962.

———. "The Apocryphal Acts of the Apostles." *VC* 37 (1983): 193–99.

———. "In Search of the Original Text of Acts." In *SLA* 103–10.

Klostermann, E. *Das Markusevangelium.* HNT. Tübingen: J. C. B. Mohr [Paul Siebeck], 1926

Knox, J. "Acts and the Pauline Letter Corpus." In *SLA* 279–87.

———. *Chapters in the Life of Paul.* Nashville: Abingdon Press, 1950.

Koester, H. *Introduction to the New Testament.* 2 vols. Berlin and New York: Walter de Gruyter, 1982.

———. "Literature, Early Christian." *IDBSup* 551–56.

Koester, H., and J. M. Robinson. *Trajectories through Early Christianity.* Philadelphia: Fortress Press, 1971.

Kraeling, E. G. "Ahikar, Book of." *IDB* 1:681.

Kremer, J., ed. *Les Actes des apôtres.* BETL 48. Louvain: Louvain Univ. Press, 1979.

Krodel, G. *Acts.* Philadelphia: Fortress Press, 1981.

Kroll, W. "Iambulos." *RE* 17:681–83.

Kümmel, W. G. "Current Theological Accusations against Luke." *Andover-Newton Theological Quarterly* 16 (1975): 131–45.

———. *Introduction to the New Testament.* Trans. H. C. Kee. Nashville: Abingdon Press, 1975.

LaDouceur, D. "Hellenistic Preconceptions of Shipwreck and Pollution as a Context for Acts 27—28." *HTR* 73 (1980): 435–50.

Laistner, M. L. W. *The Greater Roman Historians.* Sather Lectures, 1921. Berkeley and Los Angeles: Univ. of California Press, 1966.

La Piana, G. "The Roman Church at the End of the Second Century." *HTR* 18 (1925): 201–78.

Lavagnini, B. *Studi sul romanzo greco.* 1921. Messina, 1950.

Leo, F. *Die griechisch-römische Biographie.* Leipzig, 1901.

Lesky, A. *History of Greek Literature.* Trans. J. Willis and C. de Heer. New York: Thomas Y. Crowell Co., 1966.

Levick, B. *Roman Colonies in Southern Asia Minor.* Oxford: At the Clarendon Press, 1967.

Levin, D. N. "To Whom Did the Ancient Novelists Address Themselves?" *RivStudClass* 25 (1977): 18–29.

Liefeld, W. L. "The Wandering Preacher as Social Figure in the Roman Empire." Diss., Columbia Univ., 1967.

Linton, O. "The Third Aspect." *StudTheol* 3 (1951): 79–95.

Lovejoy, A. O., and G. Boas. *Primitivism and Related Ideas in Antiquity.* Vol. 1. Baltimore: Johns Hopkins Univ. Press, 1935.

Ludvikovsky, J. *Recky Roman Dobrodruzny (Le roman grec d'aventures).* Prague, 1925.

McCasland, S. V. "Ships and Sailing in the New Testament." *IDB* 4:335–37.

————. "Travel and Communication in the New Testament." *IDB* 4:690–93.

McCulloh, W. *Longus*. Boston: Twayne Pubs., 1970.

MacDonald, D. R. *The Legend and the Apostle: The Battle for Paul in Story and Canon.* Philadelphia: Westminster Press, 1983.

————, ed. *The Apocryphal Acts of Apostles*. Semeia 38. Atlanta: Scholars Press, 1986.

McLachlan, H. *St. Luke: The Man and His Work*. New York: Longmans, Green & Co., 1920.

MacMullen, R. *Christianizing the Roman Empire: A.D. 100–400*. New Haven: Yale Univ. Press, 1984.

————. *Enemies of the Roman Order: Treason, Unrest, and Alienation in the Empire.* Cambridge: Harvard Univ. Press, 1966.

————. *Paganism in the Roman Empire*. New Haven: Yale Univ. Press, 1981.

————. *Roman Social Relations: 50 B.C. to A.D. 284*. New Haven: Yale Univ. Press, 1974.

MacRae, G. "Miracle in the *Antiquities* of Josephus." In *Miracles*, ed. C. F. D. Moule, 129–47. New York: Morehouse-Barlow Co., 1966; London: A. R. Mowbray & Co., 1965.

Mähler, H. "Der Metiochus-Parthenope Roman." *ZPE* 23 (1976): 1–20.

Malherbe, A. J. *The Cynic Epistles*. SBLSBS 12. Atlanta: Scholars Press, 1977.

————. *Social Aspects of Early Christianity*. 2d ed., enl. Philadelphia: Fortress Press, 1983.

Marrou, H. I. *A History of Education in Antiquity*. Trans. G. Lamb. New York: New American Library, 1964.

Marshall, I. H. *The Acts of the Apostles*. Grand Rapids: Wm. B. Eerdmans, 1980.

————. "Recent Study of the Acts of the Apostles." *ExpTim* 80 (1968–69): 292–96.

Marxsen, W. *Introduction to the New Testament*. Trans. G. Buswell. Philadelphia: Fortress Press, 1968.

Mattill, A. J. "Luke as a Historian in Criticism since 1840." Diss., Vanderbilt Univ., 1959.

Mayer, G. "Neue Standardwerke zur jüdisch-hellenistischen Literatur." *TR* 48 (1983): 305–19.

Mealand, D. L. "Community of Goods and Utopian Allusions in Acts 2—4." *JTS* 28 (1977): 96–99.

Meeks, W. "Simon Magus." *RSR* 3 (1977): 137–42.

Mendell, C. W. "Petronius and the Greek Romance." *CP* 12 (1917): 158–72.

Merkelbach, R. "Inhalt und Form in symbolischen Erzählungen der Antike." *Eranos Jahrbuch* 35 (1966): 145–75.

————. *Roman und Mysterium in der Antike*. Berlin, 1962.

Michel, O. *Die Abschiedsrede des Paulus an die Kirche*. StANT. Munich, 1973.

Miles, G., and G. Trompf. "Luke and Antiphon." *HTR* 69 (1976): 259–67.

Millar, F., et al., eds. *The Roman Empire and Its Neighbors*. New York: Delacorte Press, 1967.

Miralles, C. "*Eros* as *Nosos* in the Greek Novel." In *EA* 20–21.

Misch, G. *Geschichte der Autobiographie*. Vol. 1. Leipzig, 1931.

Moehring, H. R. "The Census in Luke as an Apologetic Device." In *Studies in New Testament and Early Christian Literature* (A. Wikgren Festschrift), ed. D. Aune, 144–60. Leiden: E. J. Brill, 1972.

———. "The Persecution of the Jews and the Adherents of the Isis Cult at Rome, A.D. 19." *NovT* 3 (1959): 293–304.

Momigliano, A. *The Development of Greek Biography.* Cambridge: Harvard Univ. Press, 1971.

———. "Pagan and Christian Historiography in the Fourth Century, A.D." In *Conflict between Paganism and Christianity in the Fourth Century,* 79–99. Oxford: At the Clarendon Press, 1963.

———. "Second Thoughts on Greek Biography." *Medelingen van het Nederlandsch historisch te Rome* N.R. 34 (1971): 245–57.

Mommsen, T. "Die Rechtsverhältnisse des Apostels Paulus." *ZNW* 2 (1902): 81–96.

Morard, F. "Souffrance et martyre dans les Actes apocryphes." In *LAaa* 109–19.

Morgan, J. R. "History, Romance, and Realism in the Aithiopika." *CLAnt* 1 (1982): 221–65.

Moule, C. F. D. *The Birth of the New Testament.* 3d ed. San Francisco: Harper & Row, 1982.

Mueller, C. W. "Chariton V. Aphrodisias und die Theorie des Romans." *AntAbend* 22 (1976): 115–36.

Munck, J. *Paul and the Salvation of Mankind.* Trans. F. Clarke. Richmond: John Knox Press, 1959.

Murray, G. *The Literature of Ancient Greece.* 3d ed. Chicago: Univ. of Chicago Press, 1956.

Nestle, W. "Legenden vom Tod der Gottesverächter." *ARW* 33 (1936): 246–69.

Neyrey, J. "The Forensic Defense Speech and Paul's Trial Speeches in Acts 22—26." In *Luke-Acts,* ed. Talbert, 210–24.

Nickelsburg, G. W. *Jewish Literature between the Bible and the Mishnah.* Philadelphia: Fortress Press, 1981.

Niese, B. *Kritik der beiden Makkabaeerbucher.* Berlin, 1960.

Nigg, W. *Die Kirchengeschichtschreibung.* Munich, 1934.

Nilsson, M. P. *Geschichte der griechischen Religion.* Vol. 2. Munich, 1961.

———. *Greek Piety.* Trans. H. J. Rose. New York: W. W. Norton & Co., 1969.

Nock, A. D. "Alexander of Abonuteichos." *CQ* 22 (1928): 160–62.

———. *Conversion: The Old and the New in Religion from Alexander the Great to Augustine of Hippo.* London: Oxford Univ. Press, 1969 [1933].

———. *Essays on Religion and the Ancient World.* 2 vols. Ed. Z. Stewart. Cambridge: Harvard Univ. Press, 1972.

———. "*Isopoliteia* and the Jews." In *Essays* 2:960–62.

———. Review of Dibelius, *Aufsätze.* In *Essays* 2:821–32.

———. Review of Kerenyi, *Die griechisch-orientalische Romanliteratur.* In *Essays* 1: 169–76.

Norden, E. *Agnostos Theos.* Darmstadt, 1974.

———. *Die antike Kunstprosa.* 2 vols. Stuttgart, 1958.

Ogle, M. B. "The Trance of Lover and of Saint." *TAPA* 71 (1940): 296–301.

O'Neill, J. C. *The Theology of Acts in Its Historical Setting.* London: SPCK, 1970.

Ormerod, H. A. *Piracy in the Ancient World.* New York: Barnes & Noble, 1924.

Oster, R. "The Ephesian Artemis as an Opponent of Early Christianity." *JAC* 19 (1976): 24–44.

O'Sullivan, J. N., and W. A. Beck. "P. Oxy 3319: The Sesonchosis Romance." *ZPE* 45 (1982): 71–83.

Overbeck, F. *Über die Anfänge der patristischen Literatur*. 1882. Basel, n.d.

Perry, B. E. *The Ancient Romances: A Literary Historical Account of Their Origins.* Sather Lectures, 1951. Berkeley and Los Angeles: Univ. of California Press, 1967.

———. "Chariton and His Romance from a Literary Point of View." *AJP* 51 (1930): 93–134.

———. "The Egyptian Legend of Nectanebus." *TAPA* 97 (1966): 327–33.

———. "Literature in the Second Century." *ClassJ* 50 (1955): 295–98.

———. "Petronius and the Comic Romance." *ClassPhil* 20 (1925): 31–49.

———. Review of Braun, *History and Romance. ClassJ* 37 (1942): 537–40.

———. Review of Lavagnini, *Le origini del romanzo greco. AJP* 44 (1923): 371–73.

———. Review of Trenkner, *Greek Novella. AJP* 81 (1960): 442–47.

———. *Studies in the Text History of the Life and Fables of Aesop.* APA Mon 7. Haverford, Pa., 1936.

Pervo, R. I. "Entertainment and Early Christian Literature." *Explor* 7 (1984): 29–39.

———. "Joseph of Asenath and the Greek Novel." In *SBLSP 1976*, ed. G. MacRae, 171–81. Missoula, Mont.: Scholars Press, 1976.

———. "The Literary Genre of the Acts of the Apostles." Diss., Harvard Univ., 1979.

———. Review of Anderson, *Eros Sophistes. SecCent* 5 (1985): 51–52.

———. Review of Davies, *The Revolt of the Widows. SecCent* 2 (1982): 47–49.

———. Review of Fitzmyer, *The Gospel according to Luke I—IX. ATR* 66 (1984): 443–45.

———. Review of Gasque, *History of the Criticism. ATR* 59 (1977): 108–13.

———. Review of Hengel, *Acts and the History of Earliest Christianity. ATR* 63 (1981): 92–93.

———. Review of Mattil, *Luke and the Last Things*, and Tiede, *Prophecy and History in Luke-Acts. ATR* 64 (1982): 98–99.

———. "Social and Religious Aspects of the Western Text." In *The Living Text* (E. W. Saunders Festschrift), ed. D. Groh and R. Jewett, 229–41. Lanham, Md.: Univ. Press of America, 1985.

———. "The Testament of Joseph and Greek Romance." In *Studies on the Testament of Joseph*, ed. G. W. Nickelsburg, 15–28. Missoula, Mont.: Scholars Press, 1975.

———. "Wisdom and Power." *ATR* 67 (1985): 307–25.

Peter, H. *Wahrheit und Kunst: Geschichte und Plagiat im klassischen Altertums.* Leipzig, 1911.

Petersen, N. *Literary Criticism for New Testament Critics.* Ed. Dan Via. Philadelphia: Fortress Press, 1978.

Peterson, E. "Heis Theos." Diss., Univ. of Göttingen, 1920.

Peterson, J. "Missionary Methods of the Religions in the Early Roman Empire." Diss., Univ. of Chicago, 1942.

Petzke, G. *Die Traditionen über Apollonius von Tyrana und das Neues Testament.* Studia ad Corpus Hellenisticum N.T. Leiden: E. J. Brill, 1970.

Pfeiffer, R. H. *History of New Testament Times: With an Introduction to the Apocrypha.* New York: Harper & Bros., 1949.

Pfister, F. "Apostelgeschichten." In *Neutestamentliche Apokryphen*, 2d ed., ed. E. Hennecke, 163–71. Tübingen, 1924.

Plümacher, E. "Acta-Forschung 1974–1982." *TRu* 48 (1983): 1–56.

———. "Apokryphe Apostelakten." *RESup* 15:11–70.

————. "Die Apostelgeschichte als historische Monographie." In *Les Actes*, ed. Kremer, 457–66.

————. "Lukas als griechischer Historiker." *RESup* 14:235–64.

————. *Lukas als hellenistischer Schriftsteller: Studien zur Apostelgeschichte.* SUNT 9. Göttingen: Vandenhoeck & Ruprecht, 1972.

————. "Wirklichkeitserfahrung und Geschichtsschreibung bei Lukas." *ZNW* 68 (1977): 2–22.

Pöhlmann, R. *Geschichte der sozialen Frage.* Vol. 2. Munich, 1925.

Pokorny, P. "Die Romfahrt des Paulus und der antike Roman." *ZNW* 64 (1973): 233–44.

Poland, F. *Geschichte des griechischen Vereinswesens.* Leipzig: Teubner, 1909.

Poupon, G. "L'accusation de magie dans les Actes apocryphes." In *LAaa* 71–94.

Praeder, S. M. "Acts 27:1–28:16: Sea Voyages in Ancient Literature and the Theology of Luke-Acts." *CBQ* 46 (1984): 683–706.

————. "Jesus-Paul, Peter-Paul, and Jesus-Peter Parallelisms." In *SBLSP 1984,* 23–39. Chico, Calif.: Scholars Press, 1984.

————. "Luke-Acts and the Ancient Novel." In *SBLSP 1981,* 269–92. Chico, Calif.: Scholars Press, 1981.

————. "Narrative Voyage: An Analysis and Interpretation of Acts 27—28." Diss., Graduate Theological Union, Berkeley, Calif., 1980.

Preuschen, E. *Die Apostelgeschichte.* HNT. Tübingen, 1912.

Prieur, J.-M. "La figure de l'apôtre dans les Actes apocryphes d'André." In *LAaa* 121–39.

Quinn, J. D. "The Last Volume of Luke." In *Perspectives on Luke-Acts,* ed. Talbert, 76–98.

Radl, W. *Paulus und Jesus im Lukanischen Doppelwerk.* Bern, 1975.

Ramsay, W. *The Bearing of Recent Discovery on the Trustworthiness of the New Testament.* Reprint. Grand Rapids: Baker Book House, 1953.

————. *The Church in the Roman Empire.* New York, 1893.

————. *St. Paul the Traveller and Roman Citizen.* New York, 1906.

Rattenbury, R. M. "Chastity and Chastity Ordeals in Ancient Greek Romance." *Proc. Leeds Phil. Lit. Soc.* 1 (1926): 59–71.

————. Review of Helm, *Antike Roman. Gnomon* 22 (1950): 74–77.

Reardon, B. P. "Aspects of the Greek Novel." *Greece and Rome* 23 (1976): 118–31.

————. *Courants littéraires grecs des IIe et IIIe siècles.* Ann Litt Univ Nantes 3. Paris, 1971.

————. "The Greek Novel." *Phoenix* 23 (1969): 291–310.

————. "The Second Sophistic and the Novel." In *Approaches to the Second Sophistic,* ed. G. Bowersock, 23–29. University Park: Pennsylvania State Univ. Press, 1974.

————. "Theme, Structure, and Narrative in Chariton." *YCS* 27 (1982): 1–28.

————, ed. *Erotica Antiqua.* Bangor, Wales, 1977. Acta of the International Conference on the Ancient Novel.

Reitzenstein, R. *Hellenistische Wundererzählungen.* Darmstadt, 1974.

Renie, R. P. J. "L'élection de Mathias." *RevBib* 55 (1948): 42–53.

Richlin, A. *The Garden of Priapus: Sexuality and Aggression in Roman Humor.* New Haven: Yale Univ. Press, 1983.

Riefstahl, H. *Der Roman des Apuleius.* FSRKA 15. Frankfurt am Main, 1938.

Robbins, V. "By Land and by Sea." In *Perspectives on Luke-Acts,* ed. Talbert, 215–42.

Robinson, J. M., and H. Koester. *Trajectories through Early Christianity.* Philadelphia: Fortress Press, 1971.

Robinson, W. C. "The Theological Context for Interpreting Luke's Travel Narrative." *JBL* 79 (1960): 20–31.

Rohde, E. *Der griechische Roman und seine Vorläufer.* Hildesheim, 1960. Reprint, 1974.

———. Review of Schwartz, *Fünf Vorträge.* In *Kleine Schriften*, 5–9. Tübingen, 1901.

Rohrbach, R. "Methodological Considerations in the Debate over the Social Class Status of Early Christians." *JAAR* 52 (1984): 519–46.

Roloff, J. *Die Apostelgeschichte.* NTD 5. Göttingen: Vandenhoeck & Ruprecht, 1981.

Saint-Denis, E. de. *Essais sur le rire et le sourire des latins.* Paris, 1965.

Sanday, G. N. *Heliodorus.* Boston: Twayne Pubs., 1982.

Sanders, H. "A Fragment of the *Acta Pauli* in the Michigan Collection." *HTR* 31 (1938): 113–42.

Scheller, P. "De Hellenistica Historiae Conscribendae Arte." Diss., Univ. of Leipzig, 1911.

Schiering, S. P., and M. J. Schiering. "The Influence of the Ancient Romances on the Acts of the Apostles." *Classical Bulletin* 54 (1978): 81–88.

Schille, G. "Die Fragwürdigkeit eines Itinerars der Paulusreisen." *TheolLit* 89 (1959): 165–74.

Schissel von Fleschenberg, O. *Entwicklungsgeschichte des griechischen Romanes.* Halle, 1913.

Schmeling, G. *Chariton.* Boston: Twayne Pubs., 1974.

———. *Xenophon of Ephesus.* Boston: Twayne Pubs., 1980.

Schmid, W. "Chariton." *RE* 3:2168–71.

Schmidt, K. L. "Die Stellung der Evangelien in der allgemeinen Literaturgeschichte." In *Eucharisterion* (H. Gunkel Festschrift), ed. H. Schmidt, 50–134. Göttingen, 1923.

Schneemelcher, W. "Die Apostelgeschichte des Lukas und die *Acta Pauli.*" In *Apophoreta* (E. Haenchen Festschrift), ed. W. Eltester and F. Kettler, 236–50. Tübingen, 1964.

Schneider, C. "Mastigoō, ktl." *TDNT* 4:515–19.

Schneider, G. *Die Apostelgeschichte.* 2 vols. Freiburg: Herder & Herder, 1980–82.

Schulz, S. "Gottes Vorsehung bei Lukas." *ZNW* 54 (1963): 104–16.

Schürer, E. *A History of the Jewish People in the Time of Jesus Christ.* Rev. and ed. G. Vermes and F. Millar. 3 vols. Edinburgh: T. & T. Clark, 1973–86.

Schwartz, E. *Fünf Vorträge über den griechischen Roman.* Berlin, 1896.

———. "Artapanus." *RE* 2:1306.

Schweizer, E. "Concerning the Speeches in Acts." In *SLA* 208–16.

———. *Luke: A Challenge to Present Theology.* Atlanta: John Knox Press, 1982.

Scobie, A. *Aspects of the Ancient Romance and Its Heritage.* Meisenheim am Glan, 1969.

———. *More Essays on the Ancient Romance.* Meisenheim am Glan, 1973.

Scott, K. "Ruler Cult and Related Problems in the Greek Romances." *ClassPhil* 33 (1938): 380–89.

Seaford, R. *Pompeii.* New York: Thames & Hudson, 1979.

Segal, E. *Roman Laughter: The Comedy of Plautus.* New York: Harper & Row, 1971.

Seltman, C. *Riot in Ephesus.* London: Dufour Editions, 1958.

Sherwin-White, A. N. *Roman Society and Roman Law in the New Testament*. Oxford: At the Clarendon Press, 1963.

Sinko, T. "De Ordine quo Erotici Scriptores Graeci sibi Successisse Videantur." *Eos* 41 (1946): 23–45.

Smallwood, E. M. *The Jews under Roman Rule*. SJLA 20. Leiden: E. J. Brill, 1976.

Smith, E. M. "The Egypt of the Greek Romance." *ClassJ* 23 (1927): 531–37.

Smith, J. *The Voyage and Shipwreck of St. Paul*. 4th ed. London, 1880.

Smith, M. "Prolegomena to a Discussion of Aretalogies." *JBL* 90 (1971): 174–98.

———. "The Reason for the Persecution of Paul and the Obscurity of Acts." In *Studies in Mysticism and Religion* (G. Scholem Festschrift), 261–68. Jerusalem, 1967.

———. Review of Merkelbach, *Roman*. *CW* 27 (1964): 378.

Soady, A. "Romance Elements in Vergil's *Aeneid* 1–4." In *EA* 40–42.

Soeder, R. *Die apokryphen Apostelgeschichten und die romanhafte Literatur der Antike*. Stuttgart, 1969.

Steichele, H. "Vergleich der Apostelgeschichte mit der antiken Geschichtsschreibung." Diss., Univ. of Munich, 1971.

Stengel, A. *De Luciani Veris Historiis*. Berlin, 1911.

Stevenson, L. *The English Novel*. Boston: Houghton Mifflin, 1960.

Stone, M., ed. *Jewish Writings of the Second Temple Period*. CRINT 2/2. Philadelphia: Fortress Press, 1984.

Stowers, S. "Social Status, Public Speaking, and Private Teaching: The Circumstances of Paul's Preaching Activity." *NovT* 26 (1984): 59–82.

Streeter, B. H. *The Primitive Church*. New York: Macmillan Co., 1929.

Suess, W. *Lachen, Komik und Witz in der Antike*. Stuttgart, 1969.

Sullivan, J. P. "Petron in der neueren Forschung." *Helikon* 17 (1977): 137–54.

———. *The Satyricon of Petronius: A Literary Study*. Bloomington: Indiana Univ. Press, 1968.

Syme, R. *The Roman Revolution*. Oxford: At the Clarendon Press, 1939.

Tacitus. *De vita agricolae*. Ed. R. M. Ogivie and I. Henderson. Oxford: At the Clarendon Press, 1967.

Talbert, C. *Acts*. KPG. Atlanta: John Knox Press, 1984.

———. "An Introduction to Acts." *Rev. and Exp.* 71 (1974): 437–49.

———. *Literary Patterns, Theological Themes, and the Genre of Luke-Acts*. SBLMS 20. Missoula, Mont.: Scholars Press, 1974.

———. *Reading Luke*. New York: Crossroad, 1983.

———, ed. *Luke-Acts*. New York: Crossroad, 1984.

———, ed. *Perspectives on Luke-Acts*. Danville, Va.: National Assn. of Baptist Professors of Religion, 1978.

Tatum, J. *Apuleius and the Golden Ass*. Ithaca, N.Y.: Cornell Univ. Press, 1979.

Tcherikover, V. "Ideology of the Letter of Aristeas." *HTR* 51 (1958): 59–85.

———. "Jewish Apologetic Literature Reconsidered." *Eos* 48 (1956): 169–93.

Theissen, G. *The Miracle Stories of the Early Christian Tradition*. Trans. F. McDonagh; ed. J. Riches. Philadelphia: Fortress Press, 1983.

———. *The Social Setting of Pauline Christianity: Essays on Corinth*. Trans. and ed. with intro. J. Schütz. Philadelphia: Fortress Press, 1982.

Thiele, G. "Zum griechischen Roman." In *Aus der Anomia*, ed. C. Robert, 124–33. Berlin, 1890.

Tiede, D. L. *The Charismatic Figure as Miracle Worker*. SBLDS 1. Missoula, Mont.: Scholars Press, 1972.

————. *Prophecy and History in Luke-Acts.* Philadelphia: Fortress Press, 1980.

Tissot, Y. "Encratisme et Actes apocryphes." In *LAaa* 109–19.

Torrey, C. C. *The Composition and Date of Acts.* HTS. Cambridge: Harvard Univ. Press, 1916.

Trenkner, S. *The Greek Novella in the Classical Period.* Cambridge: At the Univ. Press, 1958.

Trocme, E. *Le livre des Actes et l'histoire.* Paris, 1957.

Turcan, R. "Le roman 'Initiatique.'" *RHR* 163 (1963): 147–99. Review of Merkelbach, *Roman.*

Turner, P. "Novels, Ancient and Modern." *Novel* 2 (1968): 15–24.

Ullmann, B. "History and Tragedy." *TAPA* 73 (1942): 25–53.

Unnik, W. C. van. "Luke's Second Book and the Rules of Hellenistic Historiography." In *Les Actes,* ed. Kremer, 37–60.

————. *Tarsus or Jerusalem.* Trans. G. Ogg. Naperville, Ill.: Alec R. Allenson, 1962.

van der Meer, F. *Augustine the Bishop.* New York: Sheed & Ward, 1961.

Veltman, F. "The Defense Speeches of Paul in Acts." In *Perspectives on Luke-Acts,* ed. Talbert, 243–56.

Vergilius, Publius. *Die grossen Gedichte.* Ed. and intro. H. Holtorf. Munich, 1959.

Veyne, P. de. "Le 'je' dans le Satyricon." *REL* 42 (1964): 301–24.

Vielhauer, P. *Geschichte der Urchristlichen Literatur.* Berlin: Walter de Gruyter, 1975.

————. "On the 'Paulinism' of Acts." In *SLA* 33–50.

Volten, A. "Der demotische Petubastisroman." *Mitt. aus der Papyrussammlung der Oesterreich. Nat.* 5 (1956): 147–52.

Wacht, M. "Gütergemeinschaft." *RAC* 13:1–61.

Walbank, F. W. "History and Tragedy." *Historia* 9 (1960): 216–34.

Waldstein, W. "Geisselung." *RAC* 9:470–90.

Walsh, P. G. *The Roman Novel.* New York and Cambridge: Cambridge Univ. Press, 1970.

Warren, F. M. *A History of the Novel Previous to the Seventeenth Century.* Folcroft, Pa.: Folcroft Press, 1895.

Watt, I. *The Rise of the Novel.* Berkeley and Los Angeles: Univ. of California Press, 1965.

Wehrli, F. "Einheit und Vorgeschichte der griechischen-römischen Romanliteratur." *MusHelv* 22 (1965): 133–54.

Weil, H. "La Ninopédie." In *Etudes de littérature,* 90–106. Paris, 1902.

Weinreich, O. *Antike Heilungswunder.* Giessen, 1909.

————. *Gebet und Wunder.* Stuttgart, 1929.

————. *Der griechische Liebesroman.* Zurich, 1962.

Welles, H. B. *Royal Correspondence in the Hellenistic Period.* Chicago: Ares Pubs., 1974.

Wellhausen, J. *Kritische Analyse der Apostelgeschichte.* Abh. Koen. Ges. Wiss. Göttingen, Phil-Hist. Klasse. Berlin, 1914.

Wendland, P. *De Fabellis Antiquis.* Göttingen, 1911.

————. "Der Roman." In *Einleitung in die Altertumswissenschaft.* Ed. A. Gercke and E. Norden, 1:240–42. Berlin, 1912.

————. Urchristliche Literaturformen. HNT. Tübingen, 1912.

Werner, H. "Zum *Loukios E Onos.*" *Hermes* 53 (1918): 225–61.

West, S. "Joseph and Asenath: A Neglected Greek Novel." *CQ* 68 (1974): 70–81.

Wilkenhauser, A. *Die Apostelgeschichte und ihr Geschichtswert.* NTAbh. Münster,

1921.

———. "Doppelträume." *Biblica* 29 (1948): 100–111.

———. "Religionsgeschichtliche Parallelen zu Apg. 16, 9." *BZ* 23 (1935): 180–86.

———. "Die Traumgeschichte des Neuen Testaments in religionsgeschichtlicher Sicht." In *Piscisculi* (F. Dölger Festschrift), 320–33. Münster, 1939.

Wilamowitz-Moellendorf, U. von. *Die griechische undlateinische Literatur und Sprache.* Leipzig, 1907–12.

Wild, R. Review of Bovon et al., *Les Actes apocryphes. CBQ* 45 (1983): 153–54.

Williams, C. S. C. *The Acts of the Apostles.* HNTC. New York: Harper & Bros., 1957.

———. "Luke-Acts in Recent Study." *ExpTim* 73 (1961–62): 133–36.

Wilson, S. G. "Lukan Eschatology." *NTS* 16 (1970): 330–47.

———. *Luke and the Pastorals.* London, 1979.

Winkler, J. "The Mendacity of Kalasiris." *YCS* 27 (1982): 93–158.

Wolff, S. L. *The Greek Romances in Elizabethan Prose Fiction.* New York, 1932.

Zahn, T. *Die Apostelgeschichte.* KNT. 2 vols. Leipzig, 1922.

Zehnle, R. *Peter's Pentecost Discourse: Tradition and Lukan Reinterpretation in Peter's Speeches of Acts 2 and 3.* SBLMS 15. Nashville: Abingdon Press, 1971.

Zeller, E. *The Contents and Origin of the Acts of the Apostles.* Trans. J. Dare. 2 vols. London, 1875–76.

———. "Eine griechische Parallele zu der Erzählung Apostelgeschichte 16,9ff." *ZWT* 10 (1865): 103–8.

———. *Die Philosophie der Griechen.* Leipzig: Teubner, 1868.

Zimmermann, F. *The Book of Tobit.* New York: Harper & Bros., 1958.

Zimmermann, Fr. "Aus der Welt des griechischen Romans." *Antike* (1935): 292–316.

———. "Chariton und die Geschichte." In *Sozialoekonomische Verhältnisse im alten Orient und im klassischen Altertum,* ed. R. Günther and G. Schrot, 329–45. Berlin, 1961.

———. "Lukians Toxaris und das kairener Roman Fragment." *PhilWoch* 43 (1935): 1211–16.

———. "Das neue Bruchstück des Ninos-Romans." *Wiss. Zeit. U. Rostock* 3 (1954): 175–81.

———. Review of Soeder, *Die apokryphen Apostelgeschichten und die romanhafte Literatur der Antike,* and Blumenthal, *Formen und Motive in den apokryphen Apostelgeschichten. PhilWoch* 52 (1938): 1405–10.

———. "Zum Stand der Forschung über den Roman." *Forschung und Fortschritte* 26 (1950): 59–62.

Zumstein, J. "L'apôtre comme martyr." *RevTheolPhil* 112 (1980): 371–90.

———. Review of Bovon et al., *Les Actes apocryphes. RevTheolPhil* 113 (1981): 415–20.

INDEXES

CHRISTIAN SCRIPTURE

OTHER WRITERS AND WRITINGS OF ANTIQUITY